Learning Django Web Development

From idea to prototype, a learner's guide for web development with the Django application framework

Sanjeev Jaiswal

Ratan Kumar

BIRMINGHAM - MUMBAI

Learning Django Web Development

First published: June 2015

Production reference: 1150615

Published by Packt Publishing Ltd.
Livery Place
35 Livery Street
Birmingham B3 2PB, UK.

ISBN 978-1-78398-440-4

www.packtpub.com

Credits

About the Authors

Sanjeev Jaiswal is a computer graduate with 5 years of industrial experience. He basically uses Perl and GNU/Linux for his day-to-day work. He also teaches Drupal and WordPress CMS to bloggers. He first developed an interest in web application penetration testing in 2013; he is currently working on projects involving penetration testing, source code review, and log analysis, where he provides the analysis and defense of various kinds of web-based attacks.

Sanjeev loves teaching technical concepts to engineering students and IT professionals and has been teaching for the last 6 years in his leisure time. He founded Alien Coders (`http://www.aliencoders.org`), based on the learning through sharing principle for computer science students and IT professionals in 2010, which became a huge hit in India among engineering students.

He usually uploads technical videos on YouTube under the Alien Coders tag. He has got a huge fan base at his site because of his simple but effective way of teaching and his philanthropic nature toward students. You can follow him on Facebook at `http://www.facebook.com/aliencoders` and on Twitter at `@aliencoders`.

He wrote *Instant PageSpeed Optimization*, *Packt Publishing*, and looks forward to authoring or reviewing more books for Packt Publishing and other publishers.

Ratan Kumar is a computer science and engineering graduate with more than a year of start-up experience. He received the Technical Excellence Memento from the Association of Computer Engineering Students (ACES), Cochin University of Science and Technology.

When he was a product engineer at Profoundis, he worked on an international project based on services using Django. He was also part of the Microsoft accelerator program with Profoundis that was responsible for building the product iTestify, which was built using Django.

He then moved to Tracxn!, an organization that works on building platforms that can help venture capitalists, investment banks, and corporate developers find new and interesting start-ups in their investment sector. As a software developer and engineer, he majorly contributed to the development of the core product platform of Tracxn using Python for the initial scraping work, such as building cron scrappers to crawl millions of pages daily, cleaning them up, and analyzing them.

He also built the company's first product, which is called Tracxn Extension—a Chrome extension using AngularJS. He contributed to the Tracxn product platform using Grails as the framework. He also worked on Bootstrap—a frontend framework—to design the home page of `tracxn.com`.

About the Reviewers

Michael Giuliano has been programming software in various languages and technologies for the past 15 years. Having used Python in the fields of web services, machine learning, and big data since 2008, he finds it to be one of the most versatile, elegant, and productive programming languages.

Michael is currently based in London, where he leads the Python development team at Zoopla Property Group Plc.

Danijel Pančić is a JavaScript ninja and a passionate Django enthusiast. He is currently working at Bitstamp as a senior developer. He also works on various projects, including online games, and experiments with new approaches and techniques in search of better ways to achieve the desired results. You can find him at http://www.panco.si/.

Martin Pernica is currently a lead programmer and a cofounder of a new game studio called Soulbound Games in Czech Republic. He started programming very young on old PCs and, after that, he started working mainly as a web developer on PHP, Python, and Ruby for various companies. After some years of web development, Martin switched to the game development industry and started his own game studio. He also started teaching at local universities on mobile, web, and game development. He always tries to look under the hood of problems and challenges and then solves and optimizes them, which is still his passion.

Vikash Verma is a young and enthusiastic software professional who has had a wide exposure to open source technologies. His experience involves both client-side programming and server-side programming through Python, Django, and many other demanding technologies.

He has been a vital part of interesting projects from start-ups to leading IT companies as an individual leader. He has experience in the fields of data analytics, web crawling, web scraping, web application development, automation, ETL, and many more technical tracks.

I would like to thank my family and peers who always inspired me to be a go-getter. Not to mention the support and motivation I get from my soul mate, Smriti, who ensures that my work and life are in perfect balance with each other.

www.PacktPub.com

Support files, eBooks, discount offers, and more

For support files and downloads related to your book, please visit www.PacktPub.com.

Did you know that Packt offers eBook versions of every book published, with PDF and ePub files available? You can upgrade to the eBook version at www.PacktPub.com and as a print book customer, you are entitled to a discount on the eBook copy. Get in touch with us at service@packtpub.com for more details.

At www.PacktPub.com, you can also read a collection of free technical articles, sign up for a range of free newsletters and receive exclusive discounts and offers on Packt books and eBooks.

https://www2.packtpub.com/books/subscription/packtlib

Do you need instant solutions to your IT questions? PacktLib is Packt's online digital book library. Here, you can search, access, and read Packt's entire library of books.

Why subscribe?

- Fully searchable across every book published by Packt
- Copy and paste, print, and bookmark content
- On demand and accessible via a web browser

Free access for Packt account holders

If you have an account with Packt at www.PacktPub.com, you can use this to access PacktLib today and view 9 entirely free books. Simply use your login credentials for immediate access.

Table of Contents

Preface

Django, written in Python, is a web application framework designed to build complex web applications quickly without any hassle. It loosely follows the MVC pattern and adheres to the Don't Repeat ourself principle, which makes a database-driven application efficient and highly scalable, and is by far the most popular and mature Python web framework.

This book is a manual that will help you build a simple yet an effective Django web application. It starts by introducing Django to you and teaches you how to set it up and code simple programs. You will then learn to build your first Twitter-like application. Later on, you will be introduced to hashtags, Ajax (to enhance the user interface), and tweets. You will then move on to create an administration interface, learn database connectivity, and use third-party libraries. Then, you will learn to debug and deploy Django projects and will also get a glimpse of Django with AngularJS and Elasticsearch. By the end of this book, you will be able to leverage the Django framework to develop a fully functional web application with minimal effort.

What this book covers

Chapter 1, Introduction to Django, gives you an introduction to MVC web development frameworks and the history of Django and explains why Python and Django are the best tools to use to achieve the aim of this book.

Chapter 2, Getting Started, shows you how to set up our development environment on Unix/Linux, Windows, and Mac OS X. We will also see how to create our first project and connect it to a database.

Chapter 3, Code Style in Django, covers all the basic topics that you need to follow for building a website, such as coding practices for better Django web development, which IDE you should use, and version control.

Chapter 4, Building an Application Like Twitter, takes you through a tour of the main Django components and develops a working prototype for your Twitter application.

Chapter 5, Introducing Hashtags, teaches you how to design the algorithm to build a hashtag model and the mechanism to use a hashtag in your post.

Chapter 6, Enhancing the User Interface with AJAX, will help you enhance the UI experience using Ajax with Django.

Chapter 7, Following and Commenting, shows you how to create login, logout, and registration page templates. It will also show you how to allow another user to follow you and how to display the most followed user.

Chapter 8, Creating an Administration Interface, shows you the features of administrator interface using Django's inbuilt features and how we can show tweets in a customized way with a sidebar or pagination enabled.

Chapter 9, Extending and Deploying, prepares your application for deployment into a production environment by utilizing various features of the Django framework. It also shows you how to add support for multiple languages, improve performance by caching, automate testing, and configure the project for a production environment.

Chapter 10, Extending Django, speaks about how to improve the various aspects of your application, mainly performance and localization. It also teaches you how to deploy your project on a production server.

Chapter 11, Database Connectivity, covers the various forms of database connectivity, such as MySQL, NoSQL, PostgreSQL, and so on, which is required for any database-based application.

Chapter 12, Using Third-party Packages, talks about open source and how to use and implement open source third-party packages in your project.

Chapter 13, The Art of Debugging, shows you how to log and debug your code for better and efficient coding practice.

Chapter 14, Deploying Django Projects, shows you how to move a Django project from development to a production environment and the things that need to be taken care of before you go live.

Chapter 15, What's Next?, will take you to the next level where you will be introduced to the two most important and preferred components, AngularJS and Elasticsearch, used in the Django project.

What you need for this book

For this book, you will need the latest (preferably) Ubuntu/Windows/Mac operation system running on your PC/laptop with Python version 2.7.X installed.

In addition to this, you need Django 1.7.x and any one of your favorite text editors, such as Sublime Text editor, Notepad++, Vim, Eclipse, and so on.

Who this book is for

This book is for web developers who want to get started with Django for web development. Basic knowledge of Python programming is required, but no knowledge of Django is expected.

Conventions

In this book, you will find a number of text styles that distinguish between different kinds of information. Here are some examples of these styles and an explanation of their meaning.

Code words in text, database table names, folder names, filenames, file extensions, pathnames, dummy URLs, user input, and Twitter handles are shown as follows: "The username variable is the owner of the tweets that we want to see."

A block of code is set as follows:

```python
#!/usr/bin/env python
import os
import sys
if __name__ == "__main__":
    os.environ.setdefault("DJANGO_SETTINGS_MODULE",
    "django_mytweets.settings")
    from django.core.management import execute_from_command_line
    execute_from_command_line(sys.argv)
```

Any command-line input or output is written as follows:

```
Python 2.7.6 (default, Mar 22 2014, 22:59:56)
[GCC 4.8.2] on linux2
Type "help", "copyright", "credits" or "license" for more information.
```

New terms and **important words** are shown in bold. Words that you see on the screen, for example, in menus or dialog boxes, appear in the text like this: " In that link, we will find download button, after clicking on download, click on **Download Bootstrap**."

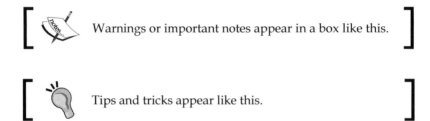

> Warnings or important notes appear in a box like this.

> Tips and tricks appear like this.

Reader feedback

Feedback from our readers is always welcome. Let us know what you think about this book—what you liked or disliked. Reader feedback is important for us as it helps us develop titles that you will really get the most out of.

To send us general feedback, simply e-mail feedback@packtpub.com, and mention the book's title in the subject of your message.

If there is a topic that you have expertise in and you are interested in either writing or contributing to a book, see our author guide at www.packtpub.com/authors.

Customer support

Now that you are the proud owner of a Packt book, we have a number of things to help you to get the most from your purchase.

Downloading the example code

You can download the example code files from your account at http://www.packtpub.com for all the Packt Publishing books you have purchased. If you purchased this book elsewhere, you can visit http://www.packtpub.com/support and register to have the files e-mailed directly to you.

Errata

Although we have taken every care to ensure the accuracy of our content, mistakes do happen. If you find a mistake in one of our books—maybe a mistake in the text or the code—we would be grateful if you could report this to us. By doing so, you can save other readers from frustration and help us improve subsequent versions of this book. If you find any errata, please report them by visiting http://www.packtpub. com/submit-errata, selecting your book, clicking on the **Errata Submission Form** link, and entering the details of your errata. Once your errata are verified, your submission will be accepted and the errata will be uploaded to our website or added to any list of existing errata under the Errata section of that title.

To view the previously submitted errata, go to https://www.packtpub.com/books/ content/support and enter the name of the book in the search field. The required information will appear under the **Errata** section.

Piracy

Piracy of copyrighted material on the Internet is an ongoing problem across all media. At Packt, we take the protection of our copyright and licenses very seriously. If you come across any illegal copies of our works in any form on the Internet, please provide us with the location address or website name immediately so that we can pursue a remedy.

Please contact us at copyright@packtpub.com with a link to the suspected pirated material.

We appreciate your help in protecting our authors and our ability to bring you valuable content.

Questions

If you have a problem with any aspect of this book, you can contact us at questions@packtpub.com, and we will do our best to address the problem.

1
Introduction to Django

Welcome to version 2.0 of Development with Django!

Django is a web development framework, and web development is a skill. To master any skill one can follow the famous "10,000 hours" rule, which says that if you practice anything for that amount of time you will certainly become an expert at it. But that's a lot of time, and without a proper plan, this can go wrong. Terribly wrong.

So, is there any better way to achieve your goal? Yes! Break the skill you want to learn into smaller subskills and then master them one at a time. (Programmers call this the "divide and conquer" rule.) You will need to identify the most important subskills by researching them. The more the frequent mentions of the subskill, the more important it becomes to master.

As you have decided to learn a new skill, as the author of this book, I request that you make a commitment, that you will stick with this book in the early frustrating hours. Frustration happens when you are learning a new thing, and trust me on this: when you feel it's too simple, you are doing it right.

In this chapter, we will cover the following topics:

- Why web development in the first place?
- What has changed in web development
- The MVC pattern in web development
- Why Django
- Inside Django

Why web development in the first place?

A website makes the first impression about the company or product directly on a global audience. Every startup now has a website, which helps to pitch their idea to their potential clients or investors.

Everything is online now, so instead of just sitting and watching the change, why not participate and learn to code it? Learning web development is one of the most valuable investments you can make with your time. It will not only benefit you by getting you a better job, but you will also be able to code your idea into a prototype in a very simple and straightforward manner.

Must-have ingredients for web development include user interface and user experience, but they are unfortunately out of the scope of this book.

What has changed in web development

Web development has made great progress during the last few years. Some of the improvements are listed as follows:

- **JavaScript**: Evolved from writing complex selectors to manipulating **Document Object Model (DOM)**. Libraries such as **jQuery** and **AngularJs** have made frontend dynamics much simpler. JavaScript has even evolved to build a production-ready server-side framework called **node.js**.

- **Browsers**: Evolved from being as simplistic as breaking the page across browsers to now intelligently restoring the connection, telling you which tab is playing music, or flawlessly rendering a real-time game.

- **Open source**: Using code written by someone else has finally become preferable than writing your own code. This helped a lot of projects to stop reinventing the wheel, **Django** being one of the best examples.

- **API as spinal cord**: Web technologies today might not be the same tomorrow, or data might not be represented in the same way or in the same place tomorrow. In other words, more devices will come with different screen sizes. Therefore, its always best to have text separated from visuals.

- **User Interface**: In the past, the precious time of the development team was consumed by User Interface design. But frameworks such as **Bootstrap** and **Foundation** have made web development a lot easier.

- **Agile development**: Moving fast in the development cycle is acceptable to most startup companies. The complete requirement is never asked for at the beginning of the software development cycle. Therefore, continuous customer or stakeholder involvement is very important. The Django framework is the most suitable framework for this kind of development. As Django's slogan says, "*the web framework for perfectionists with deadlines*".

- **Evolution of cloud computing**: This has played a significant role at the hosting end of web applications and enables faster, more reliable, and cheaper solutions for getting online.

- **Birth of NoSQL**: Cutting costs much further, NoSQL gave freedoms such as **Store it Now, Find The Value Later** and **Store Anything Together** to developers being cloud friendly and more fault tolerant.

The MVC pattern in web development

In this book, you will learn about employing a **Model-View-Controller** (**MVC**) web framework called Django, which is written in **Python**, a powerful and popular programming language.

MVC works on the idea of separate presentation. The idea behind separated presentation is to make a clear division between domain objects that model our perception of the real world and presentation objects that are the **user interface** (**UI**) elements we see on the screen. Domain objects should be completely self-contained and should work without reference to the presentation or data-handling logic (controller). They should also be able to support multiple presentations, possibly simultaneously.

The benefits of this pattern are obvious. With it, designers can work on the interface without worrying about data storage or management. And developers are able to program the logic of data handling without getting into the details of presentation. As a result, the MVC pattern quickly found its way into web languages, and serious web developers started to embrace it over previous techniques.

This book emphasizes on utilizing Django and Python to create a Web 2.0 microblogging web application with many common features found in today's Web 2.0 sites. The book follows a tutorial style to introduce concepts and explain solutions to problems. It is not meant to be a reference manual for Python or Django, for both have plenty of resources already. The book only assumes working knowledge of standard web technologies (HTML and CSS) and the Python programming language. Django, on the other hand, will be explained as we build features throughout the chapters, until we realize our goal of having a working Web 2.0 application.

Multilingual support

Django supports multilingual websites through its built-in internationalization system. This can be very valuable for those working on websites with more than one language. The system makes translating the interface a very simple task.

So, to conclude, Django provides a set of integrated and mature components, with excellent documentation, at `http://www.djangoproject.com/documentation/`.

Thanks to its large community of developers and users, there has never been a better time to start learning a web development framework!

Why Django?

Since the spread of the MVC pattern into web development, and unlike most of the other languages, Python has enjoyed quite a few choices when it comes to web frameworks. Although choosing one from many can be confusing at first, having several competing frameworks can only be a good thing for the Python community.

Django is one of the available frameworks for Python, so the question is: what sets it apart to become the topic of this book?

First of all, Django provides a set of tightly integrated components. All of these components are developed by the Django team itself. Django was originally developed as an in-house framework to manage a series of news-oriented websites. Later, its code was released on the Internet and the Django team continued its development using the open source model. Because of its roots, Django's components were designed for integration, reusability, and speed from the start.

Django's database component, the Object-relational Mapper (ORM), provides a bridge between the data model and the database engine. It supports a large set of database systems, and switching from one engine to another is a matter of changing a configuration file. This gives the developer great flexibility if a decision is made to change from one database engine to another. If you are in trouble, you can find the driver (binary Python package) here: `http://www.lfd.uci.edu/~gohlke/pythonlibs/`.

In addition, Django provides a neat development environment. It comes with a lightweight web server for development and testing. When debugging mode is enabled, Django provides very thorough and detailed error messages with a lot of debugging information. All of this makes isolating and fixing bugs very easy.

Django supports multilingual websites through its built-in internationalization system. This can be very valuable for those working on websites with more than one language. The system makes translating the interface a very simple task.

The standard features expected of a web framework are all available in Django. These include the following:

- A template and text-filtering engine with simple but extensible syntax
- A form generation and validation API
- An extensible authentication system
- A caching system for speeding up the performance of applications
- A feed framework for generating RSS feeds

Even though Django does not provide a JavaScript library to simplify working with Ajax, choosing one and integrating it with Django is a straightforward matter, as we will see in later chapters.

So, to conclude, Django provides a set of integrated and mature components with excellent documentation, thanks to its large community of developers and users. With Django available, there has never been a better time to start learning a web development framework!

Inside Django

We will mention some important reasons why we use Django for better web development. Some of the most important features are explained in the following subsections.

Django is mature

Many corporations are directly using Django in their production and with constant contributions from developers around the world. Some famous sites include **Pinterest** and **Quora**. It has established itself as the perfect web development framework.

Batteries included

Django follows Python's **batteries included** philosophy, which means Django comes with many extra features and options that are important in solving common problems faced during web development.

Tight integration between the component and modular framework

Django is very flexible in terms of its integration with their party module. The chances of there existing a popular project (for example, **mongoDB** in database domain or **SocialAuth** in **OpenID** main) that does have an **Appliaction Program Interface** (**API**) or complete plugin for Django integration are very few.

Object-relational mapper

This is one of the most important parts of the Django project. Django's database component, the ORM, provides a bridge between the data model and the database engine. The ORM layer provides features such as encapsulation, portability, safety, and expressiveness to Django's **Modal Class**, which are mapped to the configured database of choice.

Clean URL design

The URL system in Django is very flexible and powerful. It lets you define patterns for the URLs in your application and to define Python functions to handle each pattern.

This enables developers to create URLs that are both human-friendly (avoiding URL ending patterns such as `.php`, `.aspx`, and so on) and search engine-friendly.

Automatic administration interface

Django comes with an administration interface that is ready to be used. This interface makes the management of your application's data a breeze. It is also highly flexible and customizable.

Advanced development environment

In addition, Django provides a neat development environment. It comes with a lightweight web server for development and testing. When the debugging mode is enabled, Django provides very thorough and detailed error messages with a lot of debugging information. All of this makes isolating and fixing bugs very easy.

What's new in Django 1.6 and 1.7

With the latest release, version 1.6, Django has brought some major changes and a few of them are as follows:

- Python 3 is officially supported with this release, which means it is stable and can be used in production.
- The layout is simple. New defaults have been added, the Django Admin template has been added by default, and the Sites package has been removed.
- Clickjacking prevention has been added.
- The default Database is SQLite3.
- As old APIs are deprecated, the biggest change is that the transactions have been improved. The DB layer auto-commit is enabled by default.

- The DB connection in this release is persistant. Until Django 1.5, a new connection was made for every HTTP request, but from 1.6, the same connection will be reused between requests.

- Time zone defaults to UTC.

- Simple application integration.

- Scalable.

- Powerful configuration mechanism.

- There is no need to have a `models.py` file if you don't have a model.

- A new method has been added for its subclasses.

- It allows a cursor to be used as a context manager.

- Many features have been added for internationalization, form, and file upload.

- It has a better feature to avoid CSRF.

- Apart from these, a binary field has been introduced, as have HTML 5 input fields (e-mail, URL, and number).

  You can read the newly added features in detail here: `https://docs.djangoproject.com/en/1.7/releases/1.7/`.

Supported databases

Django has a great and powerful respect for data. Model the data correctly, and the rest of the site will just fall into place. With the convention that Django was designed for relational database, unofficial NoSQL implementation exists for Django as well. Here is the list of relational databases that Django supports:

- **SQL**: SQLite, MySQL, and PostgreSQL.

- **SQLite**: This is the default database for Django applications and is mainly used for testing purposes.

- **PostgreSQL**: This is an open source, widely used RDBS. We will build our microblogging example based on this.

 MySQL and PostgreSQL are the two most common databases used in the Django community, and PostgreSQL is the most popular in the Django community.

- **NoSQL**: How about having a single table for your data, whether it contains user's information or their comments, and so on? In other words, how about having no rules for the structure of inserted data or nesting data, like Articles with subdocument array with comments? Sound strange? Yes, it is. In the early days, people were using the one and only relational database concept, but since the dawn of the cloud computing era, programmers love to implement NoSQL architecture for every possible single project. It doesn't store and doesn't follow any normal forms. You can't use joins, but there are many other advantages of using it.

  App Engine, MongoDB, Elasticsearch, Cassandra, and Redis are some famous NoSQL DBs that Django supports. MongoDB is getting popular among the Django community these days.

- **MongoDB**: This is an open source, widely used NoSQL document-based database. We will be using it for creating our second small application for URL shortener.

In this book, we will mainly deal with three databases from the preceding list, but implementation of others can be almost identical with minimal configuration changes.

There are many famous websites powered by Django. Some of them are as follows:

- **Pinterest**: A content sharing service, especially for images and videos
- **Disqus**: A blog comment hosting service
- **Quora**: A question-and-answer based website
- **Bitbucket**: A free code hosting site for Git and mercurial
- **Mozilla Firefox**: The **Mozilla** support page

What you will learn using this book

This book focuses on building a microblogging web application and adding common Web 2.0 features to it. Some of these features are as follows:

- **Creating Django view, model, and controller**: This ideally deals with learning the Django framework, that is, how requests are handled on controllers to render the view after making the required manipulations with models that are stored on the database.

- **Tags and tag clouds**: In the microblogging site project, every message will have a hashtag in it (a tag starting with **#**). The mapping of these tags will be dealt with in this section.

- **Content customization and searching**: Searching for messages based on keywords or hashtags.
- **Ajax enhancements**: Using Ajax for autocomplete during search or tagging, and making edits in place for saved messages or tags.
- **Friend networks**: Listing all the friends of the profile and calculating other vital statistics.

Instead of concentrating on teaching various Django features, this book uses a tutorial style to teach how to implement these features using Django. Thus, it works as a complementary resource to the official Django documentation, which is freely available online.

Interested? Great! Prepare for the ride, as I guarantee that it will be both fun and interesting.

Summary

In this chapter, we have learned why web development is getting an edge and what has changed in the web technologies domain; how to leverage new web technologies using the Python and Django frameworks; what Django actually is and what we can achieve using it; and finally, the different kind of databases that support Django.

In the next chapter, we will cover the installation of Python and Django on various operating systems, such as Windows, Linux, and Mac, and setting up our first project using the Django platform.

2
Getting Started

Python and Django are available for multiple platforms. In this chapter, we will see how to set up our development environment on UNIX/Linux, Windows, and Mac OS X. We will also see how to create our first project and connect it to a database.

We will cover the following topics in this chapter:

- Installing Python
- Installing Django
- Installing the database system
- Creating your first project
- Setting up the database
- Launching the development server

Installing the required software

Our development environment consists of Python, Django, and a database system. In the following sections, we will see how to install these software packages.

Installing Python

Django is written in Python, so naturally, the first step in setting up our development environment is to install Python. Python is available for a variety of operating systems, and installing Python is no different from installing other software packages. The procedure, however, depends on your operating system.

For installation, you need to make sure that you get a recent version of Python. Django requires Python 2.7 or higher. The latest version of Python is 3.4.2 for 3.x and 2.7.9 for 2.x versions.

Please read the section relevant to your operating system for installation instructions.

Installing Python on Windows

Python has a standard installer for Windows users. Simply head to `https://www.python.org/download/` and download the latest version. Next, double-click on the `.exe` or `.msi` file and follow the installation instructions step by step. The graphical installer will guide you through the installation process and create shortcuts to Python executables in the Start menu.

Once done with the installation, we need to add the Python directory to the system path so that we can access Python while using the Command Prompt. To do so, follow these steps:

1. Open the Control Panel.

2. Double-click on the **System and Security** icon or text and then look for **System** (as seen in Windows 7), as shown in the following screenshot:

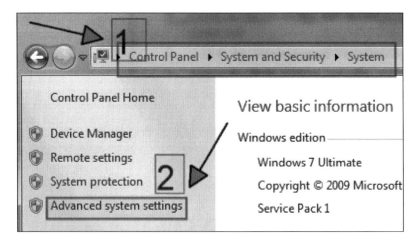

3. Click on **Advanced System Settings** and a pop-up window will appear.

4. Click on the **Environment Variables** button and a new dialog box will open.

5. Select the **Path** system variable and edit it.

6. Append the path to where you installed Python as its value (the default path is usually `c:\PythonXX`, where `XX` is your Python version), as shown in the following screenshot:

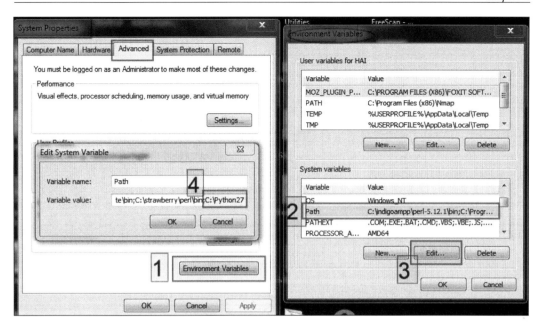

If you want to test your installation, open the **Run** dialog box, type `python`, and hit the *Enter* button. The Python interactive shell should open.

 Don't forget to separate the new path from the one before it with a semicolon (;).

Installing Python on Unix/Linux

If you use Linux or another flavor of Unix, chances are that you already have Python installed. To check, open a terminal, type `python`, and hit the *Enter* button. If you see the Python interactive shell, you already have Python installed. You should get the following output after typing `python` in the terminal:

```
Python 2.7.6 (default, Mar 22 2014, 22:59:56)
[GCC 4.8.2] on linux2
Type "help", "copyright", "credits" or "license" for more information.
```

```
● ○ ○   ratan@lenovo: ~
ratan@lenovo:~$ python
Python 2.7.6 (default, Mar 22 2014, 22:59:56)
[GCC 4.8.2] on linux2
Type "help", "copyright", "credits" or "license" for more information.
>>> █
```

The first line of the output indicates the version installed on your system (2.7.6, here).

If you receive an error message instead of seeing the preceding output, or have an old version of Python, please read on.

It is recommended that Unix/Linux users install and update Python through the system's package manager. Although the actual details vary from system to system, it won't be any different from installing any other package.

For APT-based Linux distributions, such as **Debian** and **Ubuntu**, open a terminal and type the following:

```
$ sudo apt-get update
$ sudo apt-get install python
```

If you have **Synaptic Package Manager**, simply search for Python, mark its package for installation, and click on the **Apply** button.

Users of other Linux distributions should check their system documentation for information on how to use the package manager to install packages.

Installing Python on Mac OS X

Mac OS X comes with Python preinstalled. However, due to Apple's release cycle, it's often an old version. If you start the Python interactive shell and find a version older than 2.3, please visit http://www.python.org/download/mac/ and download a newer installer for your version of Mac OS X.

Now that Python is up and running, we are almost ready. Next, we will install **virtualenv**.

Installing virtualenv

With virtualenv you can create an isolated Python environment. It's not much of a need in the beginning, but it's a lifesaver for dependency management (for example, if one of your web applications requires one version of the library and another application, due to some legacy or compatibility issues, requires another version of the same library, or if changes made in one library or application break the rest of the applications).

Virtualenv can be used to avoid such problematic situations. It will create its own environment so that it will not mess with your global settings. It usually creates its own directories and shared libraries to make virtualenv work without any external interference. If you have **pip 1.3** or greater, install it globally. You can use the following command to install virtualenv:

```
$ [sudo] pip install virtualenv
```

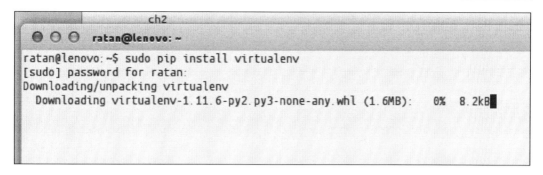

Once it has been downloaded fully, virtualenv will look like this:

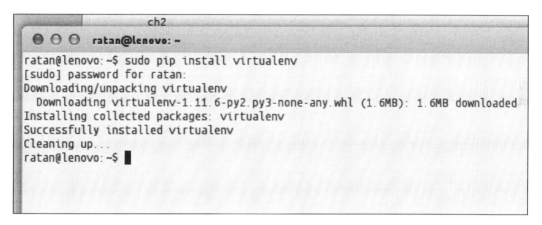

 If you have not installed pip yet, you can install it with
`sudo apt-get install python-pip`.

That's all! Now you can create your virtual environment by using the following command:

```
$ virtualenv ENV
```

```
ratan@lenovo:~$
ratan@lenovo:~$ virtualenv ENV
New python executable in ENV/bin/python
Installing setuptools, pip...done.
ratan@lenovo:~$ █
```

Virtualenv has very detailed online documentation, which you must follow for any kind of issue faced while using virtualenv. The following lines are an excerpt from that online documentation:

> *This creates* ENV/lib/pythonX.X/site-packages, *where any libraries you install will go. It also creates* ENV/bin/python, *which is a Python interpreter that uses this environment. Anytime you use that interpreter (including when a script has* #!/path/to/ENV/bin/python *in it) the libraries in that environment will be used.*

We can find the virtualenv online documentation at https://pypi.python.org/pypi/virtualenv/1.8.2.

A new virtualenv folder also includes the pip installer, so you can use the ENV/bin/pip command to install additional packages into the environment.

 Activate script: In a newly created virtual environment there will be a bin/activate shell script. For Windows systems, activate scripts are provided for **CMD** and **Powershell**.

You can read more at:

http://virtualenv.readthedocs.org/en/latest/virtualenv.html

On Unix systems, we can use the following command to activate the virtualenv script:

```
$ source bin/activate
```

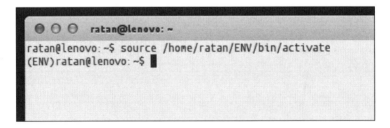

On Windows, we can use the following command to activate the virtualenv script on the command prompt:

```
: > \path\to\env\Scripts\activate
```

Type `deactivate` to undo the changes, as shown in the following screenshot:

```
●  ○  ○    ratan@lenovo: ~
ratan@lenovo: ~$ source /home/ratan/ENV/bin/activate
(ENV)ratan@lenovo: ~$ deactivate
ratan@lenovo: ~$ █
```

This changes your `$PATH` variable.

To know more about activate scripts, such as which environment you are using or whether you need to activate the script, please visit the following link:

`http://virtualenv.readthedocs.org/en/latest/virtualenv.html`

Installing Django

Installing Django is very easy, but it depends slightly on your operating system. Since Python is a platform-independent language, Django has one package that works everywhere regardless of your operating system.

To download Django, head to `http://www.djangoproject.com/download/` and grab the latest official version. The code in this book is developed on Django 1.7 (the latest as of this writing), but most of the code should run on later official releases. Next, follow the instructions related to your platform.

Django compatibility with operating systems – Windows versus Linux

There are a few points you need to know for when you deal with operating systems. Many packages and settings need to be tweaked before running Django without any flaws. Let's take a look at them:

- Some Python packages cannot be installed correctly, or at all in Windows; if they can, they will create a lot of hassle when you do

- If you need to deploy your Django application, it makes more sense to use a Unix-flavored system, simply because 99 percent of the time, your deployment environment is the same

- If your applications are complex, it's easier to get the required dependencies, be they extensions in Linux, libraries, and so on

Installing Django on Windows

After you have downloaded the Django archive, extract it to the C drive and open the command prompt (from **Start** | **Accessories**). Now, change the current directory to where you extracted Django from by issuing the following command:

```
c:\>cd c:\Django-x.xx
```

Here, x.xx is your Django version.

Next, install Django by running the following command (you will need administrative privileges for this):

 If you do not have a program to handle the .tar.gz files on your system, I recommend using **7-Zip**, which is free and available at http://www.7-zip.org/.

```
c:\Django-x.xx>python setup.py install
```

If, for some reason, the preceding instructions didn't work, you can manually copy the django folder inside the archive to the Lib\site-packages folder located in the Python installation directory. This will do the job of running the setup.py installation command.

The last step is copying the django-admin.py file from Django-x.xx\django\bin to somewhere in your system path, such as c:\windows or the folder where you installed Python.

Once done, you can safely remove the c:\Django-x.xx folder because it is no longer needed.

That's it! To test your installation, open a command prompt and type the following command:

```
c:\>django-admin.py --version
```

If you see the current version of Django printed on screen, then everything is set.

Installing Django on Unix/Linux and Mac OS X

The installation instructions for all Unix and Linux systems are the same. You need to run the following commands in the directory where the Django-x.xx.tar.gz archive is located. These commands will extract the archive and install Django for you:

```
$ tar xfz Django-x.xx.tar.gz
$ cd Django-x.xx
$ sudo python setup.py install
```

The preceding instructions should work on any Unix/Linux system, as well as Mac OS X. However, it may be easier to install Django through your system's package manager if it has a package for Django. Ubuntu has one; so to install Django on Ubuntu, simply look for a package called `python-django` in Synaptic, or run the following command:

```
$ sudo apt-get install python-django
```

You can test your installation by running the following command:

```
$ django-admin.py --version
```

If you see the current version of Django printed on screen, then everything is set.

Installing a database system

While Django does not require a database to function, the application we are going to develop does. So, in the final step of software installation, we are going to make sure that we have a database system for handling our data.

It's worth noting that Django supports several database engines: **MySQL**, **PostgreSQL**, **MS SQL Server**, **Oracle**, and **SQLite**. Interestingly, however, you only need to learn one API in order to use any of these database systems. This is possible because of Django's database layer that abstracts access to the database system. We will learn about this later, but, for now, you only need to know that, regardless of what database system you choose, you will be able to run Django applications developed in this book (or elsewhere) without modification.

If you have Python 2.7 or higher, you don't need to install anything. Python 2.7 comes with the SQLite database management system contained in a module named `sqlite3`. Unlike client-server database systems, SQLite does not require a resident process in memory and it stores the database in a single file, which makes it ideal for our development environment.

If you don't have Python 2.7, you can install the Python module for SQLite manually by downloading it at `http://www.pysqlite.org/` (Windows users) or through your package manager (Unix/Linux).

On the other hand, if you already have another Django-supported database server installed on your system, you can also use this. We will tell Django what database system to use by editing a configuration file, as we will see in later sections.

Don't I need Apache or some other web server?

Django comes with its own web server, which we are going to use during the development phase because it is lightweight and comes pre-configured for Django. However, Django does support Apache and other popular web servers, such as light tpd, nginx, and so on. We will see how to configure Django for Apache when we prepare our application for deployment later in this book.

The same applies to the database manager. During the development phase, we will use SQLite because it is easy to set up, but when we deploy the application, we will switch to a database server such as MySQL.

As I said earlier, regardless of what components we use, our code will stay the same; Django handles all the communication with the web and database servers for us.

Creating your first project

Now with the software we need in place, the time has come for the fun part–creating our first Django project!

If you recall from the Django installation section, we used a command called `django-admin.py` to test our installation. This utility is the heart of Django's project management facilities, as it enables the user to do a range of project management tasks, including these:

- Creating a new project
- Creating and managing the project's database
- Validating the current project and testing for errors
- Starting the development web server

We will see how to use some of these tasks in the rest of this chapter.

Creating an empty project

To create your first Django project, open a terminal (or Command Prompt for Windows users; that is, **Start** | **Run** | **cmd**), and type the following command. Then, hit *Enter*.

```
$ django-admin.py startproject django_bookmarks
```

This command will make a folder named `django_bookmarks` in the current directory and create the initial directory structure inside it. Let's see what kind of files are created:

```
django_bookmarks/
|-- django_bookmarks
|    |-- __init__.py
|    |-- settings.py
|    |-- urls.py
|    `-- wsgi.py
`-- manage.py
```

Here is a quick explanation of what these files are:

- `__init__.py`: Django projects are Python packages, and this file is required to tell Python that this folder is to be treated as a package.

  A package in Python's terminology is a collection of modules, and they are used to group similar files together and prevent naming conflicts.

- `manage.py`: This is another utility script used to manage our project. You can think of it as your project's version of the `django-admin.py` file. Actually, both `django-admin.py` and `manage.py` share the same backend code.

- `settings.py`: This is the main configuration file for your Django project. In it, you can specify a variety of options, including the database settings, site language(s), what Django features need to be enabled, and so on. Various sections of this file will be explained as we progress with building our application during the next chapters, but for this chapter, we will only see how to enter the database settings.

- `url.py`: This is another configuration file. You can think of it as a mapping between the URLs and Python functions that handle them. This file is one of Django's powerful features, and we will see how to utilize it in the next chapter.

When we start writing code for our application, we will create new files inside the project's folder; so the folder also serves as a container for our code.

Now that you have a general idea of the structure of a Django project, let's configure our database system.

Setting up the database

In this section, we will start working with setting up the database with various options and configuration files.

Okay, now that we have a source code editor ready, let's open the `settings.py` file in the project folder and see what it contains:

```
"""
Django settings for django_bookmarks project.

For more information on this file, see
https://docs.djangoproject.com/en/1.7/topics/settings/

For the full list of settings and their values, see
https://docs.djangoproject.com/en/1.7/ref/settings/
"""

# Build paths inside the project like this: os.path.join(BASE_DIR,
...)
import os
BASE_DIR = os.path.dirname(os.path.dirname(__file__))


# Quick-start development settings - unsuitable for production
# See https://docs.djangoproject.com/en/1.7/howto/deployment/
checklist/

# SECURITY WARNING: keep the secret key used in production secret!
SECRET_KEY = ')9c8g--=vo2*rh$9f%=)=e+@%7e%xe8jptgpfe+(90t7uurfy0'

# SECURITY WARNING: don't run with debug turned on in production!
DEBUG = True

TEMPLATE_DEBUG = True

ALLOWED_HOSTS = []


# Application definition

INSTALLED_APPS = (
    'django.contrib.admin',
    'django.contrib.auth',
    'django.contrib.contenttypes',
    'django.contrib.sessions',
    'django.contrib.messages',
    'django.contrib.staticfiles',
)
```

```python
MIDDLEWARE_CLASSES = (
    'django.contrib.sessions.middleware.SessionMiddleware',
    'django.middleware.common.CommonMiddleware',
    'django.middleware.csrf.CsrfViewMiddleware',
    'django.contrib.auth.middleware.AuthenticationMiddleware',
    'django.contrib.auth.middleware.SessionAuthenticationMiddleware',
    'django.contrib.messages.middleware.MessageMiddleware',
    'django.middleware.clickjacking.XFrameOptionsMiddleware',
)


ROOT_URLCONF = 'django_bookmarks.urls'

WSGI_APPLICATION = 'django_bookmarks.wsgi.application'



# Database
# https://docs.djangoproject.com/en/1.7/ref/settings/#databases

DATABASES = {
    'default': {
        'ENGINE': 'django.db.backends.sqlite3',
        'NAME': os.path.join(BASE_DIR, 'db.sqlite3'),
    }
}

# Internationalization
# https://docs.djangoproject.com/en/1.7/topics/i18n/

LANGUAGE_CODE = 'en-us'

TIME_ZONE = 'UTC'

USE_I18N = True

USE_L10N = True

USE_TZ = True



# Static files (CSS, JavaScript, Images)
# https://docs.djangoproject.com/en/1.7/howto/static-files/

STATIC_URL = '/static/'
```

As you may have already noticed, the file contains a number of variables that control various aspects of the application. Entering a new value for a variable is as simple as doing a Python assignment statement. In addition, the file is extensively commented, and comments explain what variables control in detail.

What concerns us now is configuring the database. As mentioned before, Django supports several database systems, so first of all, we have to specify what database system we are going to use. This is controlled by the DATABASE_ENGINE variable. If you have SQLite installed, set the variable to 'sqlite3'. Otherwise, pick the value that matches your database engine from the comment next to the variable name.

Next is the database name. Keep the database name default, as it is. On the other hand, if you are using a database server, you need to do the following:

- Enter the relevant information for the database: username, password, host, and port. (SQLite does not require any of these.)
- Create the actual database inside the database server, as Django won't do this by itself. In MySQL, for example, this is done through the mysql command line utility or phpMyAdmin.

Finally, we will tell Django to populate the configured database with tables. Although we haven't created any tables for our data yet (and won't do so until the next chapter), Django requires several tables in the database for some of its features to function properly. Creating these tables is as easy as issuing the following command:

```
$ python manage.py syncdb
```

If everything is correct, status messages will scroll on the screen, indicating that tables are being created. When prompted for the superuser account, enter your preferred username, email, and password. If, on the other hand, the database is misconfigured, an error message will be printed to help you troubleshoot the issue.

With this done, we are ready to launch our application.

Using python manage.py

When running a command that starts with python manage.py, make sure that you are currently in the project's directory where manage.py is located.

Launching the development server

As discussed before, Django comes with a lightweight web server for developing and testing applications. This server is pre-configured to work with Django, and, more importantly, it restarts whenever you modify the code.

To start the server, run the following command:

```
$ python manage.py runserver
```

Next, open your browser and navigate to this URL: `http://localhost:8000/`. You should see a welcome message, as shown in the following screenshot:

Congratulations! You have created and configured your first Django project. This project will be the base on top of which we will build our bookmarking application. During the next chapter, we will start developing our application, and the page displayed by the web server will be replaced by something we wrote ourselves!

As you may have noticed, the web server runs on port 8000 by default. If you want to change the port, you can specify it on the command line by using the following command:

```
$ python manage.py runserver <port number>
```

Also, the development server is only accessible from the local machine by default. If you want to access the development server from another machine on your network, use the following command-line arguments:

```
$ python manage.py runserver 0.0.0.0:<port number>
```

Downloading the example code

You can download the example code files for all Packt books you have purchased from your account at http://www.packtpub.com. If you purchased this book elsewhere, you can visit http://www.packtpub.com/support and register to have the files e-mailed directly to you.

Summary

In this chapter, we have prepared our development environment, created our first project, and learned how to launch the Django development server. We learned how to install Django and virtualenv in Windows and Linux. We learned the basic mechanisms of how Django settings work and even learned how to install a database.

We are now ready to start building our social bookmarking application! The next chapter takes you through a tour of the main Django components and develops a working prototype for our bookmark sharing application. It's going to be a fun chapter with many new things to learn, so keep reading!

3
Code Style in Django

As you are coming from the Python background, you must already have written lots of code, and, of course have enjoyed it too.

Python code is easy to maintain and works on both small projects or in solving any competitive programming contest; you can do either by storing Python code locally or by storing it in a public folder for easier sharing. But, if you are working on a collaborative project, especially web development, then it makes everything different from other traditional coding. This not only needs discipline, like following the project's code syntax, but you may also end up writing extensive documentation for your code. While working with any version control tools, such as GIT, your commit messages (which play an important role in making it easier for other developers to understand what you have been working on or have completed) also broadcast the current progress of project.

This chapter will cover all the basic topics which you would require to follow, such as coding practices for better Django web development, which IDE to use, version control, and so on.

We will learn the following topics in this chapter:

- Django coding style
- Using IDE for Django web development
- Django project structure
- Best practices—using version control
- Django rescue team (where to ask Django questions)
- Faster web development—using Twitter-Bootstrap

This chapter is based on the important fact that code is read much more often than it is written. Thus, before you actually start building your projects, we suggest that you familiarize yourself with all the standard practices adopted by the Django community for web development.

Django coding style

Most of Django's important practices are based on Python. Though chances are you already know them, we will still take a break and write all the documented practices so that you know these concepts even before you begin. Of course, you can come back to this chapter for a quick look when you are building your projects.

To mainstream standard practices, Python enhancement proposals are made, and one such widely adopted standard practice for development is PEP8, the style guide for Python code–the best way to style the Python code authored by Guido van Rossum.

The documentation says, "PEP8 deals with semantics and conventions associated with Python docstrings." For further reading, please visit `http://legacy.python.org/dev/peps/pep-0008/`.

Understanding indentation in Python

When you are writing Python code, indentation plays a very important role. It acts as a block like in other languages, such as **C** or **Perl**. But it's always a matter of discussion amongst programmers whether we should use tabs or spaces, and, if space, how many–two or four or eight. Using four spaces for indentation is better than eight, and if there are a few more nested blocks, using eight spaces for each indentation may take up more characters than can be shown in single line. But, again, this is the programmer's choice.

The following is what incorrect indentation practices lead to:

```
>>> def a():
...     print "foo"
...         print "bar"
IndentationError: unexpected indent
```

So, which one we should use: tabs or spaces?

Choose any *one* of them, but never mix up tabs and spaces in the same project or else it will be a nightmare for maintenance. The most popular way of indention in Python is with spaces; tabs come in second. If any code you have encountered has a mixture of tabs and spaces, you should convert it to using spaces exclusively.

Doing indentation right – do we need four spaces per indentation level?

There has been a lot of confusion about it, as of course, Python's syntax is all about indentation. Let's be honest: in most cases, it is. So, what is highly recommended is to use four spaces per indentation level, and if you have been following the two-space method, stop using it. There is nothing wrong with it, but when you deal with multiple third party libraries, you might end up having a spaghetti of different versions, which will ultimately become hard to debug.

Now for indentation. When your code is in a continuation line, you should wrap it vertically aligned, or you can go in for a hanging indent. When you are using a hanging indent, the first line should not contain any argument and further indentation should be used to clearly distinguish it as a continuation line.

 A hanging indent (also known as a negative indent) is a style of indentation in which all lines are indented except for the first line of the paragraph. The preceding paragraph is the example of hanging indent.

The following example illustrates how you should use a proper indentation method while writing the code:

```
bar = some_function_name(var_first, var_second,
                                     var_third, var_fourth)
# Here indentation of arguments makes them grouped, and stand clear from
others.
def some_function_name(
        var_first, var_second, var_third,
        var_fourth):
    print(var_first)
# This example shows the hanging intent.
```

We do not encourage the following coding style, and it will not work in Python anyway:

```
# When vertical alignment is not used, Arguments on the first line are
forbidden
foo = some_function_name(var_first, var_second,
    var_third, var_fourth)
# Further indentation is required as indentation is not distinguishable
between arguments and source code.
def some_function_name(
    var_first, var_second, var_third,
    var_fourth):
    print(var_first)
```

Although extra indentation is not required, if you want to use extra indentation to ensure that the code will work, you can use the following coding style:

```
# Extra indentation is not necessary.
if (this
    and that):
    do_something()
```

> Ideally, you should limit each line to a maximum of 79 characters. It allows for a + or – character used for viewing difference using version control. It is even better to limit lines to 79 characters for uniformity across editors. You can use the rest of the space for other purposes.

The importance of blank lines

The importance of two blank lines and single blank lines are as follows:

- **Two blank lines**: A double blank lines can be used to separate top-level functions and the class definition, which enhances code readability.
- **Single blank lines**: A single blank line can be used in the use cases–for example, each function inside a class can be separated by a single line, and related functions can be grouped together with a single line. You can also separate the logical section of source code with a single line.

Importing a package

Importing a package is a direct implication of code reusability. Therefore, always place imports at the top of your source file, just after any module comments and document strings, and before the module's global and constants as variables. Each import should usually be on separate lines.

The best way to import packages is as follows:

```
import os
import sys
```

It is not advisable to import more than one package in the same line, for example:

```
import sys, os
```

You may import packages in the following fashion, although it is optional:

```
from django.http import Http404, HttpResponse
```

If your import gets longer, you can use the following method to declare them:

```
from django.http import (
Http404, HttpResponse, HttpResponsePermanentRedirect
)
```

Grouping imported packages

Package imports can be grouped in the following ways:

- **Standard library imports**: Such as `sys`, `os`, `subprocess`, and so on.

  ```
  import re
  import simplejson
  ```

- **Related third party imports**: These are usually downloaded from the Python cheese shop, that is, **PyPy** (using pip install). Here is an example:

  ```
  from decimal import *
  ```

- **Local application / library-specific imports**: This included the local modules of your projects, such as models, views, and so on.

  ```
  from models import ModelFoo
  from models import ModelBar
  ```

Naming conventions in Python/Django

Every programming language and framework has its own naming convention. The naming convention in Python/Django is more or less the same, but it is worth mentioning it here. You will need to follow this while creating a variable name or global variable name and when naming a class, package, modules, and so on.

This is the common naming convention that we should follow:

- **Name the variables proper**ly: Never use single characters, for example, 'x' or 'X' as variable names. It might be okay for your normal Python scripts, but when you are building a web application, you must name the variable properly as it determines the readability of the whole project.

- **Naming of packages and modules**: Lowercase and short names are recommended for modules. Underscores can be used if their use would improve readability. Python packages should also have short, all-lowercase names, although the use of underscores is discouraged.

- Since module names are mapped to file names (`models.py`, `urls.py`, and so on), it is important that module names be chosen to be fairly short as some file systems are case insensitive and truncate long names.

- **Naming a class**: Class names should follow the **CamelCase** naming convention, and classes for internal use can have a leading underscore in their name.

- **Global variable names**: First of all, you should avoid using global variables, but if you need to use them, prevention of global variables from getting exported can be done via __all__, or by defining them with a prefixed underscore (the old, conventional way).

- **Function names and method argument**: Names of functions should be in lowercase and separated by an underscore and `self` as the first argument to instantiate methods. For classes or methods, use CLS or the objects for initialization.

- **Method names and instance variables**: Use the function naming rules— lowercase with words separated by underscores as necessary to improve readability. Use one leading underscore only for non-public methods and instance variables.

Using IDE for faster development

There are many options on the market when it comes to source code editors. Some people prefer full-fledged IDEs, whereas others like simple text editors. The choice is totally yours; pick up whatever feels more comfortable. If you already use a certain program to work with Python source files, I suggest that you stick to it as it will work just fine with Django. Otherwise, I can make a couple of recommendations, such as these:

- **SublimeText**: This editor is lightweight and very powerful. It is available for all major platforms, supports syntax highlighting and code completion, and works well with Python. The editor is open source and you can find it at `http://www.sublimetext.com/`

- **PyCharm**: This, I would say, is most intelligent code editor of all and has advanced features, such as code refactoring and code analysis, which makes development cleaner. Features for Django include template debugging (which is a winner) and also quick documentation, so this look-up is a must for beginners. The community edition is free and you can sample a 30-day trial version before buying the professional edition.

Setting up your project with the Sublime text editor

Most of the examples that we will show you in this book will be written using **Sublime text editor**. In this section, we will show how to install and set up the Django project.

1. **Download and installation**: You can download Sublime from the download tab of the site `www.sublimetext.com`. Click on the downloaded file option to install.

2. **Setting up for Django**: Sublime has a very extensive plug-in ecosystem, which means that once you have downloaded the editor, you can install plug-ins for adding more features to it.

After successful installation, it will look like this:

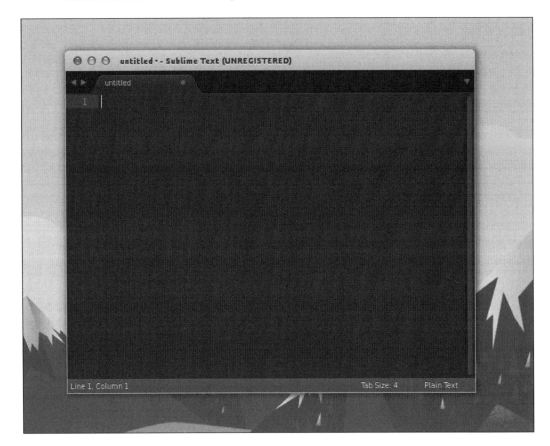

 Most important of all is **Package Control**, which is the manager for installing additional plugins directly from within Sublime. This will be your only manual installation of the package. It will take care of the rest of the package installation ahead.

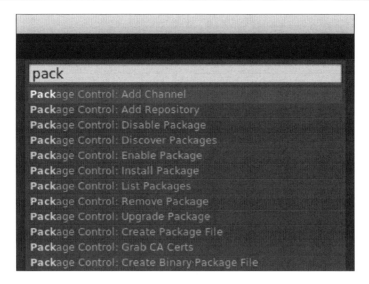

Some of the recommendations for Python development using Sublime are as follows:

- **Sublime Linter**: This gives instant feedback about the Python code as you write it. It also has PEP8 support; this plugin will highlight in real time the things we discussed about better coding in the previous section so that you can fix them.

- **Sublime CodeIntel**: This is maintained by the developer of **SublimeLint**. Sublime CodeIntel have some of advanced functionalities, such as directly go-to definition, intelligent code completion, and import suggestions.

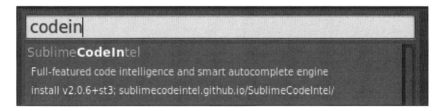

You can also explore other plugins for Sublime to increase your productivity.

Setting up the PyCharm IDE

You can use any of your favorite IDEs for Django project development. We will use pycharm IDE for this book. This IDE is recommended as it will help you at the time of debugging, using breakpoints that will save you a lot of time figuring out what actually went wrong.

Here is how to install and set up **pycharm** IDE for Django:

1. **Download and installation**: You can check the features and download the pycharm IDE from the following link:

   ```
   http://www.jetbrains.com/pycharm/
   ```

2. **Setting up for Django**: Setting up pycharm for Django is very easy. You just have to import the project folder and give the manage.py path, as shown in the following figure:

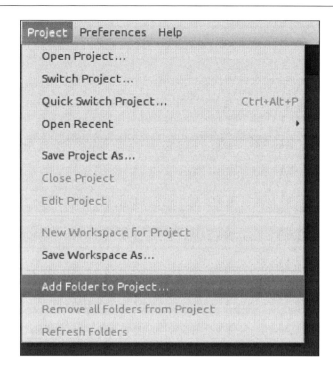

The Django project structure

The Django project structure has been changed in the 1.6 release version. Django (`django-admin.py`) also has a `startapp` command to create an application, so it is high time to tell you the difference between an application and a project in Django.

A **project** is a complete website or application, whereas an **application** is a small, self-contained Django application. An application is based on the principle that it should do one thing and do it right.

To ease out the pain of building a Django project right from scratch, Django gives you an advantage by auto-generating the basic project structure files from which any project can be taken forward for its development and feature addition.

Thus, to conclude, we can say that a project is a collection of applications, and an application can be written as a separate entity and can be easily exported to other applications for reusability.

To create your first Django project, open a terminal (or Command Prompt for Windows users), type the following command, and hit *Enter*:

```
$ django-admin.py startproject django_mytweets
```

This command will make a folder named `django_mytweets` in the current directory and create the initial directory structure inside it. Let's see what kind of files are created.

The new structure is as follows:

```
django_mytweets///
django_mytweets/
manage.py
```

This is the content of `django_mytweets/`:

```
django_mytweets/
__init__.py
settings.py
urls.py
wsgi.py
```

Here is a quick explanation of what these files are:

- `django_mytweets` (the outer folder): This folder is the project folder. Contrary to the earlier project structure in which the whole project was kept in a single folder, the new Django project structure somehow hints that every project is an application inside Django.

  This means that you can import other third party applications on the same level as the Django project. This folder also contains the `manage.py` file, which include all the project management settings.

- `manage.py`: This is utility script is used to manage our project. You can think of it as your project's version of `django-admin.py`. Actually, both `django-admin.py` and `manage.py` share the same backend code.

 Further clarification about the settings will be provided when are going to tweak the changes.

Let's have a look at the `manage.py` file:

```python
#!/usr/bin/env python
import os
import sys
if __name__ == "__main__":
    os.environ.setdefault("DJANGO_SETTINGS_MODULE", "django_
mytweets.settings")
    from django.core.management import execute_from_command_line
    execute_from_command_line
    execute_from_command_line(sys.argv)
```

The source code of the `manage.py` file will be self-explanatory once you read the following code explanation.

```
#!/usr/bin/env python
```

The first line is just the declaration that the following file is a Python file, followed by the import section in which `os` and `sys` modules are imported. These modules mainly contain system-related operations.

```
import os
import sys
```

The next piece of code checks whether the file is executed by the main function, which is the first function to be executed, and then loads the Django setting module to the current path. As you are already running a virtual environment, this will set the path for all the modules to the path of the current running virtual environment.

```
if __name__ == "__main__":
    os.environ.setdefault("DJANGO_SETTINGS_MODULE",
    "django_mytweets.settings")
django_mytweets/ ( Inner folder)
__init__.py
```

Django projects are Python packages, and this file is required to tell Python that this folder is to be treated as a package. A package in Python's terminology is a collection of modules, and they are used to group similar files together and prevent naming conflicts.

- `settings.py`: This is the main configuration file for your Django project. In it, you can specify a variety of options, including database settings, site language(s), what Django features need to be enabled, and so on. Various sections of this file will be explained as we progress with building our application during the following chapters.

  By default, the database is configured to use SQLite Database, which is advisable to use for testing purposes. Here, we will only see how to enter the database in the settings file; it also contains the basic setting configuration, and with slight modification in the `manage.py` file, it can be moved to another folder, such as `config` or `conf`.

  To make every other third-party application a part of the project, we need to register it in the `settings.py` file. INSTALLED_APPS is a variable that contains all the entries about the installed application. As the project grows, it becomes difficult to manage; therefore, there are three logical partitions for the INSTALLED_APPS variable, as follows:

  - DEFAULT_APPS: This parameter contains the default Django installed applications (such as the admin)

- ◦ THIRD_PARTY_APPS: This parameter contains other application like **SocialAuth** used for social authentication

- ◦ LOCAL_APPS: This parameter contains the applications that are created by you

- url.py: This is another configuration file. You can think of it as a mapping between URLs and the Django view functions that handle them. This file is one of Django's more powerful features, and we will see how to utilize it in the next chapter.

  When we start writing code for our application, we will create new files inside the project's folder. So, the folder also serves as a container for our code.

Now that you have a general idea of the structure of a Django project, let's configure our database system.

Best practices – using version control

Version control is a system that remembers all the changes you make to your projects as you keep progressing. At any point of time, you can see the changes made to a particular file; over a period of time, you can revert it or edit it further.

It makes much more sense for a project that has multiple contributors, mainly for those working on the same file concurrently. Version control is a lifesaver because it keeps records of both the versions of files and allows options such as saving both by merging or discarding any one copy.

We will be using distributed version control, that is, each developer has a complete copy of the project (contrary to subversion, where repositories are hosted on a system server).

Git – the latest and most popular version control tool

Git is a version control tool we will be using for our projects. It is the best available tool out there for version control and is open source too. Git works well with other types of files, apart from source code files, life images, PDFs, and so on. You can download Git from the following URL:

http://git-scm.com/downloads

Most of the modern IDEs already have built-in version control system support; like PyCharm, Sublime has a plugin that can integrate Git in the working directory. Git can be initialized form the terminal using the `git` command, and you can check out further options provided by it using the `git --help` command.

How Git works

We, as developers, have a local copy of the project synchronized with a remote server (often called repository) and can send it to a remote repository. When the other developer wants to push changes to the remote repository, they have to pull your changes first. This minimizes chances of any conflict on the central repository where every developer is in sync. This whole work flow is shown in the next section.

Setting up your Git

Any project can be added to Git for version control to creating a folder into a Git repository. To do this, use the following commands:

- `$git init`: If you want to copy an existing Git repository, which might be the case if your friend has already hosted it somewhere on **GitHub** or **Bitbucket**, use the following command:

    - `$git clone URL`: The URL of the remote repository, like `https://github.com/AlienCoders/web-development.git`.

Staging area: The staging area is the place where all your files have to be listed first before you commit them. In short, staging is needed as an intermediate step, rather than a direct commit, because, when conflicts occur, they are flagged in the staging area. Only after the conflicts are resolved can the files be committed.

Let's take a look at the following commands and their uses:

- `$git add <file-name>` or `$git add`: For adding all files to the staging area in bulk.

- `$git status`: To know the status of your working directory, which files have been added, and which files have not been added.

- `$git diff`: To get the status of what is modified and staged, or what is modified and has not been staged.

- `$ git commit -m`: To commit the changes made, first you have to add them to the staging area; then, you have to commit them using this command.

- `$ git rm <file-name>`: If you have mistakenly added any file to the staging area, you can remove it from the staging area by using this command.

- `$git stash`: Git doesn't track the renamed files. In other words, if you have renamed already staged files, you will have to add them again to the staging and then commit. You can save the changes by not actually committing to the repository by using the following command.

- `$git stash apply`: It takes all the current changes and saves it to the stack. Then, you can continue working with your changes. Once you are in a position to get your saved changes, you can do so using this command.

Branching in Git

Another concept of version control is **branching** (Git). A branch is like a path for your commits, and by default, all commits are made on the master branch. A branch is mainly used to track the feature in a project. Every feature can be made as branch to be worked on; once the feature is complete, it can be merged back to the master.

The basic work flow of branch is this: you initially have a master branch and make a new branch for each new feature. Changes are committed into the new branch, and once done with the feature, you can merge it back to the master branch. This can be visually represented as follows:

- `$git branch`: To list an existing branch using Git, we need to use this command.

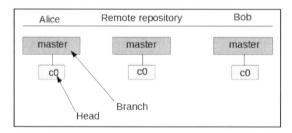

- `git checkout -b <new-branch-name>`: A new branch can be created in the existing repository using this command. We can see logically how it looks with the help of the following block diagram:

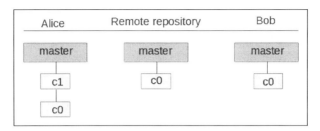

You will get a message informing you that you have switched to the new branch. If you want to switch back to the old branch, you can use the following command:

- `$git checkout <old-branch-name>`: You will see the message `Switched to branch <old-branch-name>`.

- `$git merge <branch-name>`: After the feature is complete, you can merge it to the branch of your choice using this command. This will merge the branch `<branch-name>` to your current branch. To sync the changes back to the `<branch-name>`, you can check out from your current branch to the branch `<branch-name>` and merge again. You can also mark the important points in your commit history by using tags.

- After the commit, you can tag an important commit by using the `$git tag -a v1.0` command.

- To get new changes from the remote server, you can fetch the changes from Git using the `$git fetch` command.

- To merge the changes directly to your current branch, you can use the `$git pull` command.

- After you are done with your changes, you can commit and push them to the remote repository using the `$git push` command.

Setting up the database

In this section, we will start working with code for the first time. Therefore, we will have to choose a source code editor to enter and edit code. You can use any of your favorite source code editors. As mentioned in the previous section, we have used the Sublime text editor to write code for this book.

OK, now that you have a source code editor ready, let's open `settings.py` in the project folder and see what it contains:

```
# Django settings for django_mytweets project.
DEBUG = True
TEMPLATE_DEBUG = DEBUG
ADMINS = (
    # ('Your Name', 'your_email@domain.com'),
)
MANAGERS = ADMINS
DATABASE_ENGINE = ''    # 'postgresql_psycopg2', 'postgresql',
                        # 'mysql', 'sqlite3' or 'ado_mssql'.
DATABASE_NAME = ''      # Or path to database file
                        # if using sqlite3.
DATABASE_USER = ''      # Not used with sqlite3.
DATABASE_PASSWORD = ''  # Not used with sqlite3.
DATABASE_HOST = ''      # Set to empty string for localhost.
                        # Not used with sqlite3.
DATABASE_PORT = ''      # Set to empty string for default.
                        # Not used with sqlite3.
```

There are many more lines in the `settings.py` file, but we have trimmed the remaining contents of this file.

As you may have already noticed, the file contains a number of variables that control various aspects of the application. Entering a new value for a variable is as simple as doing a Python assignment statement. In addition, the file is extensively commented, and comments explain what variables control in detail.

What concerns us now is configuring the database. As mentioned before, Django supports several database systems, so first of all, we have to specify what database system we are going to use. This is controlled by the DATABASE_ENGINE variable. If you have SQLite installed, set the variable to `sqlite3`. Otherwise, pick the value that matches your database engine from the comment next to the variable name.

Next is the database name. We will choose a descriptive name for your database; edit DATABASE_NAME and set it to django_mytweetsdb. If you are using SQLite, this is all you need to do. On the other hand, if you are using a database server, follow these instructions:

- Enter the relevant information for the database–the username, password, host, and port (SQLite does not require any of these).

- Create the actual database inside the database server, as Django won't do this by itself. In MySQL, for example, this is done through the mysql command-line utility or phpMyAdmin.

After these simple edits, the database section in settings.py now looks like this:

```
DATABASE_ENGINE = 'sqlite3'
DATABASE_NAME = 'django_mytweetsdb'
DATABASE_USER = ''
DATABASE_PASSWORD = ''
DATABASE_HOST = ''
DATABASE_PORT = ''
```

Finally, we will tell Django to populate the configured database with tables. Although we haven't created any tables for our data yet (and we won't do so until the next chapter), Django requires several tables in the database for some of its features to function properly. Creating these tables is as easy as issuing the following command:

```
$ python manage.py syncdb
```

If everything is correct, status messages will scroll on the screen, indicating that tables are being created. When prompted for the superuser account, enter your preferred username, e-mail, and password. If, on the other hand, the database is misconfigured, an error message will be printed to help you troubleshoot the issue.

With this done, we are ready to launch our application.

Using python manage.py

When you run a command that starts with python manage.py, make sure that you are currently in the project's directory where the manage.py file is located.

Launching the development server

As discussed before, Django comes with a lightweight web server for developing and testing applications. This server is pre-configured to work with Django, and more importantly, it restarts whenever you modify the code.

To start the server, run the following command:

```
$ python manage.py runserver
```

Next, open your browser and navigate to this URL: `http://localhost:8000/`. You should see a welcome message, as shown in the following screenshot:

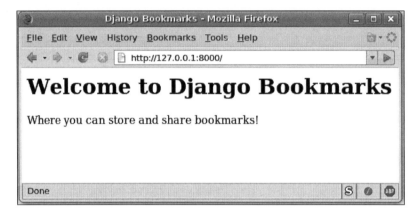

Congratulations! You have created and configured your first Django project. This project will be the basis on top of which we will build our bookmarking application. In the next chapter, we will start developing our application, and the page displayed by the web server will be replaced by something we wrote ourselves!

As you may have noticed, the web server runs on port `8000` by default. If you want to change the port, you can specify it on the command line using the following command:

```
$ python manage.py runserver <port number>
```

Also, the development server is only accessible from the local machine by default. If you want to access the development server from another machine on your network, use the following command line arguments:

```
$ python manage.py runserver 0.0.0.0:<port number>
```

Faster web development

When it comes to web development, one thing which majorly helps the success of the web project is its user interface and user experience. Although Django takes care of all the business logic at the backend, there is undoubtedly a need for an awesome frontend design framework that not only eases the developer's life while coding, but also enhances the user experience of the whole web project. Thus, we choose to explain **Twitter Bootstrap** here.

Minimal Bootstrap

Bootstrap is a complete frontend framework, and it's beyond the scope of this book to familiarize you with each and every aspect of it. What you must be wondering is why we would discuss Bootstrap in Django book. You are being told about a frontend framework. The idea here is to help you build a web application that you can directly use in production, and which you will be deploying to clouds such as **AWS** and **Heroku**. You need your project to be of a production grade once you finish this book. Thus, by keeping Bootstrap as simple as possible, you can still build a great-looking Django web application.

There are many ways to lay out your web pages based on the permutation and combination. To help you to get an understanding of that, we will take a look at a few examples.

Wire-framing is the first step in the web development, which means it has to deal with the location of the content on the page. If you already know the basics of web designing, this section will make much more sense to you. If not, first do some reading to get a basic idea of web development. Look up the difference between `div` and `span`, and then everything will make sense to you. You can learn more from here: `https://developer.mozilla.org/en-US/Learn/HTML`. Bootstrap basic page wire-framing is divided into rows and columns; each column is further divided into 12 sections. With these subsections, you can use the permutation to get your layout designed.

When we see a website from a developer's perspective, the first thing we notice is the wire-frame being used. For example, when you visit www.facebook.com, you see your news feed in the center of the page and other important links (such as links to messages, pages, and groups) on the left-hand side of the page. On the right-hand side, you see your friends who are available to chat.

The same layout can be imagined in Bootstrap as 2-8-2. The column for the left-hand side links will be a "2 column", the news feed will be an "8 column", and the chat section will be a "2 column". This is a basic wire-frame.

Remember the sum always has to be 12, as a live fluid grid system in Bootstrap works on 12-grid column principle for better and flexible layout.

Now, Bootstrap is not just for making a web page responsive–it has many other components to make web page look better and cleaner.

To use Bootstrap with Django, there are two ways:

- **The Django way**: pip install django-bootstrap3
- **The Manual way**: Downloading the Bootstrap resources and copying them to a static location

The Django way

If you want to install Bootstrap using a command, then you have to append the INSTALLED_APPS variable from the settings.py file with bootstrap3.

Here is a sample Django template using this method for a simple HTML form:

```
{% load bootstrap3 %}
{%# simple HTML form #%}
<form action="action_url">
    {% csrf_token %}
    {% bootstrap_form sample_form %}
    {% buttons %}
        <button type="submit" class="btn btn-primary">
            {% bootstrap_icon "heart" %} SUBMIT
        </button>
    {% endbuttons %}
</form>
```

To learn and explore more, you can refer to the following link: `http://django-bootstrap3.readthedocs.org/`

Manual installation of Bootstrap

This method is recommended for beginners, but once you are confident, you can make shortcuts by following the command method.

Here we will learn the basic inclusion for the project files, and the rest will be covered in the upcoming chapters. Once you have downloaded the Bootstrap from the online source (`http://getbootstrap.com`), the unzipped folder structure looks something like this:

```
|-- css
|    |-- bootstrap.css
|    |-- bootstrap.css.map
|    |-- bootstrap.min.css
|    |-- bootstrap-theme.css
|    |-- bootstrap-theme.css.map
|    `-- bootstrap-theme.min.css
|-- fonts
|    |-- glyphicons-halflings-regular.eot
|    |-- glyphicons-halflings-regular.svg
|    |-- glyphicons-halflings-regular.ttf
|    `-- glyphicons-halflings-regular.woff
`-- js
     |-- bootstrap.js
     `-- bootstrap.min.js
```

There are two types of local file conventions used in Django: one is "Static" and another is "media". Static files refers to the assets of your project, such as CSS, JavaScript, and so on. Media files are represented by uploaded files in the project, mainly consisting of images, video for display or download, and so on.

Adding static files to your project can be done by adding following lines to the `setting.py` file:

```
STATICFILES_DIRS = (
    # put absolute path here as string not relative path.
    # forward slash to be used even in windows.
    os.path.join(
```

```
        os.path.dirname(__file__),
        'static',
    ),
)
```

Now, all you have to do is to create a folder inside your project directory and copy all the Bootstrap resources.

Summary

We prepared our development environment in this chapter, created our first project, set up the database, and learned how to launch the Django development server. We learned the best way to write code for our Django project and saw the default Django project structure. We learned about the naming convention, the significance of blank lines, and which style of import we should use and where.

We saw which editor and which IDE would be better for Python- and Django-based web development. We learned how to use Git to keep our code updated at the repository. We learned a bit about Bootstrap to work on frontend development.

The next chapter will take you through a tour of the main Django components and will help develop a working prototype for our Twitter application. It's going to be a fun chapter with many new things to learn, so keep reading!

4
Building an Application
Like Twitter

In the previous chapters, we learned about better ways to write our code. Keeping those points in mind, it is high time that we get started with real Django project development and learn about views, models, and templates.

The first part of each section in this chapter will be about the basics and how things work in the particular subject it deals with. This will include proper practices, standard methods, and important terminology.

The second part of each section will be the application of that concept in our mytweets Django application development. The first parts can be thought of as chapter descriptions of the subjects and the second parts as exercises in the form of our Django project, which is really going to be a unique learning experience.

The following topics are covered in this chapter:

- A word about Django terminology
- Setting up the Basic Template Application
- Creating Django's template structure of the project
- Setting up the basic bootstrap for the Application
- Creating the Main Page
- Introduction to class-based views
- Django settings for our mytweets project
- Generating user pages
- Designing an initial database schema
- User registration and account management
- Creating a template for the Main Page

A word about Django terminology

Django is an MVC framework. However, throughout the code, the controller is called **view**, and the view is called **template**. The view in Django is the component which retrieves and manipulates the data, whereas the template is the component that presents data to the user. For this reason, Django is sometimes called a **Model Template View** (**MTV**) framework. This different terminology neither changes the fact that Django is an MVC framework, nor does it affect how applications are developed, but keep the terminology in mind to avoid possible confusion if you have worked with other MVC frameworks in the past.

You can think of this chapter as an in-depth tour of the main Django components. You will learn how to create dynamic pages using views, how to store and manage data in the database using models, and how to simplify page generation using templates.

While learning about these features, you will form a solid idea of how Django components work and interact with each other. Later chapters will explore these components more deeply, as we develop more features and add them to our application.

Setting up a basic template application

Our project is going to be a microblogging site, where there will be a public page for every user, which will have a timeline of the tweets they have posted.

The first thing that comes to mind after seeing the welcome page of the development server is to ask how we can change it. To create our own welcome page, we need to define an entry point to our application in the form of a URL and tell Django to call a particular Python function when a visitor accesses this URL. We will write this Python function ourselves and make it display our own welcome message.

This section basically is a redo of the configuration we did in the previous chapter, but the intent is to place all the instructions together here so that the project bootstrapping requires fewer page look-ups.

Creating a virtual environment

We will set up the virtual environment for Django to work properly by using the following command:

```
$ virtualenv django_env
```

The output will be as follows:

```
New python executable in django_env/bin/python
Installing setuptools, pip...done.
```

We need to activate the virtual environment now and set up all the environment variables so that all Python installs will be routed to this environment directory without affecting other settings:

```
$ source django_env/bin/activate
```

The output will be as follows:

```
(django_env) ratan@lenovo:~/code$
```

Installing Django

Although you have already installed Django, we will do this again because Django will be managed by `virtualenv`, which can't be messed up by other projects or users (or yourself) working elsewhere.

```
$pip install django
```

You may get an error as follows:

```
bad interpreter: No such file or directory
```

If so, create your virtualenv environment within a path without spaces. It is most likely that, in the path to the location where you have created your virtual environment, there exists a directory whose name contains a space, for example, `/home/ratan/folder name with space$virtualenv django_env`.

If so, change the directory name to something like the following:

```
/home/ratan/folder_name_with_no_space$virtualenv django_env
```

We can proceed with the Django installation using the command `pip install django`.

The output will be as follows:

```
Downloading/unpacking django
Downloading Django-1.6.5-py2.py3-none-any.whl (6.7MB): 6.7MB downloaded
Installing collected packages: django
Successfully installed django
Cleaning up...
```

Now, before we move to create our Django application, we will make sure Git is installed. Use the following command to find out the version of Git that we have installed:

```
$git --version
```

The output will be as follows:

```
git version 1.9.1
```

This confirms that we have Git installed. Of course you must be wondering whether we are going to use version control in this project. The answer is yes: as we go along, we will version-control most of the project files.

Creating Django's template structure of the project

In this section, we will create the structure for the project, for example, creating a folder called `mytweets` for our project, installing the required package for our project, and so on. Run the following command:

```
$django-admin.py startproject mytweets
```

This will create the folder called `mytweets`, which we will be using as our project directory. In the current folder, we see two subfolders: `environment` and `mytweets`. The question right now is whether we are going to version control our environment folder. We are not, because those files are very specific to your current system. They are not going to help anyone to set up the same environment as ours. However, there is another way of doing this in Python: by using the `pip freeze` command. This actually takes a snapshot of all the current libraries installed in your Django application, and then you can save that list in a text file and version control it. Thus your fellow developer can download the same version of the libraries. That's really a Pythonic way of doing it, isn't it?

The most common method for you to install the new packages is by using the `pip` command. There are the three versions of the `pip install` command, they are as follows:

```
$ pip install PackageName
```

This is the default and installs the latest version of the package:

```
$ pip install PackageName==1.0.4
```

Using the `==` parameter, you can install a specific version of the package. In this case, that is 1.0.4. Use the following command to install the package with a version number:

```
$ pip install 'PackageName>=1.0.4' # minimum version
```

Use the above command when you are not sure of the package version you are going to install but have an idea that you need the minimum version of the library.

It is very easy to use the `pip` command to install the libraries. You can do this by just typing the following into the command line:

```
$pip install -r requirements.txt
```

Now we need to freeze the libraries from the current project:

```
$pip freeze > requirements.txt
```

This command freezes the current libraries installed in the project along with the version number, if specified, and stores them in a file named `requirements.txt`.

At this stage of our project, `pip freeze` command will look something like this.

```
Django==1.6.5
argparse==1.2.1
wsgiref==0.1.2
```

To install these libraries back to your fresh environment along with the project, we can run the following command:

```
$pip install -r requirements.txt
```

Thus we can proceed with initializing only our code directory as a Git repository and changing the current path to `$cd mytweets`. Execute the following command to build a Git repository in your project folder:

```
$git init
```

The output will be as follows:

```
Initialized empty Git repository in /home/ratan/code/mytweets/.git/
```

If we run all commands on a Linux-based system for detailed directory listing we can see the following output:

```
...
drwxrwxr-x 7 ratan ratan 4096 Aug 2 16:07 .git/
...
```

This is the `.git` folder, which, as by its naming convention (starting with a dot), is hidden from the normal listing of the directory, that is, the directory where all Git-related files such as branches, commits, logs, and so on are stored. Deleting that particular directory will make your directory Git-free (free of version control) and as normal as any other directory in your current system.

We can add all our current files in the directory to the staging area by using the following command:

```
$git add .
```

Use the following command for our first commit of the project:

```
$git commit -m "initial commit of the project."
```

The output will be as follows:

```
[master (root-commit) 597b6ec] initial commit of the project.
5 files changed, 118 insertions(+)
create mode 100755 manage.py
create mode 100644 mytweets/__init__.py
create mode 100644 mytweets/settings.py
create mode 100644 mytweets/urls.py
create mode 100644 mytweets/wsgi.py
```

The first line (here, its master) says that we are in the master's branch and the others that follow are the files being committed.

So far, we have set up the basic Django template and added it to our version control. The same thing can be verified with the following command:

```
$git log
```

The output will be as follows:

```
commit 597b6ec86c54584a758f482aa5a0f5781ff4b682

Author: ratan <mail@ratankumar.org>

Date: Sat Aug 2 16:50:37 2014 +0530

initial commit of the project.
```

Instructions on setting up the author and generating SSH keys for a remote repository push can be found at the following links:

https://help.github.com/articles/set-up-git

https://help.github.com/articles/generating-ssh-keys

Setting up the basic Twitter Bootstrap for the application

As introduced in the previous chapter, bootstrap is the basic framework for the user interface design. We will proceed with the second method mentioned, that is, by manually downloading the bootstrap files and linking them in the static folder.

The method we are skipping means that we are not going to execute the following command:

```
$pip install django-bootstrap3
```

Detailed documentation for this implementation can be found at http://django-bootstrap3.readthedocs.org/.

The method that we will be following is that of downloading the bootstrap files and placing them in the static folder of our project.

To start with bootstrap, we have to start by downloading the static files from the following official bootstrap web address:

http://getbootstrap.com/

When you visit this link, you will find a download button. After clicking on **Download**, click on **Download Bootstrap**. This will give you the bootstrap resource files in zipped format. This downloaded file will have a name something like bootstrap-3.2.0-dist.zip. Extract the content of this zip file. After extraction, the folder bootstrap-3.2.0-dist will have a structure as follows:

```
|-- css
|   |-- bootstrap.css
|   |-- bootstrap.css.map
|   |-- bootstrap.min.css
|   |-- bootstrap-theme.css
|   |-- bootstrap-theme.css.map
|   |-- bootstrap-theme.min.css
|-- fonts
|   |-- glyphicons-halflings-regular.eot
|   |-- glyphicons-halflings-regular.svg
|   |-- glyphicons-halflings-regular.ttf
|   |-- glyphicons-halflings-regular.woff
|-- js
|-- bootstrap.js
|-- bootstrap.min.js
```

Application-specific static files are stored in the static subdirectory within the application.

Django will also look in any directories listed in the STATICFILES_DIRS setting. Let's update our project settings to specify a static file directory in the settings.py file.

We can update our project's `setting.py` file as follows to use Twitter bootstrap:

```
STATICFILES_DIRS = (
os.path.join(
os.path.dirname(__file__),
'static',
),
)
```

Here, the `static` variable will be the folder we will be keeping our bootstrap files in. We will create the `static` folder inside our current project directory and will copy all bootstrap's unzipped files to that folder.

For development purposes, we will keep most of the settings as there are, for example, the default database SQLite; we can later move this while deploying our test application to MySQL or any other database of our choice.

Now, before we actually use bootstrap in our projects, there are some underlying concepts we must know to understand bootstrap as a front-end framework.

Bootstrap designs the web pages based on the grid system, and there are three main components of this grid, as follows:

- **Container**: A container is used for giving a base to the whole web page, that is, generally, all the components of the bootstrap will be direct or nested child objects of the container. In other words, containers provide the width constraints on responsive widths. When the screen resolution changes, it's the container which is changing its width across the device screen. The rows and columns are percentage based so they get automatically modified.

  The container also provides a padding to the contents from browser edges so that they do not touch the side of the view area. The default padding is 15 px. You never need another container inside a container. The following image shows the structure of the container:

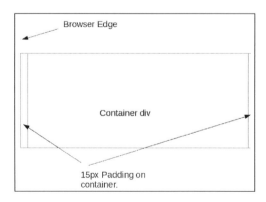

- **Row**: A row is placed inside the container and contains the column. The hierarchy is `container | row | column` for bootstrap's basic design. The row also acts like a wrapper for the columns, so in situations where columns are getting weird due to their default float left property, keep them separately grouped so that this problem is not reflected outside the row.

  Rows have 15 px of negative margin on each side, which pushes them out over the top of the container's 15 px padding. As a result, they are negated and the row touches the edge of the container, the negative margin is overlapped by padding. Thus, the row is not pushed by the container's padding. Never use a row outside a container.

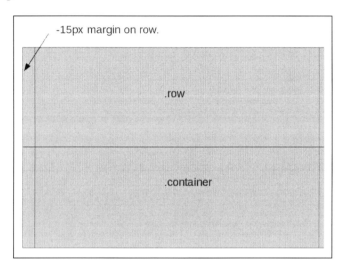

- **Column**: Columns have a 15 px padding. This means that the columns actually touch the edge of the row, which is already touching the edge of the container because of the negation property with the container discussed in the previous paragraph.

Columns again have the 15 px padding, so the content of the columns is placed 15 px away from the view edge of a container.

Therefore, we don't need a special first and last column with padding on the left and right. There is now a consistent 15 px gap across all columns.

Content inside the columns are pushed to the columns location and are also separated by 30 px of gutter between them. We can use rows inside the column for nested layouts.

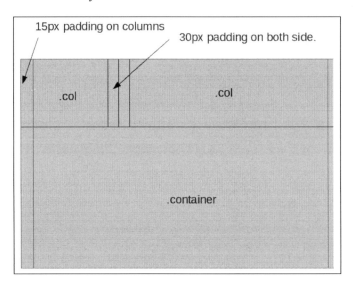

Never use a column outside of a row.

With these points in mind, we can go ahead and design our first layout.

URLs and views – creating the main page

A view in Django terminology is a regular Python function that responds to a page request by generating the corresponding page. To write our first Django view for the main page, we first need to create a Django application inside our project. You can think of an application as a container for views and data models. To create it, issue the following command within our django_mytweets folder:

```
$ python manage.py startapp tweets
```

The syntax of application creation is very similar to that of project creation. We used the startapp command as the first parameter of the python manage.py command, and provided tweets as the name of our application.

After running this command, Django will create a folder named `tweets` inside the project folder with these three files:

- `__init__.py`: This file tells Python that `tweets` is a Python package
- `views.py`: This file will contain our views
- `models.py`: This file will contain our data models

Now let's create the main page view. We will first create a `template` folder inside the project to keep all the HTML files:

$mkdir templates

Now create a base HTML file inside it named `base.html` with the following content:

```
{% load staticfiles %}
<html>
<head>
<link href="{% static 'bootstrap/css/bootstrap.min.css' %}"
rel="stylesheet" media="screen" />">
</head>

<body>
{% block content %}
<h1 class="text-info">">HELLO DJANGO!</h1>
{% endblock %}

<script src="{% static 'bootstrap/js/bootstrap.min.js' %}"></script>
</body>
</html>
```

Our directory structure will look something like this now (use the `tree` command if you are on Linux OS):

```
mytweets/
|-- manage.py
|-- mytweets
|   |-- __init__.py
|   |-- __init__.pyc
|   |-- settings.py
|   |-- settings.pyc
|   |-- urls.py
|   |-- urls.pyc
|   |-- wsgi.py
|   `-- wsgi.pyc
|-- static
```

```
|   |-- css
|   |   |-- bootstrap.css
|   |   |-- bootstrap.css.map
|   |   |-- bootstrap.min.css
|   |   |-- bootstrap-theme.css
|   |   |-- bootstrap-theme.css.map
|   |   `-- bootstrap-theme.min.css
|   |-- fonts
|   |   |-- glyphicons-halflings-regular.eot
|   |   |-- glyphicons-halflings-regular.svg
|   |   |-- glyphicons-halflings-regular.ttf
|   |   `-- glyphicons-halflings-regular.woff
|   `-- js
|   |-- bootstrap.js
|   `-- bootstrap.min.js
|-- templates
|   `-- base.html
`-- tweets
|-- admin.py
|-- __init__.py
|-- models.py
|-- tests.py
`-- views.py
```

Introduction to class-based views

Class-based views are the new way of defining views in Django. They do not replace function-based views. They are just an alternative way to implement views as Python objects instead of functions. There are two advantages they have over function-based views. With a class-based view, different HTTP requests can be mapped to a different function, as opposed to a function-based view where the branching takes place based on the `request.method` parameter. Object-oriented techniques can be used to reuse the code component, such as **mixins** (multiple inheritance).

Although we will be using class-based views for our project, to understand the exact difference between the two, here we will present the code for both.

We will have to update the `url.py` file of our project so that the `base.html` file will be served if the user requests the website.

Function-based view:

Update the view.py file as follows:

```
from django.http import HttpResponse

def index(request):
if request.method == 'GET':
return HttpResponse('I am called from a get Request')
elif request.method == 'POST':
return HttpResponse('I am called from a post Request')
```

Update the urls.py file as follows:

```
from django.conf.urls import patterns, include, url
from django.contrib import admin
from tweets import views
admin.autodiscover()

urlpatterns = patterns('',
url(r'^$', views.index, name='index'),
url(r'^admin/', include(admin.site.urls)),
)
```

Run the development server by using the following command:

$python manage.py runserver

We will see a response saying **I am called from a get Request**.

Class-based view:

Update the views.py file as follows:

```
from django.http import HttpResponse
from django.views.generic import View

class Index(ViewV iew):
def get(self, request):
return HttpResponse('I am called from a get Request')
def post(self, request):
return HttpResponse('I am called from a post Request')

urls.py
from django.conf.urls import patterns, include, url
from django.contrib import admin
from tweets.views import Index
admin.autodiscover()
```

```
urlpatterns = patterns('',
url(r'^$', Index.as_view()),
url(r'^admin/', include(admin.site.urls)),
)
```

This will also generate the same result on the browser after the development server is hit. We will be using class-based views throughout the project.

What we have rendered is just a string, which was kind of simple. We have created a `base.html` file in our template folder and will now move ahead with our class-based view and render our `base.html` file.

In Django, there is more than one way to render our page. We can render our page using any of these three functions: `render()`, `render_to_response()`, or `direct_to_template()`. However, let us first see what the difference between them is and which one we should be using:

- `render_to_response(template[, dictionary][, context_instance][, mimetype])`: The `render_to_response` command is the standard render function, and to use `RequestContext`, we will have to specify `context_instance=RequestContext(request)`.

- `render(request, template[, dictionary][, context_instance][, content_type][, status][, current_app])`. This is the new shortcut for the `render_to_response` command and is available from version 1.3 of Django. This will automatically use `RequestContext`.

- `direct_to_template()`: This is a generic view. It automatically uses `RequestContext` and all its `context_processor` parameters.

However, the `direct_to_template` command should be avoided as function-based generic views are deprecated.

We will choose the second one, the `render()` function, for rendering our `base.html` template.

The next step is the inclusion of the template folder in our Django application (the template folder we have created with the base file named `base.html`). To include the template, we will update the `settings.py` file in the following manner:

```
TEMPLATE_DIRS = (
BASE_DIR + '/templates/'
)
TEMPLATE_LOADERS = (
'django.template.loaders.filesystem.Loader',
'django.template.loaders.app_directories.Loader',
)
```

This defines the template directory and initializes the basic TEMPLATE_LOADER parameters.

Django settings for the mytweets project

Let's update the settings.py file with the minimal settings that we need for our mytweets project. Before starting our mytweets application we will add many settings which we will see with the following changes. For more information on this file, visit https://docs.djangoproject.com/en/1.6/topics/settings/.

For the full list of settings and their values, visit https://docs.djangoproject.com/en/1.6/ref/settings/.

Update the settings.py file of our project with the following content:

```
# Build paths inside the project like this: os.path.join(BASE_DIR,
...)
import os
BASE_DIR = os.path.dirname(os.path.dirname(__file__))

# Quick-start development settings - unsuitable for production
# See https://docs.djangoproject.com/en/1.6/howto/deployment/
checklist/

# SECURITY WARNING: keep the secret key used in production secret!
SECRET_KEY = 'XXXXXXXXXXXXXXXXXXXXXXXXXX'

# SECURITY WARNING: don't run with debug turned on in production!
DEBUG = True
TEMPLATE_DEBUG = True
ALLOWED_HOSTS = []

# Application definition
INSTALLED_APPS = (
'django.contrib.admin',
'django.contrib.auth',
'django.contrib.contenttypes',
'django.contrib.sessions',
'django.contrib.messages',
'django.contrib.staticfiles',
)

MIDDLEWARE_CLASSES = (
'django.contrib.sessions.middleware.SessionMiddleware',
'django.middleware.common.CommonMiddleware',
'django.middleware.csrf.CsrfViewMiddleware',
'django.contrib.auth.middleware.AuthenticationMiddleware',
'django.contrib.messages.middleware.MessageMiddleware',
```

```
'django.middleware.clickjacking.XFrameOptionsMiddleware',
)

ROOT_URLCONF = 'mytweets.urls'
WSGI_APPLICATION = 'mytweets.wsgi.application'

# Database
# https://docs.djangoproject.com/en/1.6/ref/settings/#databases

DATABASES = {
'default': {
'ENGINE': 'django.db.backends.sqlite3',
'NAME': os.path.join(BASE_DIR, 'db.sqlite3'),
}
}

#static file directory inclusion
STATICFILES_DIRS = (
os.path.join(
os.path.dirname(__file__),
'static',
),
)

TEMPLATE_DIRS = (
BASE_DIR + '/templates/'
)

# List of callables that know how to import templates from various
sources.
TEMPLATE_LOADERS = (
'django.template.loaders.filesystem.Loader',
'django.template.loaders.app_directories.Loader',
# 'django.template.loaders.eggs.Loader',
)

# Internationalization
# https://docs.djangoproject.com/en/1.6/topics/i18n/

LANGUAGE_CODE = 'en-us'
TIME_ZONE = 'UTC'
USE_I18N = True
USE_L10N = True
USE_TZ = True

# Static files (CSS, JavaScript, Images)
# https://docs.djangoproject.com/en/1.6/howto/static-files/

STATIC_URL = '/static/'
```

Now if we start our development server, our screen will look like the following screenshot:

In our `base.html` file, we have written `class="h1"` instead of `<h1></h1>`. This was knowingly done to check at runtime whether the bootstrap files are being loaded, that is, with the `Header 1` properties.

As you may have noticed, we haven't passed any variables to the template, which is what roughly differentiates static pages and dynamic pages. Let's get ahead and do that too. All we need is some changes in the `views.py` and `base.html` files, as follows:

- Changes in the `views.py` file:

```
from django.views.generic import View
from django.shortcuts import render
class Index(View):
def get(self, request):
params = {}
params["name"] = "Django"
return render(request, 'base.html', params)
```

- Changes in the `base.html` file

```
{% load staticfiles %}
<html>
<head>
<link href="{% static 'bootstrap/css/bootstrap.min.css' %}"
```

```
rel="stylesheet" media="screen">
</head>

<body>
{% block content %}
<h1>Hello {{name}}!</h1>
{% endblock %}

<script src="{% static 'bootstrap/js/bootstrap.min.js' %}"></
script>
</body>
</html>
```

We can see how simple it is. All we did is just create a map (called **dictionary** in Python) and assigned the name property to it as Django and added it in the render() function as a new parameter. It gets rendered to the base of the HTML and is easily called {{name}}. When it is rendered, it replaces itself with Django.

We will be committing all the changes we have made until now. Before we do that, let's create a .gitignore file. What this does is, whatever content there is in this file (or wildcard for the files that we have written inside the .gitignore file), it will prevent all of them from committing and will send them to the repository server.

How does it help? It helps in many important use cases. Suppose we don't want to put any local configuration files onto the production server. The .gitignore file can be a savior in such situations, as also in a case when .py files generate their .pyc files, which are compiled at runtime. We don't need those binary files on the server, as they will be separately generated each time the code changes.

On the Linux command line, just type the $vim .gitignore command in the root folder of the project directory and write *.pyc. Then, save and exit in the usual way.

Now, if we execute the $git status command, we will not see any file with the .pyc extension, which means that Git has ignored tracking files that end with the .pyc extension.

The result of the $git status command is as follows:

```
Changes not staged for commit:
(use "git add <file>..." to update what will be committed)
(use "git checkout -- <file>..." to discard changes in working
directory)

modified: mytweets/settings.py
modified: mytweets/urls.py
```

```
Untracked files:
(use "git add <file>..." to include in what will be committed)

  .gitignore
  static/
  templates/
  tweets/
```

This is quite clear, as it should be. We have previously committed the settings.py and urls.py files, and now we've made some changes in them and the mentioned untracked files are not even added to Git for tracking.

We can use the git add . command to add all the changes to the directory. However, to avoid any unwanted files being pushed to Git tracking, it is recommended that files be added one by one when we are in an advanced phase of development. For the current situation, adding files all in one go is fine. To add the required file to our project, use the following command:

```
$git add .
```

The output will be as follows:

```
On branch master
Changes to be committed:
(use "git reset HEAD <file>..." to unstage)

new file: .gitignore
modified: mytweets/settings.py
modified: mytweets/urls.py
new file: static/css/bootstrap-theme.css
new file: static/css/bootstrap-theme.css.map
new file: static/css/bootstrap-theme.min.css
new file: static/css/bootstrap.css
new file: static/css/bootstrap.css.map
new file: static/css/bootstrap.min.css
new file: static/fonts/glyphicons-halflings-regular.eot
new file: static/fonts/glyphicons-halflings-regular.svg
new file: static/fonts/glyphicons-halflings-regular.ttf
new file: static/fonts/glyphicons-halflings-regular.woff
new file: static/js/bootstrap.js
new file: static/js/bootstrap.min.js
```

```
new file: templates/base.html
new file: tweets/__init__.py
new file: tweets/admin.py
new file: tweets/models.py
new file: tweets/tests.py
new file: tweets/views.py
```

Commit the changes with proper messages, such as "*basic bootstrap template added*":

```
$git commit -m "basic bootstap template added"
```

The output will be as follows:

```
[master 195230b] basic bootstap template added
21 files changed, 9062 insertions(+), 1 deletion(-)
create mode 100644 .gitignore
create mode 100644 static/css/bootstrap-theme.css
create mode 100644 static/css/bootstrap-theme.css.map
create mode 100644 static/css/bootstrap-theme.min.css
create mode 100644 static/css/bootstrap.css
create mode 100644 static/css/bootstrap.css.map
create mode 100644 static/css/bootstrap.min.css
create mode 100644 static/fonts/glyphicons-halflings-regular.eot
create mode 100644 static/fonts/glyphicons-halflings-regular.svg
create mode 100644 static/fonts/glyphicons-halflings-regular.ttf
create mode 100644 static/fonts/glyphicons-halflings-regular.woff
create mode 100644 static/js/bootstrap.js
create mode 100644 static/js/bootstrap.min.js
create mode 100644 templates/base.html
create mode 100644 tweets/__init__.py
create mode 100644 tweets/admin.py
create mode 100644 tweets/models.py
create mode 100644 tweets/tests.py
create mode 100644 tweets/views.py
```

Putting it all together – generating user pages

So far, we have covered a lot of material, such as introduction to the concepts of views and templates. In the final section, we will write another view and make use of all the information that we have learned so far. This view will display a list of all the tweets that belong to a certain user.

Familiarization with the Django models

Models are the standard Python classes with some added features. They are subclasses of `django.db.models.Model`. In the background, an **Object-Relational Mapper (ORM)** gets bound with these classes and their objects. This makes them communicate with the underlying database. ORM is one of the important features of Django, without which we will end up writing our own queries (SQL, if its MySQL) to access the database content. Each attribute of a model is represented by a database field. Without its fields, a model will be just like an empty container, with no meaning whatsoever.

The following are Django's model attributes explained with their intended use. A complete list of fields can be found on the stranded documentation at `https://docs.djangoproject.com/en/dev/ref/models/fields/`.

Following is a partial table of these types:

Field type	Description
IntegerField	An integer
TextField	A large text field
DateTimeField	A date-and-time field
EmailField	An e-mail field with 75 characters maximum
URLField	A URL field with 200 characters maximum
FileField	A file-upload field

Each model field takes a set of field-specific arguments. For example, if we want a field to be a `CharField` field, we must pass its `max_length` parameter as its argument, which is mapped to the field size in `varchar` to the database.

The following are the arguments that can be applied to all the field types (they are optional):

- `null`: By default, it is set to `false`. When set to `true`, the associated field is allowed to have a value of `null` stored in the database.

- `blank`: By default, it is set to `false`. When set to `true`, the associated field is allowed to have a value of `blank` stored in the database.

> The difference between the `null` and `blank` parameters is that the `null` parameter is mainly database-related, whereas the `blank` parameter is used for validating the field. In other words, if the attribute is set to `false`, the empty value (`blank`) for the attribute will not get saved.

- `choices`: This can be a list or a tuple and must be iterable. If this is in the form of a tuple, the first element is the value that will get stored to the database and the second value is used for display in widget-like forms or `ModelChoiceField`.

  For example:

  ```
  USER_ROLE = (
  ('U', 'USER'),
  ('S', 'STAFF'),
  ('A', 'ADMIN')
  )
  user_role = models.CharField(max_length=1,
  choices=USER_ROLE)
  ```

- `default`: Values that are assigned to the attribute every time an object of the class is instantiated.

- `help_text`: Help text displayed in the form of a widget.

- `primary_key`: If set to `True`, this field is made primary key for the model. If there is no primary key in the model, Django will create an integer field and mark that as the primary key.

Relationships in models

There are three major types of relationships: many-to-one, many-to-many, and one-to-one.

Many-to-one relationships

In Django, the `django.db.models.ForeignKey` parameter is used to define a model as a foreign key to another model's attribute, which results in a many-to-many relationship.

It is used as any other attribute of a model class, after including the class in which it is present. For example, if students study in a particular school, the relationship is that the school has many students but a student goes to only one school, making this a many-to-one relationship. Let's take a look at the following code snippet:

```
from django.db import models
class School(models.Model):
# ...
ass
class Student(models.Model):
school = models.ForeignKey(School)
# ...
```

One-to-one relationships

One-to-one relationships are very similar to many-to-one relationships. The only difference is that reverse mapping results in a single object in the case of one-to-one as opposed to many-to-one relationships.

For example:

```
class EntryDetail(models.Model):
entry = models.OneToOneField(Entry)
details = models.TextField()
```

In the preceding example, the `EntryDetail()` class has an attribute called `entry`, which is mapped one-to-one with the `Entry` model. This means that every `Entry` object has been mapped to the `EntryDetail` model.

Many-to-many relationships

As the name itself suggests, model attributes with many-to-many relationships provide access to both the models it's been pointed to (like backward one-to-many relationships). Attribute naming is the only significant difference between the two relationships.

This will be clearer if we go through the following example:

```
class Product(models.Model):
name = models.CharField(_(u"Name"), max_length=50)
class Category(models.Model):
name = models.CharField(_(u"Name"), max_length=50)
products = models.ManyToManyField("Product", blank=True,
null=True)
```

With the idea of attribute and primary relationships, we can now straightaway create our projects model, which we will soon be doing in the coming sections.

If we are going to design the model for an application, we should break up the applications if it has too many models. If we have more than roughly 15 models in our application, we should think about the ways in which to break our application into smaller applications. This is because, with the existing 15-model application, we are probably doing way too many things. This doesn't go with the Django philosophy of an *app should do one thing and do it right*.

Models – designing an initial database schema

Coming back to our project, we will need two models in the initial phase: the `user` model and the `tweet` model. The `user` model will be used for storing the basic user details of the users that have accounts in our project.

Then comes the `tweet` model, which will store data related to the tweet, such as the tweet text, the user who has created that tweet, and other important details such as the timestamps of the tweet posted, and so on.

To list the tweets of a user, it will be better if we create a separate user application specific to all the users of our project. Our user models will be created by extending Django's `AbstractBaseUser` user model class.

 Changing the actual `user` class in your Django source tree and/or copying and altering the `auth` module is never recommended.

This will be the first application of using a framework for web development instead of writing the whole authentication by ourselves, which is pretty common to all web development scenarios. Django comes with predefined libraries so that we don't have to reinvent the wheel. It comes with both authentication and authorization together and is called the authentication system.

Django's user objects

An additional configurable user model is shipped with Django 1.5, which is the easier method for storing user-specific data in the application.

We will create a user application and then import the Django's default user model into it:

```
$python manage.py startapp user_profile
```

We will extend the Django user model according to our need in the current project by creating a custom `User()` class that inherits from the `AbstractBaseUser` class. Therefore, our `models.py` file will look like this:

```
from django.db import models
from django.contrib.auth.models import AbstractBaseUser

class User(AbstractBaseUser):

Custom user class.
```

Now that we have created our custom `user` class for the project, we can add all the basic attributes to this `user` class that we would like to be in the user model.

Now `models.py` looks like this:

```
from django.db import models
from django.contrib.auth.models import AbstractBaseUser

class User(AbstractBaseUser):

Custom user class.

username = models.CharField('username', max_length=10,
unique=True, db_index=True)
email = models.EmailField('email address', unique=True)
joined = models.DateTimeField(auto_now_add=True)
is_active = models.BooleanField(default=True)
is_admin = models.BooleanField(default=False)
```

In the preceding code snippet, the custom user model `email` field has a property `unique` that is set to `True`. This means that a user can only register once with the given e-mail address, the verification can be done on the registration page. You will see a `db_index` option also in the `username` attribute with value `True`, which will index the user table on the `username` attribute.

`joined` is the `dateTimeField` parameter populated automatically when a new user profile is created; the `is_active` field is set to `True` by default when a new user account is created, and the `is_admin` field is initialized to `False` at the same time.

One more field is needed to make this almost the same as the default Django user model, which is the `username` field.

Add the `USERNAME_FIELD` field in the `models.py` file as follows:

```
USERNAME_FIELD = 'username'
def __unicode__(self):
return self.username
```

`USERNAME_FIELD` also works as the unique identifier for a user model in Django. We have mapped our `username` parameter with Django's `username` field. This field must be unique (`unique=True`) in its definition, which our `username` field already is.

The `__unicode__()` method is also added as the definition that displays a human-readable representation of our user model object.

Thus, the final `models.py` file will look like this:

```
from django.db import models
from django.contrib.auth.models import AbstractBaseUser

class User(AbstractBaseUser):
"""
Custom user class.
"""
username = models.CharField( 'username', max_length=10,
unique=True, db_index=True)
email = models.EmailField('email address', unique=True)
joined = models.DateTimeField(auto_now_add=True)
is_active = models.BooleanField(default=True)
is_admin = models.BooleanField(default=False)

USERNAME_FIELD = 'username'
def __unicode__(self):
return self.username
```

Now, after defining our user model, we can move ahead to design the tweet model. This is the same application that we created to check out the basic class-based view. We will add content to its `models.py` file, as follows:

```
from django.db import models
from user_profile import User
class Tweet(models.Model):
"""
Tweet model
"""
```

```
user = models.ForeignKey(User)
text = models.CharField(max_length=160)
created_date = models.DateTimeField(auto_now_add=True)
country = models.CharField(max_length=30)
is_active = models.BooleanField(default=True)
```

The tweet model is designed as to be as simplistic as possible for the user. The `attribute` parameter is a foreign key to the `User` object we have already created. The `text` attribute is the tweet content and it will mostly consist of plain text. The `created_Date` attribute, which is automatically added to the database when the `tweet` object is uninitialized, stores the name of the country from where the tweet has actually been posted. In most cases, it will be the same as the user's country. The `is_active` flag is used to represent the tweet's current status, whether it's active and can be displayed or has been deleted by the user.

We need to create the tables in the database for both the models we just created, `user_profile` and `tweet`. We will have to update the `INSTALLED_APPS` variable of your project's `settings.py` file to tell Django to include these two applications in the Django project.

Our updated `INSTALLED_APPS` variable will be as follows:

```
INSTALLED_APPS = (
'django.contrib.admin',
'django.contrib.auth',
'django.contrib.contenttypes',
'django.contrib.sessions',
'django.contrib.messages',
'django.contrib.staticfiles',
'user_profile',
'tweet'
)
```

You can see the last two entries we made to add our models.

Now to create the database table for our project, we will run the command from our root project folder in the terminal:

$python manage.py syncdb

The output will be as follows:

```
Creating tables ...
Creating table django_admin_log
Creating table auth_permission
Creating table auth_group_permissions
Creating table auth_group
```

```
Creating table auth_user_groups
Creating table auth_user_user_permissions
Creating table auth_user
Creating table django_content_type
Creating table django_session
Creating table user_profile_user
Creating table tweet_tweet
```

You just installed Django's auth system, which means you don't have any superusers defined. You can see the following on the terminal:

```
Would you like to create one now? (yes/no): yes
Username (leave blank to use 'ratan'):
Email address: mail@ratankumar.org
Password: XXXX
Password (again): XXXX
Superuser created successfully.
Installing custom SQL ...
Installing indexes ...
Installed 0 object(s) from 0 fixture(s)
```

As a result, our database has been populated with a table. There will appear a database file for our project called db.sqlite3.

As with Django 1.6, the administrator panel comes by default. All we need for our models to be available in Django's admin panel is to add the admin.site.register parameter with the model name as argument for both the applications.

Thus, after addition of admin.site.register(parameter) to both the admin.py, that is, under mytweets and user_profile files will look as the following:

- The admin.py file of the tweet application would look as follows:

  ```
  from django.contrib import admin
  from models import Tweet

  admin.site.register(Tweet)
  ```

- The admin.py file of the user_profile application would look as follows:

  ```
  from django.contrib import admin
  from models import User
  admin.site.register(User)
  ```

Start the server using the following command:

$python manage.py runserver

Then visit the URL http://127.0.0.1:8000/admin; it will ask for login information. As you may remember, we have created the default user at the time of running the $python manage.py syncdb command; use the same username and password.

After successful login, the admin dashboard looks like the following screenshot:

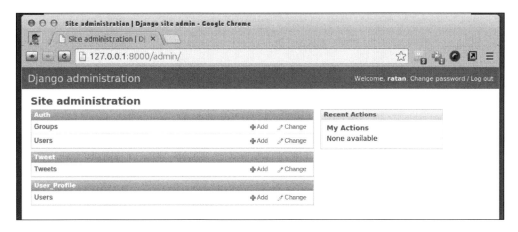

Let's play with the admin dashboard and create a `user` and a `tweet` object that we will be using next for home page views. To add a new user to the project just click on the **Add** button in front of the user model box as shown in the following screenshot:

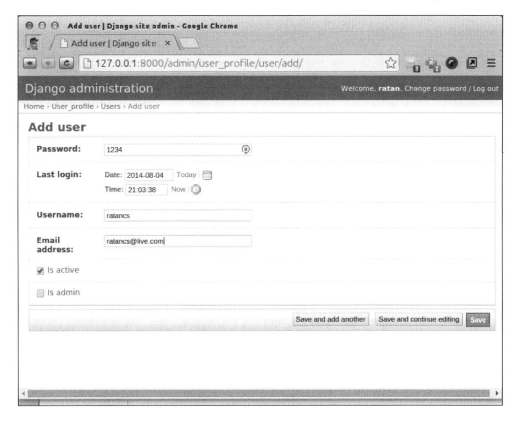

Then fill up the details and save it. You will see a **"user successfully created"** message as shown in the following screenshot:

We will follow a similar process for creating a tweet. First go back to http://127.0.0.1:8000/admin/. Then, click on the **Add** button in front of the tweet box.

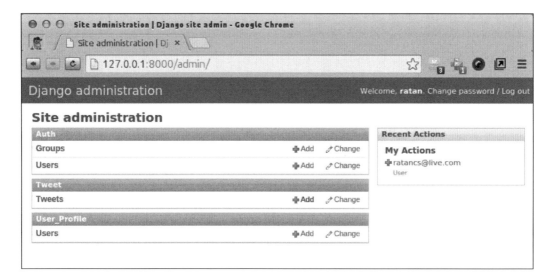

Compose a new tweet by filling out the boxes and selecting the user from the dropdown. This user list is already populated as we have mapped the user to the user object. As we keep on adding users, the dropdown will get populated with all the user objects.

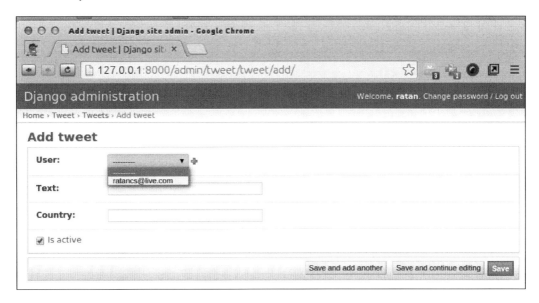

Finally, after composing the tweet, click on the **Save** button. You will see the same screen shown in the following screenshot:

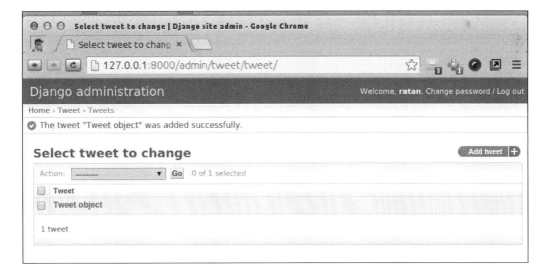

If you look closely, the administrator listing page says every tweet is a `tweet` object, which is not very human-friendly. It can easily be customized for this case. In fact, the same rule is applicable for all the model base representations in the Django admin view or wherever they are displayed.

Add the following code snippet in the `admin.py` file of our project:

```
def __unicode__(self):
return self.text
```

Our admin view will now show the exact text instead of writing tweet object.

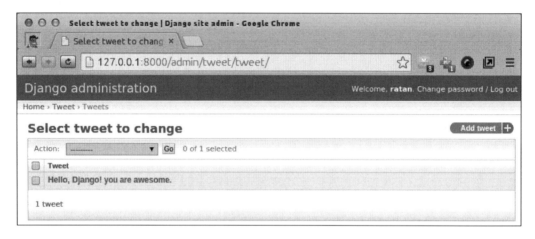

Creating a URL

Every user in our project will have a profile with a unique URL in the following format: `http://127.0.0.1:8000/user/<username>`. Here, the `username` variable is the owner of the tweets that we want to see. This URL is different from the first URL we added earlier because this contains a dynamic portion, so we will have to employ the power of regular expressions in order to express this URL. Open the `urls.py` file and edit it so that the URL table looks like this:

```
url(r'^user/(\w+)/$', Profile.as_view()), urls.py
from django.conf.urls import patterns, include, url
from django.contrib import admin
from tweet.views import Index,Profile
admin.autodiscover()

urlpatterns = patterns('',
url(r'^$', Index.as_view()),
url(r'^user/(\w+)/$', Profile.as_view()),
url(r'^admin/', include(admin.site.urls)),
)
```

The pattern here looks more complicated than the first one. The annotation \w means an alphanumeric character or the underscore. The + sign after it causes the regular expression to match one or more repetitions of what precedes the sign. So, in effect,\w+ means any string that consists of alphanumeric characters and possibly the underscore. We have surrounded this portion of the regular expression with parentheses. This will cause Django to capture the string that matches this portion and pass it to the view.

One last thing needs explaining before we see the view in action. The regular expression that we used will look a bit strange if you haven't used regular expressions before. It is a raw string that contains two characters, ^ and $. The annotation r'' is the Python syntax for defining raw strings. If Python encounters such a raw string, backslashes and other escape sequences are retained in the string, rather than being interpreted in any way. In this syntax, backslashes are left in the string without change and escape sequences are not interpreted. This is useful while working with regular expressions because they often contain backslashes.

In regular expressions, ^ means the beginning of the string and $ means the end of the string. So ^$ basically means a string that doesn't contain anything, that is, an empty string. Given that we are writing the view of the main page, the URL of the page is the root URL and it should indeed be empty.

Python documentation of the re module covers regular expressions in detail. I recommend reading it if you want a thorough treatment of regular expressions. You can find the documentation online at http://docs.python.org/lib/module-re.html. Here is a table that summarizes regular expression syntax for those who want a quick refresher:

Symbol /expression	Matched string
. (Dot)	Any character
^ (Caret)	Start of string
$	End of string
*	0 or more repetitions
+	1 or more repetitions
?	0 or 1 repetitions
		A	B means A or B
[a-z]	Any lowercase character
\w	Any alphanumeric character or _
\d	Any digit

We will now be creating a `Profile()` class with GET functions in the `view.py` file of our tweet application. The important thing to learn here is how the `get()` function handles the dynamic parameter passed through the URL, which is the `username` variable.

The `view.py` of our tweet application would look as follows:

```
class Profile(View):
"""User Profile page reachable from /user/<username> URL"""
def get(self, request, username):
params = dict()()()
user = User.objects.get(username=username)
tweets = Tweet.objects.filter(user=user)
params["tweets"] = tweets
params["user"] = user
return render(request, 'profile.html', params)
```

Templates – creating a template for the Main Page

We are almost done with the model creation for our project. We will now move ahead and create the view page.

The first page we are going to create is the basic page which will list out all the tweets posted by a user. This can be a so-called public profile page that can be accessed without any authentication.

As you might have noticed, we have used a `profile.html` file in the `Profile` class of the `views.py` file, which belongs to our tweet application.

The `views.py` file of our project will look as follows:

```
class Profile(View):
"""User Profile page reachable from /user/<username> URL"""
def get(self, request, username):
params = dict()
user = User.objects.get(username=username)
tweets = Tweet.objects.filter(user=user)
params["tweets"] = tweets
params["user"] = user
return render(request, 'profile.html', params)
```

We will use the Bootstrap framework, which we have already imported in our `base.html` file, to design the `Profile.html` file.

We will first restructure the base.html file which we created for our application. Now this base.html file will be used as a template or theme of our project. We will import this file across the project, which results in constant user interface across the project.

We will just remove the div tag we placed inside the block content from our base.html file.

We also need jQuery, which is a JavaScript library for complete functioning of bootstrap. It can be downloaded from http://jquery.com/download/. For our current project, we will download the latest version of jQuery in production-ready phase. We will be adding it before bootstrap's JavaScript import.

The base.html file should look like this now:

```
{% load staticfiles %}
<html>
<head>
<link href="{% static 'bootstrap/css/bootstrap.min.css' %}"
rel="stylesheet" media="screen">
</head>

<body>
{% block content %}
{% endblock %}

<script src="{% static 'js/jquery-2.1.1.min.js' %}"></script>
<script src="{% static 'bootstrap/js/bootstrap.min.js'
%}"></script>
</body>
</html>
```

In this case the block is as follows:

```
{% block content %}
{% endblock %}
```

This means that, whichever template we are going to extend the base.html file, currently in the profile.html file, the content of the profile.html file will be rendered between these block quotes. To understand this better, consider this: you have a header (in some cases, navigation bar) and footer on every page and the page content changes depending upon the view. With the preceding template, we generally need to place the header code before the block content and footer content below the block content.

Using a header is much easier now as we have the advantage of frontend framework. We will first choose the layout of our project. For simplicity, we will divide the whole page into three sections. The first will be the header, which will be constant as we navigate throughout the project. The same will apply to the bottom of the page, which is our footer.

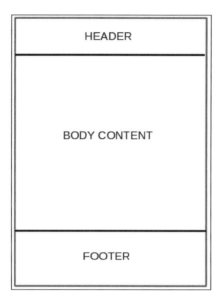

To achieve the preceding layout, our bootstrap code will be built in this way: we will use bootstrap's `navbar` for our header section as well as for the footer section. Then we will place the container `div` tag. Our updated code for the `base.html` file will be changed to the following:

```
{% load staticfiles %}
<html>
<head>
<link href="{% static 'css/bootstrap.min.css' %}"
rel="stylesheet" media="screen">
</head>
<body>
<nav class="navbar navbar-default navbar-fixed-top"
role="navigation">
<a class="navbar-brand" href="#">MyTweets</a>
<p class="navbar-text navbar-right">User Profile Page</p>
</nav>
<div class="container">
{% block content %}
```

```
{% endblock %}
</div>
<nav class="navbar navbar-default navbar-fixed-bottom"
role="navigation">
<p class="navbar-text navbar-right">Footer </p>

</nav>
<script src="{% static 'js/bootstrap.min.js' %}"></script>
</body>
</html>
```

The `navbar` parameter will start in the body, but before the container, so that it can wrap the whole container. We use Django block content to render the rows which we will define in the extended templates, in this case, the `profile.html` file. The footer section comes in last, which is after the `endblock` statement.

This will render the following page:

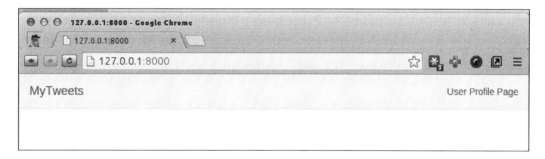

 Note that if you do not get the static file included, replace the STATICFILES_DIRS variable with the following in your settings.py file:

```
STATICFILES_DIRS = (
BASE_DIR + '/static/',
)
```

The design for the profile page is as follows:

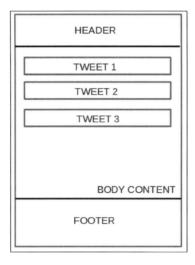

This can easily be designed again with the help of a bootstrap component called well. The `well` or `wellbox` components are used with an element to give it an inset effect. The `profile.html` file will just extend the `base.html` file and only contain rows and further elements.

The `profile.html` file of our project would look as follows:

```
{% extends "base.html" %}
{% block content %}
<div class="row clearfix">
<div class="col-md-12 column">
{% for tweet in tweets %}
<div class="well">
<span>{{ tweet.text }}</span>
</div>
{% endfor %}
</div>
</div>
{% endblock %}
```

This will show the tweets of a user we pass via a parameter in the URL. The example we have taken is the user `ratancs`, who we created during the initial setup. You can see their tweets in the following screenshot:

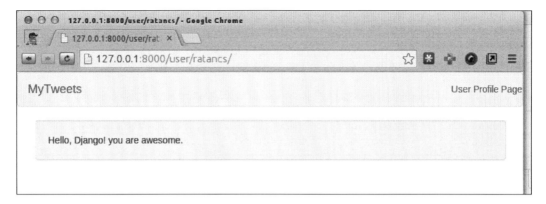

Summary

We learned the basic terminology related to our Django project, what we need to set up the basic template structure of our project, and how to set up the bootstrap for our tweet-like application. We also saw how MVC works here and the role of URL and views while creating the main page.

Then, we introduced class-based views to generate user pages. We saw how models work in Django and how to design the database schema for the project. We also learned to build a user registration page, an account management page, and a template for the main page.

We will learn to design the algorithm for building a hashtag model and the mechanism to use hashtags in your post in the following chapters.

5
Introducing Hashtags

Tags are one of the most prominent features in Web 2.0 applications. A **tag** is a keyword associated with a piece of information, such as an article, image, or link. **Tagging** is the process of assigning tags to content. It is usually done by the author or users and allows for user-defined categorization of content.

We will also be using tags in our project, and we will be calling it **hashtags**. Tags have become very popular in web applications because they enable users to classify, view, and share content easily. If you are not familiar with tags, you can see examples by visiting social sites such as Twitter, Facebook, or Google Plus, where tags are pinned to each status or conversation to help us find trending topics. Since we are going to build a micro blogging site, tags will help us to categorize the conversations between users.

To introduce tags into our system, we need a mechanism that enables users to submit tweets to the database along with hashtags. Later, we will also need a method for browsing tweets classified under a certain tag.

In this chapter, you will learn about the following:

- Designing a hashtag data model
- Building an algorithm that separates hashtags from a tweet form
- Creating pages for listing tweets under a certain hashtag
- Building a tag cloud

The hashtag data model

Hashtags need to be stored in the database and associated with tweets. So, the first step to introducing tags into our project is to create a data model for hashtags. A hashtag object will only hold one piece of data, a string that represents the hashtag. In addition, we need to maintain the list of hashtags associated with a particular tweet.

You may recall from *Chapter 4, Building an Application Like Twitter,* that we used foreign keys to associate tweets with users, and we called this a one-to-many relationship. However, the relationship between hashtags and tweets is not one-to-many, because one hashtag can be associated with many tweets, and one tweet can also have many hashtags associated with it. This is called a many-to-many relationship, and it is represented in Django models using the models.ManyToManyField parameter.

You should be well aware by now that data models go into the mytweet | models. py file. So, open the file and add the following HashTag class to it:

```
class HashTag(models.Model):
    """
    HashTag model
    """
    name = models.CharField(max_length=64, unique=True)
    tweet = models.ManyToManyField(Tweet)
    def __unicode__(self):
        return self.name
```

Pretty straightforward, isn't it? We simply defined a data model for hashtags. This model holds the tag name and its tweet in its ManyToManyField parameter. When you have finished entering the code, don't forget to run the following command in order to create a table for the model in the database:

$ python manage.py syncdb

output:

```
Creating tables ...
Creating table tweet_hashtag_tweet
Creating table tweet_hashtag
Installing custom SQL ...
Installing indexes ...
Installed 0 object(s) from 0 fixture(s)
```

Now, to see the detailed SQL query of how Django creates and implements all the relationships, and also how it creates the table for them, we can just issue the command `sql` with the model name to `manage.py`. It will show the SQL queries it will run to create the instance of the object. Those who are already familiar with SQL know that many-to-many relationships are usually implemented in SQL by creating a third table that connects the two related tables. Now, let's see how Django implements this type of relationship. In the terminal, issue the following command:

```
$ python manage.py sql tweet
```

output:

```
BEGIN;
CREATE TABLE "tweet_tweet" (
    "id" integer NOT NULL PRIMARY KEY,
    "user_id" integer NOT NULL REFERENCES "user_profile_user" ("id"),
    "text" varchar(160) NOT NULL,
    "created_date" datetime NOT NULL,
    "country" varchar(30) NOT NULL,
    "is_active" bool NOT NULL
)
;
CREATE TABLE "tweet_hashtag_tweet" (
    "id" integer NOT NULL PRIMARY KEY,
    "hashtag_id" integer NOT NULL,
    "tweet_id" integer NOT NULL REFERENCES "tweet_tweet" ("id"),
    UNIQUE ("hashtag_id", "tweet_id")
)
;
CREATE TABLE "tweet_hashtag" (
    "id" integer NOT NULL PRIMARY KEY,
    "name" varchar(64) NOT NULL UNIQUE
)
;
COMMIT;
```

The output may slightly differ depending on your database engine. Indeed, Django automatically creates an extra table called `tweet_hashtag_tweet` to maintain the many-to-many relationship.

It is worth noting that when we define a many-to-many relationship in Django's model API, the `models.ManyToMany` field can be placed in either of the two related models. We could have put this field in the tweet model instead of hashtag; since we created the hashtag model later, we put the `models.ManyToMany` field in it.

For testing purposes, we will move to the admin panel and create a tweet with hashtags, as we did for both user and tweet creation. But, first, we will have to register the hashtags for the administration panel in the `admin.py` file.

The modified `admin.py` file will look like this:

```
from django.contrib import admin
from models import Tweet,Hashtag
# Register your models here.
admin.site.register(Tweet)
admin.site.register(HashTag)
```

Now we can move to the administration panel with /administration URL.

Before we create a hashtag for a tweet, we need to create a tweet with a hashtag. Later, we will write a program that will parse the tweet and automatically create the hashtag instance associated with it.

Refer to the demo diagram for creating the tweet that we have shown in *Chapter 4, Building an Application Like Twitter*, and create a tweet with the following text:

```
Hello, #Django! you are awesome.
```

With the same user we used, `ratancs`, then move on to the hashtag model and create the hashtag `#Django` and associate it with the tweet we created. This will give you an idea of how we assign a hashtag to the tweet.

Let us create a proper tweet submission form, which will ask users to write the tweet as input. It will create all the hashtags associated with the tweet and will save the tweet.

Have a look at the user profile page we have created. At the top center of the page, there will be an input box already associated with the user; thus, when he writes a tweet and hits the button to submit, the tweet will be saved with his ID.

Now, visit this URL: `http://localhost:8000/user/ratancs/`. You will see both the tweets we created earlier.

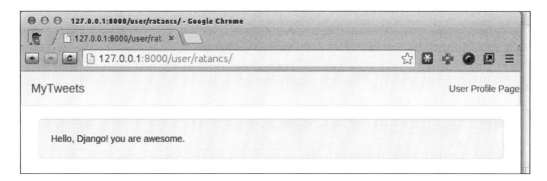

We will go back to the `profile.html` code and append a text area with a submit button to post a tweet for the user. The design will be the same as we chose to display the tweet–that is, we will be using the same well box of `Twitter bootstrap`.

Our `profile.html` file template is as follows:

```
{% extends "base.html" %}
{% block content %}
<div class="row clearfix">
  <div class="col-md-12 column">
    {% for tweet in tweets %}
    <div class="well">
      <span>{{ tweet.text }}</span>
    </div>
    {% endfor %}
  </div>
</div>
{% endblock %}
```

This `{%for ...}` block is used to represent multiple tweets, one below each other, as they have the `div` tag.

Now we will create a `div` tag just above the `{% for ...}` block, and will add our tweet submission form.

Before we write out the form, let us understand about Django forms and how they can be used.

Django forms

Creating, validating and processing forms is an all-too-common task. Web applications receive input and collect data from users by means of web forms. So, naturally, Django comes with its own library to handle these tasks. All you have to do is to import the library and start writing your forms:

```
from django import forms
```

The Django forms library handles three common tasks:

- HTML form generation
- Server-side validation of user input
- HTML form redisplay in case of input errors

The way in which this library works is similar to the way in which Django's data models work. You start by defining a class that represents your form. This class must be derived from the `forms.Form` base class. Attributes in this class represent form fields. The `forms` package provides many field types.

When you create an object from a class that is derived from the `forms.Form` base class, you can interact with it using a variety of methods. There are methods for HTML code generation, methods to access the input data, and methods to validate the form.

We will learn about the forms library by creating a tweet post form in the next section.

Designing the tweet post form

Let's start by creating our first Django form. Create a new file in the tweets application folder and call it `forms.py`. Then, open the file in your code editor and enter the following code:

```
from django import forms
class TweetForm(forms.Form):
  text = forms.CharField(widget=forms.Textarea(attrs={'rows': 1,
  'cols': 85}), max_length=160)
  country = forms.CharField(widget=forms.HiddenInput())
```

After examining the code, you will notice that the way in which we defined this class is similar to the way in which we defined the model classes. We derived the `TweetForm` class from `forms.Form`. All form classes need to inherit from this class. Next, we define the fields that this form contains:

```
text = forms.CharField(widget=forms.Textarea(attrs={'rows': 1,
'cols': 85}), max_length=160)
```

The form contains a text field which will have an HTML tag for text area, an additional attribute for rows and column, and a maximum size limit for input, which is same as the maximum length of the tweet.

```
country = forms.CharField(widget=forms.HiddenInput())
```

Please note that the form also contains a hidden field called `country`, which will be a char field.

There are many field types in the `forms` package. There are several parameters, listed as follows, which can be passed to the constructor of any field type. Some specialized field types can take other parameters in addition to these ones.

- `label`: The label of the field when HTML code is generated.
- `required`: Whether the user must enter a value or not. It is set to `True` by default. To change it, pass `required=False` to the constructor.
- `widget`: This parameter lets you control how the field is rendered in HTML. We used it just now to make the `CharField` parameter of the password become a password input field.
- `help_text`: A description of the field will be displayed when the form is rendered.

The following is a table of commonly used field types:

Field type	Description
CharField	Returns a string.
IntegerField	Returns an integer.
DateField	Returns a Python datetime.date object.
DateTimeField	Returns a Python datetime.datetime object.
EmailField	Returns a valid e-mail address as a string.
URLField	Returns a valid URL as a string.

Here is a partial list of available form widgets:

Widget type	Description
PasswordInput	A password text field.
HiddenInput	A hidden input field.
Textarea	A text area that enables text entry on multiple lines.
FileInput	A file upload field.

Now, we need to modify the `profile.html` file as per the `form.py` file. Update the `profile.html` file as follows:

```
{% extends "base.html" %}
{% block content %}
<div class="row clearfix">
  <div class="col-md-12 column">
    <form method="post" action="post/">{% csrf_token %}
      <div class="col-md-8 col-md-offset-2 fieldWrapper">
        {{ form.text.errors }}
        {{ form.text }}
      </div>
      {{ form.country.as_hidden }}
      <div>
        <input type="submit" value="post">
      </div>
    </form>
  </div>
  <h3> </h3>
  <div class="col-md-12 column">
    {% for tweet in tweets %}
    <div class="well">
      <span>{{ tweet.text }}</span>
    </div>
    {% endfor %}
  </div>
</div>
{% endblock %}
```

Posting the tweet is achieved by a simple form, which is `<form method="post" action="post/">{% csrf_token %}`. The method with which the form will be posted is `"post"` and the relative URL to post a tweet form will be `post/`,

```
{% csrf_token %}
```

This code generated the CSRF token, which actually addresses a security issue; it protects this `post` URL from attacks from another server; details on this will be explained in a later section in this chapter.

We have added a `div` tag just before the tweet `<div>`, and this `div` tag contains a form that will save the tweets when the post button is clicked on.

```
<div class="col-md-8 col-md-offset-2 fieldWrapper">
  {{ form.text.errors }}
  {{ form.text }}
</div>
```

This `fieldWrapper` class in the `div` tag is used by Django's form library to render the HTML tag that we have mentioned for text in form class (which is Text area), followed by the cases of form renders for any error.

This will render the form as shown in the following screenshot:

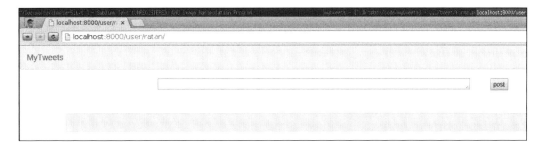

Now, we need to do two things to make this form work:

1. We have to define a method in a controller that is going to take this form submission request and save the tweet data to our tweet model class object.

2. We have to define a URL pattern to which this form will be submitted with the tweet as content.

To handle the request, we will add a new class which will accept the tweet from the form. We will name this class `PostTweet`. This class is added in `tweet/view.py` with an import dependency `from tweet.forms import TweetForm`.

```python
class PostTweet(View):
  """Tweet Post form available on page /user/<username> URL"""
  def post(self, request, username):
    form = TweetForm(self.request.POST)
    if form.is_valid():
      user = User.objects.get(username=username)
      tweet = Tweet(text=form.cleaned_data['text'],
      user=user,
      country=form.cleaned_data['country'])
      tweet.save()
      words = form.cleaned_data['text'].split(" ")
      for word in words:
      if word[0] == "#":
        hashtag, created = 
        HashTag.objects.get_or_create(name=word[1:])
        hashtag.tweet.add(tweet)
      return HttpResponseRedirect('/user/'+username)
```

We only need to define the post method as we only need this class to accept the data. This logic is pretty clear here; if the form is valid, only then will the data be persisted. Redirection always happens. The code also does one more special task; that is, the separation of all the hashtags from a tweet. This is done in a similar way to splitting all the words in a tweet, and if the word starts with # (hash), it will create a hashtag of that word (think of a regular expression here). For the second part, we are going to add an entry in our `urls.py` file, as follows:

```python
from django.conf.urls import patterns, include, url
from django.contrib import admin
from tweet.views import Index, Profile, PostTweet

admin.autodiscover()

urlpatterns = patterns('',
    url(r'^$', Index.as_view()),
    url(r'^user/(\w+)/$', Profile.as_view()),
    url(r'^admin/', include(admin.site.urls)),
    url(r'^user/(\w+)/post/$', PostTweet.as_view())
)
```

If you look carefully at the last line, we have:

```python
url(r'^user/(\w+)/post/$', PostTweet.as_view())
```

This means that all the requests of the form `/user/<username>/post` will be rendered by `PostTweet`.

With this, we have made a simple Django form that can make the user post the tweet from his Twitter page, as shown in the following image:

Once the tweet is posted, the page will show all tweets, as shown in the following image:

Creating a tag page

Next, we will create a page that is similar to the Twitter listing for hashtags. For this task, we will almost follow the same architecture that we followed for the user profile. Let's start by adding a URL entry for the hashtag page. Open the `urls.py` file and insert the following entry (preferably below the user page entry so as to keep the table organized):

```
url(r'^hashTag/(\w+)/$', HashTagCloud.as_view()),
```

The captured part of this regular expression is the same as that of the user page. We will only allow alphanumeric characters in a hashtag.

We will define the `hashtag` class in the controller as follows:

```
class HashTagCloud(View):
    """Hash Tag  page reachable from /hastag/<hashtag> URL"""
    def get(self, request, hashtag):
        params = dict()
        hashtag = HashTag.objects.get(name=hashtag)
        params["tweets"] = hashtag.tweet
        return render(request, 'hashtag.html', params)
```

The HTML template page we will use will be almost the same as that of the profile, except for the form part that we used for posting the tweet.

We need to create the `hashtag.html` file with the following code:

```
{% extends "base.html" %}
{% block content %}
<div class="row clearfix">
  <div class="col-md-12 column">
    {% for tweet in tweets.all %}
    <div class="well">
      <span>{{ tweet.text }}</span>
    </div>
    {% endfor %}
  </div>
</div>
{% endblock %}
```

This will list all the tweets with the hashtag passed from the URL.

Summary

We have learned how to design a hashtag data model and an algorithm required to separate hashtags from a tweet form. Then, we created pages for listing tweets under a certain hashtag. We saw a code snippet for how to build a tweet with hashtag like a tag cloud seen in many blogging sites.

In the next chapter, we will see how to enhance the UI experience using AJAX with Django.

6

Enhancing the User Interface with AJAX

The coming of **AJAX** was an important landmark in the history of Web 2.0. AJAX is a group of technologies that enables developers to build interactive, feature-rich Web applications. Most of these technologies were available many years before AJAX itself. However, the advent of AJAX represents the transition of the Web from static pages that needed to be refreshed whenever data was exchanged to dynamic, responsive, and interactive user interfaces.

Since our project is a Web 2.0 application, it should be heavily focused on user experience. The success of our application depends on getting users to post and share content on it. Therefore, the user interface of our application is one of our major concerns. This chapter will improve the interface of our application by introducing AJAX features, making it more user-friendly and interactive.

In this chapter, you will learn about the following topics:

- AJAX and its advantages
- Using AJAX in Django
- How to use the open source jQuery framework
- Implementing the searching of tweets
- Editing a tweet in place without loading a separate page
- Auto completion of hashtags while submitting a tweet

AJAX and its advantages

AJAX, which stands for **Asynchronous JavaScript and XML**, consists of the following technologies:

- HTML and CSS to structure and style information
- JavaScript to access and manipulate information dynamically
- An XMLHttpRequest object, which is an object provided by modern browsers to exchange data with the server without reloading the current web page
- A format to transfer data between the client and server

XML is used sometimes, but it could be in the HTML, plain text, or JavaScript-based format called JSON.

AJAX technologies let you code the client-side exchange data with the server behind the scenes, without reloading the entire page each time the user makes a request. By using AJAX, Web developers are able to increase the interactivity and usability of Web pages.

AJAX offers the following advantages when implemented in the right places:

- **Better user experience**: With AJAX, the user can do a lot without refreshing the page, which brings Web applications closer to the regular desktop applications
- **Better performance**: By exchanging only the required data with the server, AJAX saves the bandwidth and increases the application's speed

There are numerous examples of Web applications that use AJAX. Google Maps and Gmail are perhaps two of the most prominent examples. In fact, these two applications played an important role in spreading the use of AJAX because of the success that they enjoyed. What sets Gmail apart from other webmail services is its user interface, which enables users to manage their e-mails interactively without waiting for a page to reload after every action. This creates a better user experience and makes Gmail feel like a responsive and feature-rich application rather than a simple website.

This chapter explains how to use AJAX with Django, so as to make our application more responsive and user-friendly. We are going to implement three of the most common AJAX features found in web applications today. However, before that, we will learn about the benefits of using an AJAX framework, as opposed to working with raw JavaScript functions.

Using an AJAX framework in Django

As we have already used Bootstrap in our project, we need not configure it separately for AJAX and jQuery.

There are many advantages of using an AJAX framework:

- JavaScript implementations vary from browser to browser. Some browsers provide more complete and feature-rich implementations, whereas others contain implementations that are incomplete or don't adhere to standards.

  Without an AJAX framework, developers must keep track of browser support for the JavaScript features that they are using and must work around the limitations that are present in some browsers for the implementation of JavaScript.

  On the other hand, when using an AJAX framework, the framework takes care of this for us; it abstracts access to the JavaScript implementation and deals with the differences and quirks of JavaScript across browsers. This way, we can concentrate on developing features instead of worrying about browser differences and limitations.

- The standard set of JavaScript functions and classes is a bit lacking for full-fledged web application development. Various common tasks require many lines of code even though they could be wrapped in simple functions.

  Therefore, even if you decide not to use an AJAX framework, you will find yourself writing a library of functions that encapsulates JavaScript facilities and makes them more usable. However, why reinvent the wheel when there are many excellent open source libraries already available?

AJAX frameworks available in the market today range from comprehensive solutions that provide server-side and client-side components to light-weight client-side libraries that simplify working with JavaScript. Given that we are already using Django on the server side, we only want a client-side framework. In addition to this, the framework should be easy to integrate with Django without requiring any additional dependencies. Finally, it is preferable to pick a light and fast framework. There are many excellent frameworks that fulfill our requirements, such as **Prototype**, the **Yahoo! UI Library**, and **jQuery**.

However, for our application, I'm going to pick jQuery because it's the lightest of the three. It also enjoys a very active development community and a wide range of plugins. If you already have experience with another framework, you can continue using it during this chapter. It is true that you will have to adapt the JavaScript code in this chapter to your framework, but Django code on the server side will remain the same no matter which framework you choose.

> You need to import Bootstrap and jQuery as well. Thus, no specific installation or import is needed to use the AJAX feature in our Django project.

Using the open source jQuery framework

Before we start implementing AJAX enhancements in our project, let's go through a quick introduction to the jQuery framework.

The jQuery JavaScript framework

jQuery is a library of JavaScript functions that facilitates interaction with HTML documents and manipulates them. The library is designed to reduce the time and effort spent on writing code and achieving cross-browser compatibility, while at the same time it takes full advantage of what JavaScript offers to build interactive and responsive web applications.

The general workflow of using jQuery consists of the following two steps:

1. Selecting an HTML element or a group of elements to work on.
2. Applying a jQuery method to the selected group.

Element selectors

jQuery provides a simple approach to select elements: it works by passing a CSS selector string to a function called `$()`. Here are some examples that illustrate the usage of this function:

- If you want to select all anchor (`<a>`) elements on a page, you can use the `$("a")` function call
- If you want to select anchor elements that have the `.title` CSS class, use `$("a.title")`
- To select an element whose ID is #nav, you can use `$("#nav")`
- To select all the list item (`<li>`) elements inside #nav, use `$("#nav li")`

The $() function constructs and returns a jQuery object. After that, you can call methods on this object to interact with the selected HTML elements.

jQuery methods

jQuery offers a variety of methods to manipulate HTML documents. You can hide or show elements, attach event handlers to events, modify CSS properties, manipulate the page structure, and, most importantly, perform AJAX requests.

To debug, we are choosing the Chrome browser as the browser of our choice. Chrome is one of the most advanced JavaScript debugger in the form of its Chrome developer's tools. To launch it, press *Ctrl+Shift+J* on the keyboard.

To experiment with the methods outlined in this section, launch the development server and navigate to the user profile page (http://127.0.0.1:8000/user/ratan/). Open the Chrome developer tool (by pressing *Ctrl+Shift+J* on your keyboard) console by pressing *F12*, and try selecting the elements and manipulating them.

Hiding and showing elements

Let's start with something simple. To hide an element on the page, call the hide() method on it. To show it again, call the show() method. For example, try this on the navigation menu called navbar in Bootstrap of your application:

```
>>> $(".navbar").hide()
```

```
>>> $(".navbar").show()
```

You can also animate the element while hiding and showing it. Try the fadeOut(), fadeIn(), slideUp(), or slideDown() methods to see two of these animated effects.

Of course, these methods (like all other jQuery methods) also work if you select more than one element at once. For example, if you open a user profile and enter the following method call into the Chrome developers tools console, all of the tweets will disappear:

```
>>> $('.well').slideUp()
```

Accessing CSS properties and HTML attributes

Next, we will learn how to change the CSS properties of elements. jQuery offers a method called css() to perform CSS operations. If you call this method with a CSS property name passed as a string, it returns the value of this property:

```
>>> $(".navbar").css("display")
```

The result of this is as follows:

```
block
```

If you pass a second argument to this method, it sets the specified CSS property of the selected element to the additional argument:

```
>>> $(".navbar").css("font-size", "0.8em")
```

The result of this is as follows:

```
<div id="nav" style="font-size: 0.8em;">
```

In fact, you can manipulate any HTML attribute and not just CSS properties. To do so, use the `attr()` method, which works in a similar way as the `css()` method. Calling it with an attribute name returns the attribute value, whereas calling it with an attribute name or value pair sets the attribute to the passed value:

```
>>> $("input").attr("size", "48")
```

This results in the following:

```
<input type="hidden" name="csrfmiddlewaretoken" value="xxx" size="48">
<input id="id_country" name="country" type="hidden" value="Global"
size="48">
<input type="submit" value="post" size="48">
```

This will change the size of all the input elements on the page at once to `48`.

In addition to this, there are shortcut methods to get and set commonly used attributes, such as `val()`, which returns the value of an input field when called without arguments and sets this value to an argument if you pass one. There is also the `html()` method that controls the HTML code inside an element.

Finally, there are two methods that can be used to attach or detach a CSS class to an element: they are the `addClass()` and `removeClass()` methods. A third method is provided to toggle a CSS class and it is called as the `toggleClass()` method. All of these class methods take the name of the class to be changed as a parameter.

Manipulating HTML documents

Now that you are comfortable with manipulating HTML elements, let's see how to add new elements or remove the existing elements. To insert HTML code before an element, use the `before()` method, and to insert code after an element, use the `after()` method. Note how jQuery methods are well named and very easy to remember!

Let's test these methods by inserting parentheses around tag lists on the user page.

Open your user page and enter the following in the Chrome developer tools console:

```
>>> $(".well span").before("<strong>(</strong>")
>>> $(".well span").after("<strong>)</strong>")
```

You can pass any string you want to, the `before()` or `after()` methods. The string may contain plain text, one HTML element, or more. These methods offer a very flexible way to dynamically add HTML elements to an HTML document.

If you want to remove an element, use the `remove()` method. For example:

```
$("#navbar").remove()
```

Not only does this method hide the element, it also removes it completely from the document tree. If you try to select the element again after using the `remove()` method, you will get an empty set:

```
>>> $("#nav")
```

The result of this is as follows:

```
[]
```

Of course, this only removes the elements from the current instance of the page. If you reload the page, the elements will appear again.

Traversing the document tree

Although CSS selectors offer a very powerful way to select elements, there are times when you want to traverse the document tree starting from a particular element.

For this, jQuery provides several methods. The `parent()` method returns the parent of the currently selected element. The `children()` method returns all the immediate children of the selected element. Finally, the `find()` method returns all the descendants of the currently selected element. All of these methods take an optional CSS selector string to limit the result to elements that match the selector. For example, `$(".column").find("span")` returns all the `<span>` descendants of a class column.

If you want to access an individual element of a group, use the `get()` method, which takes the index of the element as a parameter. The `$("span").get(0)` method, for example, returns the first `<span>` element out of the selected group.

Handling events

Next we will learn about event handlers. An event handler is a JavaScript function that is invoked when a particular event happens, for example, when a button is clicked or a form is submitted. jQuery provides a large set of methods to attach handlers to events; events of particular interest in our application are mouse clicks and form submissions. To handle the event of clicking on an element, we select this element and call the `click()` method on it. This method takes an event handler function as a parameter. Let's try this in our Chrome developer console.

Open the user profile page of the application and insert a button after the tweet:

```
>>> $(".well span").after("<button id=\"test-button\">Click me!</
button>")
```

 Note that we had to escape the quotations in the strings passed to the `after()` method.

If you try to click on this button, nothing will happen, so let's attach an event handler to it:

```
>>> $("#test-button").click(function () { alert("You clicked me!"); })
```

Now, when you click on the button, a message box will appear. How did this work?

The argument that we passed to the `click()` method may look a bit complicated, so let's examine it again:

```
function () { alert("You clicked me!"); }
```

This appears to be a function declaration, but without a function name. Indeed, this construct creates what is called an anonymous function in JavaScript terminology and it is used when you need to create a function on the fly and pass it as an argument to another function. We could have avoided using anonymous functions and declared the event handler as a regular function:

```
>>> function handler() { alert("You clicked me!"); }
```
```
>>> $("#test-button").click(handler)
```

The preceding code achieves the same effect, but the first one is more concise and compact. I highly recommend you to get used to anonymous functions in JavaScript (if you are not already), as I'm sure you will appreciate this construct and find it more readable after using it for a while.

Handling form submissions is very similar to handling mouse clicks. First you select the form, then you call the `submit()` method on it, and then you pass the handler as an argument. We will use this method many times while adding AJAX features to our project in later sections.

Sending AJAX requests

Before we finish this section, let's talk about AJAX requests. jQuery provides many ways to send AJAX requests to the server. There is, for example, the `load()` method that takes a URL and loads the page at this URL into the selected element. There are also methods to send the GET or POST requests and to receive the results. We will examine these methods in more depth while implementing AJAX features in our project.

What next?

This wraps up our quick introduction to jQuery. The information provided in this section will be enough to continue with this chapter, and once you finish this chapter, you will be able to implement many interesting AJAX features on your own. However, please keep in mind that this jQuery introduction is only the tip of the iceberg. If you want a comprehensive treatment of the jQuery framework, I highly recommend you read *Learning jQuery* from Packt Publishing, as it covers jQuery in much more detail. You can find out more about this book at `http://www.packtpub.com/jQuery`.

Implementing the searching of tweets

We will start introducing AJAX in our application by implementing live searches. The idea behind this feature is simple: when the user types a few keywords into a text field and clicks on search, a script works behind the scenes to fetch the search results and presents them on the same page. The search page does not reload, thus saving bandwidth, and provides a better and more responsive user experience.

Before we start implementing this, we need to keep in mind an important rule while working with AJAX: write your application so that it works without AJAX and then introduce AJAX to it. If you do so, you ensure that everyone will be able to use your application, including users who don't have JavaScript enabled and those who use browsers without AJAX support.

Implementing a searching

So, before we work with AJAX, let's write a simple view that searches bookmarks by title. First of all, we need to create a search form, so open the `tweets/forms.py` file and add the following class to it:

```
class SearchForm(forms.Form):
query = forms.CharField(label='Enter a keyword to search for',
widget=forms.TextInput(attrs={'size': 32, 'class':'form-
control'}))
```

As you can see, it's a pretty straightforward form class with only one text field. This field will be used by the user to enter search keywords. Next, let's create a view to conduct the search. Open the `tweets/views.py` file and enter the following code into it:

```
class Search(View):
    """Search all tweets with query /search/?query=<query> URL"""
    def get(self, request):
      form = SearchForm()
      params = dict()
      params["search"] = form
    return render(request, 'search.html', params)

    def post(self, request):
      form = SearchForm(request.POST)
      if form.is_valid():
      query = form.cleaned_data['query']
      tweets = Tweet.objects.filter(text__icontains=query)
      context = Context({"query": query, "tweets": tweets})
      return_str = render_to_string('partials/_tweet_search.html',
      context)
    return HttpResponse(json.dumps(return_str),
    content_type="application/json")
    else:
      HttpResponseRedirect("/search")
```

Apart from a couple of method calls, the view should be very easy to understand. If you look at the `get` request, it is pretty simple, as it prepares the search form and then renders it.

The `post()` method is where all the magic happens. When we are rendering the search result, it is just a layout rendering with the search form, that is, if you take a look at the new file we created called `search.html`, you can see the following:

```
{% extends "base.html" %}
{% load staticfiles %}
```

```
{% block content %}

<div class="row clearfix">
  <div class="col-md-6 col-md-offset-3 column">
    <form id="search-form" action="" method="post">{% csrf_token
    %}
      <div class="input-group input-group-sm">
      {{ search.query.errors }}
      {{ search.query }}
        <span class="input-group-btn">
          <button class="btn btn-search"
          type="submit">search</button>
        </span>
      </div><!-- /input-group -->
    </form>
  </div>
  <div class="col-md-12 column tweets">
  </div>
</div>
{% endblock %}
{% block js %}
  <script src="{% static 'js/search.js' %}"></script>
{% endblock %}
```

If you look carefully, you will see the inclusion of a new section named {% block js %}. The concept used here is the same as of the {% block content %} block, that is, what is declared here will be rendered in the base.html file. Taking it further, and looking at the modified base.html file, we can see the following:

```
{% load staticfiles %}
  <html>
    <head>
      <link href="{% static 'css/bootstrap.min.css' %}"
        rel="stylesheet" media="screen">
        {% block css %}
        {% endblock %}
    </head>
    <body>
      <nav class="navbar navbar-default" role="navigation">
        <a class="navbar-brand" href="#">MyTweets</a>
        <p class="navbar-text navbar-right">User Profile Page</p>
      </nav>
      <div class="container">
        {% block content %}
        {% endblock %}
```

```
        </div>
        <nav class="navbar navbar-default navbar-fixed-bottom"
        role="navigation">
          <p class="navbar-text navbar-right">Footer </p>
        </nav>
        <script src="{% static 'js/jquery-2.1.1.min.js'
        %}"></script>
        <script src="{% static 'js/bootstrap.min.js' %}"></script>
        <script src="{% static 'js/base.js' %}"></script>
            {% block js %}
            {% endblock %}
      </body>
    </html>
```

The preceding code clearly shows the two new content blocks, which are as follows:

```
    {% block css %}
      {% endblock %}
      {% block js %}
    {% endblock %}
```

They are used to include the respective file types and to render the file types with the base, so that maintaining the project becomes much simpler using the simple rule of declaring just one CSS and JavaScript file per page. We will implement this later in the book with the concepts that call **assets pipeline**.

Now, coming back to our AJAX search feature, you will see that this `search.html` file is similar to the `tweet.html` file.

For the search feature, we will create a new URL, which we need to append to the following `urls.py` file:

```
    url(r'^search/$', Search.as_view()),
    urls.py
    from django.conf.urls import patterns, include, url
    from django.contrib import admin
    from tweet.views import Index, Profile, PostTweet, HashTagCloud,
    Search

    admin.autodiscover()

    urlpatterns = patterns('',
    url(r'^$', Index.as_view()),
    url(r'^user/(\w+)/$', Profile.as_view()),
    url(r'^admin/', include(admin.site.urls)),
    url(r'^user/(\w+)/post/$', PostTweet.as_view()),
```

```
url(r'^hashTag/(\w+)/$', HashTagCloud.as_view()),
url(r'^search/$', Search.as_view()),
)
```

In the `search.html` file, we defined the `search.js` method; let's create this JavaScript file, which actually makes the AJAX request:

`search.js`

```
$('#search-form').submit(function(e){
$.post('/search/', $(this).serialize(), function(data){
$('.tweets').html(data);
});
e.preventDefault();
});
```

This JavaScript code gets triggered when the form is submitted, it makes an AJAX post request to the `/search` user with the serialized form data, and it gets the response. Then, with the response it gets, it appends the data to the element that has the class tweets.

If we open the user search in the browser, it will look like the following screenshot:

Now, wait! What happens when this form is submitted?

The AJAX request goes to the `post()` method of the search class, which is as follows:

```
def post(self, request):
  form = SearchForm(request.POST)
  if form.is_valid():
    query = form.cleaned_data['query']
    tweets = Tweet.objects.filter(text__icontains=query)
    context = Context({"query": query, "tweets": tweets})
```

```
    return_str = render_to_string('partials/_tweet_search.html',
    context)
return HttpResponse(json.dumps(return_str),
content_type="application/json")
else:
    HttpResponseRedirect("/search")
```

We are checking the form validation after we extract from the `request.POST` method; if the form is valid, the query is extracted from the form object.

Then, the `tweets = Tweet.objects.filter(text__icontains===query)` method searches for the substring match for the given query term.

Searches are conducted using a method called `filter` in the `Tweets.objects` module. You can think of it as the equivalent of the SELECT statements in Django models. It receives the search criteria in its arguments and returns the search results. The name of each argument must adhere to the following naming convention:

```
field__operator
```

Note that the `field` and `operator` variables are separated by two underscores: the field, which is the name of the field that we want to search by, and operator, which is the lookup method that we want to use. Here is a list of the commonly used operators:

- `exact`: This is the value of the argument that is an exact match of the field
- `contains`: This field contains the value of the argument
- `startswith`: This field starts with the value of the argument
- `lt`: This field is less than the value of the argument
- `gt`: This field is greater than the value of the argument

Also, there are case-insensitive versions of the first three operators: `iexact`, `icontains`, and `istartswith` that can be included in the list as well.

One thing that we are doing is totally different now, which is the following:

```
context = Context({"query": query, "tweets": tweets})
return_str = render_to_string('partials/_tweet_search.html',
context)
return HttpResponse(json.dumps(return_str),
content_type="application/json")
```

Our goal was to load the search results without reloading or refreshing the search page. If so, how our previous render method will help us? It can't. We need some methods that can help us send the date to the browser without reloading it.

We widely use the concepts in web development called **partials**. They are generally small snippets of HTML code generated on the server side, are rendered as JSON, and then they get appended to the existing DOM with the help of JavaScript.

To implement this method, we will first create a folder called partials in the existing template folder, a `_tweet_search.html` file with the following content:

```
{% for tweet in tweets %}
  <div class="well">
    <span>{{ tweet.text }}</span>
  </div>
{% endfor %}
{% if not tweets %}
  <div class="well">
    <span> No Tweet found.</span>
  </div>
{% endif %}
```

The code will render the entire tweet object within a well box or, if no tweet object is found, it will render `No tweet Found` inside the well box.

The preceding concept is to render a partial as a string in the view, and if we need to pass any parameters for the render, we need to pass them in the first place with the call to generate the string from partials. To pass the parameters for partials, we need to create a context object and then pass our parameters:

```
context = Context({"query": query, "tweets": tweets})
return_str = render_to_string('partials/_tweet_search.html',
context)
```

First, we will create the context with the `query` (which we will use later) and `tweets` parameters and use the `render_to_string()` function. Then, we can use JSON to dump the string to the `HttpResponse()` function with the following:

```
return HttpResponse(json.dumps(return_str),
content_type="application/json")
```

The list of imports are as follows:

```
from django.views.generic import View
from django.shortcuts import render
from user_profile.models import User
from models import Tweet, HashTag
from tweet.forms import TweetForm, SearchForm
from django.http import HttpResponseRedirect
from django.template.loader import render_to_string
from django.template import Context
from django.http import HttpResponse
import json
```

That's it! We completed a basic AJAX-based search for our tweets. Searching for django listed the two tweets we created, as shown in the following screenshot:

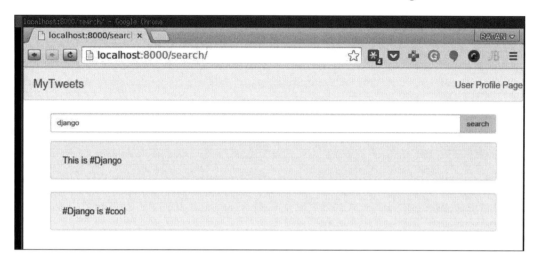

Go ahead and play with the search engine, and I'm sure you will fall more in love with Django.

We now have a functional (albeit very basic) search page. The search functionality itself will be improved during later chapters, but what matters to us now is introducing AJAX to the search form, so that results are fetched behind the scenes and are presented to the user without reloading the page. Thanks to our modular code, this task will turn out to be much simpler than it may seem.

Implementing the live searching of tweets

As we conducted a simple search in the previous section, we will now implement the live search, which is technically the same, but the only difference is that the search form will be submitted with every key stroke and the results will be loaded in real, time.

To implement live searches, we need to do the following two things:

- We need to intercept and handle the event of submitting the search form. This can be done using the submit() method of jQuery.

- We need to use AJAX to load the search results in the background and insert them in the page.

jQuery offers a method called `load()` that retrieves a page from the server and inserts its contents into the selected element. In its simplest form, the function takes the URL of the remote page to be loaded as a parameter.

We will implement the live search on hashtags, that is, we will create a new page that is the same as the search page that we just created, but this will be for hashtags and we will use a live hashtag suggestion (autocomplete for hashtag). Before we begin, we need the Twitter `typeahead` JavaScript library for the same.

Download the latest version of this library from `http://twitter.github.io/typeahead.js/`.

For this chapter, we downloaded the version 10.05 of the library. Download it and save it to your current JavaScript folder.

First of all, let's modify our search view a little, so that it only returns the search results without the rest of the search page when it receives an additional GET variable called AJAX. We do so to enable the JavaScript code on the client side to easily retrieve search results without the rest of the search page HTML format. This can be done by simply using the `bookmark_list.html` template instead of the `search.html` template when requested.

GET contains the key AJAX parameter. Open the `bookmarks/views.py` file and modify the `search_page` parameter (toward the end), so that it becomes as follows:

```
def search_page(request):
  [...]
  variables = RequestContext(request, {
    'form': form,
    'bookmarks': bookmarks,
    'show_results': show_results,
    'show_tags': True,
    'show_user': True
  })
  if request.GET.has_key('AJAX'):):):
    return render_to_response('bookmark_list.html', variables)
  else:
    return render_to_response('search.html', variables)
```

Next, create a file called `search.js` in the `site_media` directory and link it to the `templates/search.html` file like this:

```
{% extends "base.html" %}
  {% block external %}
    <script type="text/javascript" src="/site_media/search.js">
    </script>
  {% endblock %}
```

```
{% block title %}Search Bookmarks{% endblock %}
{% block head %}Search Bookmarks{% endblock %}
[...]
```

Now for the fun part! Let's create a function that loads the search results and inserts them into the corresponding `div` tag. Write the following code in the `site_media/search.js` file:

```
function search_submit() {
   var query = $("#id_query").val();
   $("#search-results").load(
     "/search/?AJAX&query=" + encodeURIComponent(query)
   );
   return false;
}
```

Let's go through this function line by line:

- The function first gets the query string from the text field using the `val()` method.

- We use the `load()` method to get the search results from the `search_page` view and to insert the search results into the `#search-results` div. The request URL is constructed by first calling the `encodeURIComponent` parameter on query, which works exactly like the `urlencode` filter we used in the Django templates. Calling this function is important to ensure that the constructed URL remains valid even if the user enters special characters into the text field, such as `&`. After the escape query, we concatenate it with the `/search/?AJAX&query=` parameter. This URL invokes the `search_page` view and passes the GET variable's AJAX parameter and query to it. The view returns the search results and the `load()` method in turn loads the results into the `#search-results` div.

- We return `False` from the function to tell the browser not to submit the form after calling our handler. If we don't return `False` in the function, the browser will continue to submit the form as usual and we don't want that.

One little detail remains: where and when should you attach the `search_submit` parameter to the submit event of the search form? A rule of thumb when writing JavaScript is that we cannot manipulate elements in the document tree before the document finishes loading. Therefore, our function must be invoked as soon as the search page is loaded. Fortunately for us, jQuery provides a method to execute a function when the HTML document is loaded. Let's utilize it by appending the following code to the `site_media/search.js` file:

```
$(document).ready(function () {
   $("#search-form").submit(search_submit);
});
```

The $(document) function selects the document element of the current page. Note that there are no quotations around the document variable; it's a variable provided by the browser, not a string.

The ready() method takes a function and executes it as soon as the selected element finishes loading. So, in effect, we are telling jQuery to execute the passed function as soon as the HTML document is loaded. We pass an anonymous function to the ready() method, and this function simply binds the search_submit parameter to the submit event of the #search-form form.

That's it. We've implemented live searches with less than fifteen lines of code. To test the new functionality, navigate to http://127.0.0.1:8000/search/, submit queries, and note how the results are displayed without reloading the page.

The information covered in this section can be applied to any form that needs to be processed in the background without reloading the page. You can, for example, create a comment form with a preview button that loads the preview in the same page without reloading. In the next section, we will enhance the user page to let users edit their bookmarks in place without navigating away from the user page.

Editing a tweet in place without loading a separate page

Editing posted content is a very common task on websites. It's usually implemented by offering an **edit** link next to the content. When clicked on, this link takes the user to a form located at another page, where the content can be edited. When the user submits the form, they are redirected back to the content page.

Imagine, on the other hand, that you could edit content without navigating away from the content page. When you click on the **edit** button, the content is replaced with a form. When you submit the form, it disappears and the updated content appears in its place. Everything happens on the same page; editing the form's rendering and submissions are done using JavaScript and AJAX. Wouldn't such a workflow be more intuitive and responsive?

The preceding technique described is called **in-place editing**. It now finds its way in Web applications and becomes more common. We will implement this feature in our application by letting the user edit their bookmarks in place on the user page.

Since our application doesn't support the editing of bookmarks yet, we will implement this first and then modify the editing procedure to work in place.

Implementing bookmark editing

We already have most of the parts that are needed to implement bookmark editing. If you recall from the previous chapter, in the `bookmarks/views.py` file, we implemented the `bookmark_save_page` view in such a way that if the user tries to save the same URL more than once, the same bookmark is updated rather than being duplicated. This was easy to do thanks to the `get_or_create()` method provided by data models. This little detail greatly simplifies the implementation of bookmark editing. Here is what we need to do:

- We pass the URL of the bookmark that we want to edit as a GET variable named URL to the `bookmark_save_page` view.

- We modify the `bookmark_save_page` view, so that it populates the fields of the bookmark form if it receives the GET variable. The form is populated with the data of the bookmark that corresponds to the passed URL.

When the populated form is submitted, the bookmark will be updated, as we explained earlier, because it will seem to be that the user submitted the same URL another time.

Before we implement the preceding described technique, let's reduce the size of the `bookmark_save_page` view by moving the part that saves a bookmark to a separate function. We will call this function `_bookmark_save`. The underscore at the beginning of the name tells Python not to import this function when the views module is imported. The function expects a request and a valid form object as parameters; it saves a bookmark out of the form data and returns this bookmark.

Open the `bookmarks/views.py` file and create the following function; you can cut and paste the code from the `bookmark_save_page` view if you like, as we will not make any changes to it except for the `return` statement at the end:

```
def _bookmark_save(request, form):
  # Create or get link.
  link, dummy = \
  Link.objects.get_or_create(url=form.clean_data['url'])
  # Create or get bookmark.
  bookmark, created = Bookmark.objects.get_or_create(
    user=request.user,
    link=link
  )
  # Update bookmark title.
  bookmark.title = form.clean_data['title']
  # If the bookmark is being updated, clear old tag list.
  if not created:
    bookmark.tag_set.clear()
    # Create new tag list.
```

```
      tag_names = form.clean_data['tags'].split()
      for tag_name in tag_names:
        tag, dummy = Tag.objects.get_or_create(name=tag_name)
        bookmark.tag_set.add(tag)
        # Save bookmark to database and return it.
        bookmark.save()
      return bookmark
      Now in the same file, replace the code that you removed from
      bookmark_save_page
      with a call to _bookmark_save :
        @login_required
        def bookmark_save_page(request):
          if request.method == 'POST':
            form = BookmarkSaveForm(request.POST)
          if form.is_valid():
            bookmark = _bookmark_save(request, form)
            return HttpResponseRedirect(
              '/user/%s/' % request.user.username
            )
          else:
            form = BookmarkSaveForm()
            variables = RequestContext(request, {
              'form': form
            })
          return render_to_response('bookmark_save.html', variables)
```

The current logic in the bookmark_save_page view works like this:

[Pseudo Code]

```
if there is POST data:
  Validate and save bookmark.
  Redirect to user page.
else:
  Create an empty form.
Render page.
```

To implement bookmark editing, we need to slightly modify the logic, as follows:

[Pseudo Code]

```
if there is POST data:
  Validate and save bookmark.
  Redirect to user page.
  else if there is a URL in GET data:
    Create a form an populate it with the URL's bookmark.
  else:
    Create an empty form.
Render page.
```

Let's translate the preceding pseudo code into Python. Modify the bookmark_save_
page view in the bookmarks/views.py file, so that it looks like the following code
(the new code is highlighted):

```python
from django.core.exceptions import ObjectDoesNotExist
@login_required
def bookmark_save_page(request):
  if request.method == 'POST':
    form = BookmarkSaveForm(request.POST)
      if form.is_valid():
        bookmark = _bookmark_save(request, form)
        return HttpResponseRedirect(
          '/user/%s/' % request.user.username
        )
      elif request.GET.has_key('url'):):):
        url = request.GET['url']
        title = ''
        tags = ''
      try:
        link = Link.objects.get(url=url)
        bookmark = Bookmark.objects.get(
          link=link,
          user=request.user
        )
      title = bookmark.title
      tags = ' '.join(
        tag.name for tag in bookmark.tag_set.all()
      )
      except ObjectDoesNotExist:
        pass
      form = BookmarkSaveForm({
        'url': url,
        'title': title,
        'tags': tags
      })
      else:
        form = BookmarkSaveForm()
        variables = RequestContext(request, {
          'form': form
        })
      return render_to_response('bookmark_save.html',
      variables)
```

This new section of the code first checks whether a GET variable called URL exists. If this is the case, it loads the corresponding Link and Bookmark objects of this URL and binds all the data to a bookmark saving form. You may wonder why we load the Link and Bookmark objects in a try-except construct that silently ignores exceptions.

Indeed, it's perfectly valid to raise an HTTP 404 exception if no bookmark was found for the requested URL. However, our code chooses to only populate the URL field in this situation, leaving the title and tags fields empty.

Now, let's add **edit** links next to each bookmark in the user page. Open the templates/bookmark_list.html file and insert the highlighted code:

```
{% if bookmarks %}
  <ul class="bookmarks">
    {% for bookmark in bookmarks %}
      <li>
        <a href="{{ bookmark.link.url }}" class="title">
        {{ bookmark.title|escape }}</a>
        {% if show_edit %}
          <a href="/save/?url={{ bookmark.link.url|urlencode }}"
          class="edit">[edit]</a>
        {% endif %}
      <br />
      {% if show_tags %}
        Tags:
          {% if bookmark.tag_set.all %}
            <ul class="tags">
              {% for tag in bookmark.tag_set.all %}
                <li><a href="/tag/{{ tag.name|urlencode }}/">
              {{ tag.name|escape }}</a></li>
              {% endfor %}
            </ul>
      {% else %}
        None.
      {% endif %}
      <br />
  [...]
```

Note how we constructed edit links by appending the bookmark's URL to /save/?url= {{ bookmark.link.url|urlencode }}.

Also, since we only want to show edit links on the user's page, the template renders these links only when the `show_edit` flag is set to `True`. Otherwise, it wouldn't make sense to let the user edit other people's links. Now open the `bookmarks/views.py` file and add the `show_edit` flag to the template variables in the `user_page` flag:

```
def user_page(request, username):
    user = get_object_or_404(User, username=username)
    bookmarks = user.bookmark_set.order_by('-id')
    variables = RequestContext(request, {
        'bookmarks': bookmarks,
        'username': username,
        'show_tags': True,
        'show_edit': username == request.user.username,
    })
    return render_to_response('user_page.html', variables)
```

The `username == request.user.username` expression evaluates to `True` only when users view their own page, and this is precisely what we want.

Finally, I suggest you reduce the font size of the edit links a little. Open the `site_media/style.css` file and append the following to its end:

```
ul.bookmarks .edit {
    font-size: 70%;
}
```

And we are done! Feel free to navigate to your user page and experiment with editing your bookmarks before we continue.

Implementing in-place editing of bookmarks

Now that we have bookmark editing implemented, let's move to the exciting part: adding in-place editing with AJAX!

Our approach to this task will be as follows:

- We will intercept the event of clicking on an edit link and use AJAX to load a bookmark editing form from the server. Then we will replace the bookmark on the page with the editing form.

- When the user submits the edit form, we will intercept the submission event and use AJAX to send the updated bookmark to the server.

- The server saves the bookmark and returns the HTML representation of the new bookmark. We will then replace the edit form on the page with the markup returned by the server.

We will implement the preceding procedure using an approach very similar to live searching. First, we will modify the `bookmark_save_page` view, so that it responds to AJAX requests when a GET variable called AJAX exits. Next, we will write JavaScript code to retrieve an edit form from the view, which posts bookmark data back to the server when the user submits this form.

Since we want to return the markup of an edit form to the AJAX script from the `bookmark_save_page` view, let's restructure our templates a little. Create a file called `bookmark_save_form.html` in templates and move the bookmark saving form from the `bookmark_save.html` file to this new file:

```
<form id="save-form" method="post" action="/save/">
  {{ form.as_p }}
  <input type="submit" value="save" />
</form>
```

Note that we also changed the action attribute of the form to `/save/` and gave it an ID. This is necessary for the form to work on the user page as well as on the bookmark submission page.

Next, include this new template in the `bookmark_save.html` file:

```
{%extends "base.html" %}
{%block title %}Save Bookmark{% endblock %}
{%block head %}Save Bookmark{% endblock %}
{%block content %}
{%include 'bookmark_save_form.html' %}
{%endblock %}
```

Ok, now we have the form in a separate template. Let's update the `bookmark_save_page` view to handle both the normal and AJAX requests. Open the `bookmarks/views.py` file and update the view, so that it looks like the following (modified with the new lines that are highlighted):

```
def bookmark_save_page(request):
  AJAX = request.GET.has_key('AJAX')))
  if request.method == 'POST':
    form = BookmarkSaveForm(request.POST)
    if form.is_valid():
      bookmark = _bookmark_save(form)
        if AJAX:
          variables = RequestContext(request, {
            'bookmarks': [bookmark],
            'show_edit': True,
            'show_tags': True
        })
```

```
        return render_to_response('bookmark_list.html', variables)
    else:
      return HttpResponseRedirect(
        '/user/%s/' % request.user.username
      )
    else:
      if AJAX:
        return HttpResponse('failure')
        elif request.GET.has_key('url'):
          url = request.GET['url']
          title = ''
          tags = ''
      try:
        link = Link.objects.get(url=url)
        bookmark = Bookmark.objects.get(link=link,
        user=request.user)
        title = bookmark.title
        tags = ' '.join(tag.name for tag in
        bookmark.tag_set.all())
      except:::
        pass
        form = BookmarkSaveForm({
          'url': url,
          'title': title,
          'tags': tags
        })
      else:
        form = BookmarkSaveForm()
        variables = RequestContext(request, {
          'form': form
        })
        if AJAX:
          return render_to_response(
            'bookmark_save_form.html',
            variables
          )
          else:
            return render_to_response(
              'bookmark_save.html',
              variables
            )
```

Let's examine each highlighted section separately:

```
AJAX = request.GET.has_key('AJAX')
```

At the beginning of the method, we will check whether a GET variable named AJAX exists. We will store the result in a variable called AJAX. Later in the method, we can check whether we are handling an AJAX request or not, using this variable:

```
if condition:
  if form.is_valid():
    bookmark = _bookmark_save(form)
    if AJAX:
      variables = RequestContext(request, {
        'bookmarks': [bookmark],
         'show_edit': True,
         'show_tags': True
      })
    return render_to_response('bookmark_list.html', variables)
    else:
      return HttpResponseRedirect('/user/%s/' %
      request.user.username)
    else:
      if AJAX:
        return HttpResponse('failure')
```

If we receive a POST request, we check whether the submitted form is valid or not. If it is valid, we save the bookmark. Next, we check whether this is an AJAX request. If it is, we render the saved bookmark using the `bookmark_list.html` template and return it to the requesting script. Otherwise, it is a normal form submission, so we redirect the user to their user page. On the other hand, if the form is not valid, we only act as if it's an AJAX request by returning the string `'failure'`, which we will respond to by displaying an error dialog in JavaScript. We don't need to do anything if it's a normal request because the page will be reloaded and the form will display any errors in the input:

```
if AJAX:
  return render_to_response('bookmark_save_form.html', variables)
  else:
    return render_to_response('bookmark_save.html', variables)
```

This is checked at the end of the method. The execution reaches this point if there is no POST data, which means that we should render a form and return it. We use the `bookmark_save_form.html` template if it's an AJAX request and the `bookmark_save` method, otherwise save it as an HTML file.

Our view is now ready to serve AJAX requests as well as normal page requests. Let's write the JavaScript code that will take advantage of the updated view. Create a new file called `bookmark_edit.js` in the `site_media` profile. However, before we add any code to it, let's link the `bookmark_edit.js` file to the `user_page.html` template. Open the `user_page.html` file and modify it as follows:

```
{% extends "base.html" %}
  {% block external %}
    <script type="text/javascript"
    src="/site_media/bookmark_edit.js">
    </script>
  {% endblock %}
  {% block title %}{{ username }}{% endblock %}
  {% block head %}Bookmarks for {{ username }}{% endblock %}
  {% block content %}
    {% include 'bookmark_list.html' %}
  {% endblock %}
```

We have to write two functions in the `bookmark_edit.js` file:

- `bookmark_edit`: This function handles the clicks on edit links. It loads an edit form from the server and replaces the bookmark with this form.

- `bookmark_save`: This function handles the submissions of edit forms. It sends form data to the server and replaces the form with the bookmark HTML returned by the server.

Let's start with the first function. Open the `site_media/bookmark_edit.js` file and write the following code in it:

```
function bookmark_edit() {
  var item = $(this).parent();
  var url = item.find(".title").attr("href");
  item.load("/save/?AJAX&url=" + escape(url), null, function () {
    $("#save-form").submit(bookmark_save);
  });
  return false;
}
```

Because this function handles click events on an edit link, the `this` variable refers to the edit link itself. Wrapping it in the jQuery `$()` function and calling the `parent()` function returns the parent of the edit link, which is the `<li>` element of the bookmark (try it in the Firebug console to see the same for yourself).

After retrieving a reference to the bookmark's `<li>` element, we obtain a reference to the bookmark's title and extract the bookmark's URL from it using the `attr()` method.

Next, we use the `load()` method to put an editing form in place of the bookmark's HTML file. This time, we are calling the `load()` method with two extra arguments in addition to the URL. The `load()` function takes two optional parameters, which are as follows:

- It takes an object of key or value pairs if we are sending a POST request. Since we get the edit form from the server-side view using a GET request, we pass null for this parameter.
- It takes a function that is called when jQuery finishes loading the URL into the selected element. The function we are passing attaches the `bookmark_save()` method (which we are going to write next) to the form that we've just retrieved.

Finally, the function returns `False` to tell the browser not to follow the edit link. Now we need to attach the `bookmark_edit()` function to the event of clicking an edit link using `$(document).ready()`:

```
$(document).ready(function () {
  $("ul.bookmarks .edit").click(bookmark_edit);
});
```

If you try to edit a bookmark in the user page after writing this function, an edit form should appear, but you should also get a JavaScript error message in the Firebug console because the `bookmark_save()` function is not defined, so let's write it:

```
function bookmark_save() {
  var item = $(this).parent();
  var data = {
    url: item.find("#id_url").val(),
    title: item.find("#id_title").val(),
    tags: item.find("#id_tags").val()
  };
  $.post("/save/?AJAX", data, function (result) {
    if (result != "failure") {
      item.before($("li", result).get(0));
      item.remove();
      $("ul.bookmarks .edit").click(bookmark_edit);
    }
    else {
      alert("Failed to validate bookmark before saving.");
    }
  });
  return false;
}
```

Here, the `this` variable refers to the edit form because we handle the event of submitting a form. The function starts by retrieving a reference to the form's parent, which is again the bookmark's `<li>` element. Next, the function retrieves the updated data from the form using the ID of each form field and the `val()` method.

Then it uses a method called `$.post()` to send data back to the server. Finally, it returns `False` to prevent the browser from submitting the form.

As you may have guessed, the `$.post()` function is a jQuery method that sends POST requests to the server. It takes three parameters, which are as follows:

- The URL of the target of the POST request.
- An object of key/value pairs that represents POST data.
- A function that is invoked when the request is done. The server response is passed to this function as a string parameter.

It's worth mentioning that jQuery provides a method called `$.get()` to send a GET request to the server. It takes the same types of parameters as the `$.post()` function. We use the `$.post()` method to send the updated bookmark data to the `bookmark_save_page` view. As discussed a few paragraphs ago, the view returns the update bookmark HTML if it succeeds in saving it. Otherwise, it returns the `failure` string.

Therefore, we check whether the result returned from the server is `failure` or not. If the request succeeds, we insert the new bookmark before the old one using the `before()` method and remove the old bookmark from the HTML document using the `remove()` method. If, on the other hand, the request fails, we display an alert box displaying the failure.

Several little things remain before we finish this section. Why do we insert the `$("li",result).get(0)` method instead of the result itself? If you check the `bookmark_save_page` view, you will see that it uses the `bookmark_list.html` template to construct the bookmark's HTML. However, the `bookmark_list.html` template returns the bookmark `<li>` element wrapped in an `<ul>` tag. Basically, the `$("li", result).get(0)` method tells jQuery to extract the first `<li>` element in the result and this is the element that we want. As you see from the preceding snippet, you can use the jQuery `$()` function to select the elements from an HTML string by passing this string as a second argument to the function.

The `bookmark_submit` template is attached to its event from within the `bookmark_edit` template, so we don't need to do anything about it in the `$(document).ready()` method.

Lastly, after loading the updated bookmark into the page, we call the `$("ul.bookmarks.edit").click(bookmark_edit)` method again to attach the `bookmark_edit` template to the newly loaded edit link. If you don't do so and try to edit a bookmark twice, the second click on the edit link will take you to a separate form page.

When you finish writing the JavaScript code, open your browser and go to your user page to experiment with the new feature. Edit the bookmarks, save them, and note how the changes are immediately reflected on the page without any reloading.

Now that you have completed this section, you should have a good understanding of how in-place editing is implemented. There are many other scenarios where this feature can be useful, for example, it can be used to edit an article or a comment on the same page without navigating away to a form located on a different URL.

In the next section, we will implement a third common AJAX feature that helps the user enter tags while submitting a bookmark.

Autocompletion of hashtags while submitting a tweet

The last AJAX enhancement that we are going to implement in this chapter is autocompletion of tags. The concept of autocompletion found its way into web applications when Google released their Suggest searching interface. Suggest works by displaying the most popular search queries below the search input field based on what the user has typed so far. It's also similar to how code editors in integrated development environments offer code completion suggestions based on what you type. This feature saves time by letting the user type a few characters of the word they want and then lets them select it from a list without having to type it in completely.

We will implement this feature by offering suggestions when the user enters tags while submitting a bookmark, but instead of writing this feature from scratch, we are going to use a jQuery plugin to implement it. jQuery enjoys a large and continually growing list of plugins that provides a variety of features. Installing a plugin is no different from installing jQuery itself. You download one (or more) files and link them to your template and then you write a few lines of JavaScript code to activate the plugin.

You can browse the list of the available jQuery plugins by navigating to `http://docs.jquery.com/Plugins`. Search for the autocomplete plugin in the list and download it, or you can directly grab it from `http://bassistance.de/jquery-plugins/jquery-plugin-autocomplete/`.

You will get a zip archive with many files in it. Extract the following files (which can be found in the `jquery/autocomplete/scroll` directory) to the `site_media` directory:

- **jquery.autocomplete.css**
- **dimensions.js**
- **jquery.bgiframe.min.js**
- **jquery.autocomplete.js**

Since we want to offer the autocomplete feature on the bookmark submission page, create an empty file called `tag_autocomplete.js` in the `site_media` folder. Then open the `templates/bookmark_save.html` file and link all of the preceding files to it:

```
{% extends "base.html" %}
  {% block external %}
  <link rel="stylesheet"
  href="/site_media/jquery.autocomplete.css" type="text/css" />
  <script type="text/javascript"
  src="/site_media/dimensions.js"> </script>
  <script type="text/javascript"
  src="/site_media/jquery.bgiframe.min.js"> </script>
  <script type="text/javascript"
  src="/site_media/jquery.autocomplete.js"> </script>
  <script type="text/javascript"
  src="/site_media/tag_autocomplete.js"> </script>
  {% endblock %}
  {% block title %}Save Bookmark{% endblock %}
  {% block head %}Save Bookmark{% endblock %}
[...]
```

We now finished installing the plugin. If you read its documentation, you will find that this plugin is activated by calling a method named `autocomplete()` on a selected input element. The `autocomplete()` function takes the following parameters:

- **A server-side URL**: For this, the plugin sends a GET request to this URL with what has been typed so far and expects the server to return a set of suggestions.

- **An object that can be used to specify various options**: Options that are of interest to us are multiple. This option has a Boolean variable that tells the plugin that the input field is used to enter multiple values (remember that we use the same text field to enter all the tags) and multiple separators that are used to tell the plugin which string separates multiple entries. In our case, it's a single space character.

So before activating the plugin, we need to write a view that receives user input and returns a set of suggestions. Open the `bookmarks/views.py` file and append the following to its end:

```
def AJAX_tag_autocomplete(request):
  if request.GET.has_key('q'):):):
    tags = \
    Tag.objects.filter(name__istartswith=request.GET['q'])[:10]
  return HttpResponse('\n'.join(tag.name for tag in tags))
return HttpResponse()
```

The `autocomplete()` plugin sends user input in a GET variable named q. Therefore, we can verify that this variable exists and build a list of tags whose names begin with the value of this variable. This is done using the `filter()` method and the `istartswith` operator that we learned about earlier in this chapter. We only take the first ten results to avoid overwhelming the user with suggestions and to reduce the bandwidth and performance costs. Finally, we join the suggestions into a single string separated by newlines, wrap the string into an `HttpResponse` object, and return it.

With the suggestion view ready, add a URL entry to the plugin in the `urls.py` file, as follows:

```
urlpatterns = patterns('',
  # AJAX
  (r'^AJAX/tag/autocomplete/$', AJAX_tag_autocomplete),
)
```

Now activate the plugin on the tags input field by entering the following code in the `site_media/tag_autocomplete.js` file:

```
$(document).ready(function () {
  $("#id_tags").autocomplete(
    '/AJAX/tag/autocomplete/',
    {multiple: true, multipleSeparator: ' '}
  );
});
```

The code passes an anonymous function to the `$(document).ready()` method. This function invokes the `autocomplete()` function on the tags input field, passing the arguments that we talked about earlier.

These few lines of code are all that we need in order to implement autocompletion of tags. To test the new feature, navigate to the bookmark submission form at `http://127.0.0.1:8000/save/` and try to enter a character or two in the tags field. Suggestions should appear based on the tags available in your database.

With this feature, we finish this chapter. We covered a lot of material and learned about many exciting technologies and techniques. After reading the chapter, you should be able to think of and implement many other enhancements to the user interface, such as the ability to delete bookmarks from the user page or to do live browsing of bookmarks by tags among, many other things.

The next chapter will shift to a different topic: we will let users vote and comment on their favorite bookmarks and the front page of our application won't remain as empty as it is now!

Summary

Phew! This was a long chapter, but hopefully you learned a lot from it! We started the chapter with learning about the jQuery framework and how to integrate it in to our Django project. After that, we implemented three exciting features in our bookmarking application: live searching, in-place editing, and autocompletion.

The next chapter is going to be another exciting one. We will let users submit bookmarks to the front page and vote for their favorite bookmarks. We will also enable users to comment on bookmarks. So, read on!

Following and Commenting

The main idea behind our application is to provide a platform for users to share their thoughts via tweets. Just letting the user create a new tweet is only one part of it, and the application is said to be incomplete if users are not able to interact with the existing tweet. In this chapter, we will do the other part, which is enabling users to follow a particular user and comment on an existing tweet. You will also learn several new Django features while working through it.

In this chapter, you will learn about:

- Letting users follow another user
- Displaying the most followed user

Letting users follow another user

So far, our users are able to discover new tweets by browsing hashtags and user pages. Let's provide a method for users to follow another user so that they can see, on their individual homepages, the aggregated tweets from all users they are following. Let's also enable users to comment on a new tweet.

We will also create a page where users can list popular users by the number of followers. This feature is important for our application because it will change the main page from a basic welcome page to a frequently updated list of users, where users will be able to find trending users and their interesting tweets.

Our strategy for implementing this feature consists of the following:

- Creating a data model to store a user and their followers. This model will keep track of various pieces of information related to the user.

- Giving each user a follow button next to their title. We will also create a view that shows counts, such as the number of tweets a user has made and their follower count. This involves a considerable amount of work, but the results will be worth it and we will learn a lot of useful information during the process.

Let's get started!

At first, what we are going to add is a retweet count to every tweet and to keep track of all the tweets voted up by the user. To implement this, we need to create a new UserFollowers data model.

The UserFollowers data model

When a user is followed by another user, we need to store the following information in the database:

- The date on which the user was followed. We need this in order to display the user who has the highest number of followers over a certain period of time.
- The number of followers a user has.
- The list of users who are following our user.

This is needed to prevent users from following the same user twice.

For this purpose, we will create a new data model called UserFollowers. Open user_profile/model.py and add the following class to it:

```
class UserFollowers(models.Model):
    user = models.ForeignKey(User, unique=True))
    date = models.DateTimeField(auto_now_add=True)
    count = models.IntegerField(default=1))
    followers = models.ManyToManyField(User,
    related_name='followers')
    def __str__(self):
        return '%s, %s' % self.user, self.count
```

This data model utilizes some important features, so we will go through its fields one by one. The user field is a foreign key that refers back to the user that is being followed. We want it to be unique so that the same user cannot be followed more than once.

The date field is of the type models.DateTimeField. As its name suggests, you can use this field to store a date/time value. The argument auto_now_add tells Django to automatically set this field to the current date/time when an object of this data model is first created.

The count field is of the type `models.IntegerField`. This field holds an integer value. By using the `default=1` parameter with this field, we tell Django to set the field's value to 1 when an object of this data model is first created.

The following `ManyToManyField` parameter contains the list of users who followed this user.

 Here, the `related_name='followers'` parameter must be given as the second parameter. Both user and follower point to the same class `user`, which if distinguished by related name, can give an error such as this, Accessor for field `user` clashes with related m2m field `User.userfollowers_set`.

After entering the data model code into `user_profile/models.py` file, run the following command to create its corresponding tables in the database:

```
$ python manage.py syncdb
```

With this, we can store all the information that we need to maintain followers.

Next, we are going to to create a view in which users can follow other users by clicking on the follow button next to their profile name.

Modify the user profile page accordingly if the visited user is not the same who has already followed you, then there should be a button to follow the user. If the user is already being followed, the same button should allow unfollowing.

Let us edit the existing user profile, `profile.html`.

Adding a user icon against the username, we can use the following Bootstrap glyphicons. This is the set of icons that is shipped with the default Bootstrap.

```
{% block navbar %}
<p class="navbar-text navbar-right">
  <span class="glyphicon glyphicon-user"></span>
  {{ user.username }}
</p>
{% endblock %}
```

We will also design a new tweet post textbox on the profile page. The updated `user_profile.html` file is as follows:

```
{% extends "base.html" %}
{% block navbar %}
<p class="navbar-text navbar-right">
  <span class="glyphicon glyphicon-user"></span>
  {{ user.username }}
```

```
    </p>
{% endblock %}
{% block content %}
<div class="row clearfix">
  <div class="col-md-6 col-md-offset-3 column">
    <form id="search-form" action="post/" method="POST">{%
    csrf_token %}
      <div class="input-group">
        {{ form.text.errors }}
        {{ form.text }}
        {{ form.country.as_hidden }}
        <span class="input-group-btn">
          <button class="btn btn-default"
          type="submit">Post</button>
        </span>
      </div><!-- /input-group -->
    </form>
  </div>
  <h1> </h1>
  <div class="col-md-12 column">
    {% for tweet in tweets %}
    <div class="well">
      <span>{{ tweet.text }}</span>
    </div>
    {% endfor %}
  </div>
</div>
{% endblock %}
```

Update the `forms.py` file to render a new form:

```
class TweetForm(forms.Form):
    text = forms.CharField(widget=forms.Textarea(attrs={'rows': 1,
    'cols': 85, 'class':'form-control', 'placeholder': 'Post a new
    Tweet'}), max_length=160)
    country = forms.CharField(widget=forms.HiddenInput())
```

The updated UI for the form will look like this:

To add the functionality to follow a user, we need to first create another user. We will follow the same method we used before, that is, via Django Administrator.

One very important thing we have been postponing is user login and registration. The follow functionality can't be used without it. We will implement Django login first, and then we will move to the follow functionality.

The user login model

To implement user login, we need to add default URLs for login and registration. We will add the following URL patterns in the `urls.py` file:

```
url(r'^login/$', 'django.contrib.auth.views.login'),
url(r'^logout/$', 'django.contrib.auth.views.logout')
```

Now, our `urls.py` file will look like this:

```
from django.conf.urls import patterns, include, url
from django.contrib import admin
from tweet.views import Index, Profile, PostTweet, HashTagCloud,
Search, SearchHashTag, HashTagJson
admin.autodiscover()

urlpatterns = patterns('',
  url(r'^$', Index.as_view()),
  url(r'^user/(\w+)/$', Profile.as_view()),
  url(r'^admin/', include(admin.site.urls)),
  url(r'^user/(\w+)/post/$', PostTweet.as_view()),
  url(r'^hashTag/(\w+)/$', HashTagCloud.as_view()),
  url(r'^search/$', Search.as_view()),
  url(r'^search/hashTag$', SearchHashTag.as_view()),
  url(r'^hashtag.json$', HashTagJson.as_view()),
  url(r'^login/$', 'django.contrib.auth.views.login'),
  url(r'^logout/$', 'django.contrib.auth.views.logout')
)
```

Both the login and logout views have default template names, `registration/login.html` and `registration/logged_out.html` respectively. Because these views are specific to the user and not our reusable application, we'll create a new template/registration directory inside the `mytweets` project using the following command:

```
$ mkdir -p mytweets/templates/registration
```

Then, create a simple login and logout page. Use the following code snippet in the `login.html` file:

```
{% extends "base.html" %}
{% block content %}
{% if form.errors %}
<p>Your username and password didn't match. Please try
again.</p>
{% endif %}
<form method="post" action="{% url
'django.contrib.auth.views.login' %}">
  {% csrf_token %}
  <table>
    <tr>
      <td>{{ form.username.label_tag }}</td>
      <td>{{ form.username }}</td>
    </tr>
    <tr>
      <td>{{ form.password.label_tag }}</td>
      <td>{{ form.password }}</td>
    </tr>
  </table>
  <input type="submit" value="login"/>
  <input type="hidden" name="next" value="{{ next }}"/>
</form>
{% endblock %}
```

Use the following code snippet in the `logout.html` file:

```
{% extends "base.html" %}
{% block content %}
  You have been Logged out!
{% endblock %}
```

We have just enabled Django's default authentication system. As this does basic authorization, it has its predefined URLs for certain redirections. For example, we already know that `/login` will take a user to the `/registration/login.html` page. Similarly, once the user is authenticated, they are redirected to the URL `accounts/profile`. In our project, we have a custom URL for each user. We will update these entries in the `settings.py` file

```
LOGIN_REDIRECT_URL = '/profile'
LOGIN_URL = 'django.contrib.auth.views.login'
```

To keep things simple, we will just create a view, which will take an authenticated user to the profile, which will then redirect the user to their profile page. Basically, we will construct the parameter of the username after valid authentication; in other words, /profile | /profile/<username> will be generated in a separate class view. For this, we also need to create a URL entry as follows:

```
url(r'^profile/$', UserRedirect.as_view()),
```

And `Profile` redirect class with a `get()` method as:

```
class UserRedirect(View):
    def get(self, request):
    return HttpResponseRedirect('/user/'+request.user.username)
```

This is it. Now every logged-in user will be redirected to his profile page.

Now, coming back to the original problem, when a user visits another user's profile, they will have the option to follow this user's profile; this means the follower will get updates about all the posted tweets on their home page.

Once following a user, the follower will have the option to unfollow the user, and if the user visits their own profile, they should see nothing at all.

The updated code for the user profile is as follows:

```
{% extends "base.html" %}
{% block navbar %}
<p class="navbar-text navbar-left">
  <span class="glyphicon glyphicon-user"> </span>
  {{ profile.username }}'s Profile Page
  {% if profile.username != user.username %}
  <span class="btn btn-xs btn-default follow-btn" title="Click
  to follow {{ profile.username }}">
  <input id="follow" type="hidden" name="follow" value="{{
  profile.username }}">
  <span class="glyphicon glyphicon-plus"> </span> {% if
  following %} Unfollow {% else %} Follow {% endif %}</span>
  {% endif %}
</p>
<p class="navbar-text navbar-right">
  <span class="glyphicon glyphicon-user"></span>
  {{ user.username }}
</p>
{% endblock %}
{% block content %}
<div class="row clearfix">
  <div class="col-md-6 col-md-offset-3 column">
```

```
<form id="search-form" action="post/" method="POST">{%
csrf_token %}
  <div class="input-group">
    {{ form.text.errors }}
    {{ form.text }}
    {{ form.country.as_hidden }}
    <span class="input-group-btn">
      <button class="btn btn-default"
      type="submit">Post</button>
    </span>
  </div>
  <!-- /input-group -->
</form>
</div>
<h1> </h1>
<div class="col-md-12 column">
  {% for tweet in tweets %}
  <div class="well">
    <span>{{ tweet.text }}</span>
  </div>
  {% endfor %}
</div>
</div>
{% endblock %}
```

The following code checks whether the user is viewing their own profile; if so, they will not be shown the follow button. It also checks whether the user logged in is following the profile they've visited; if so, the unfollow button will be shown, and if not, the follow button will be shown.

```
{% if profile.username != user.username %}
<span class="btn btn-xs btn-default follow-btn" title="Click to
follow {{ profile.username }}">
  <input id="follow" type="hidden" name="follow" value="{{
  profile.username }}">
<span class="glyphicon glyphicon-plus"> </span>
{% if following %} Unfollow {% else %} Follow {% endif %}</span>
{% endif %}
```

To render the updated view, `class Profile()` has also been updated as follows:

```
class Profile(LoginRequiredMixin, View):
  """User Profile page reachable from /user/<username> URL"""
  def get(self, request, username):
    params = dict()
    userProfile = User.objects.get(username=username))
```

```
userFollower = UserFollower.objects.get(user=userProfile)
if userFollower.followers.filter
(username=request.user.username).exists():
  params["following"] = True
else:
  params["following"] = False
  form = TweetForm(initial={'country': 'Global'})
  search_form = SearchForm()
  tweets = Tweet.objects.filter(user=userProfile)
  .order_by('-created_date')
  params["tweets"] = tweets
  params["profile"] = userProfile
  params["form"] = form
  params["search"] = search_form
  return render(request, 'profile.html', params)
```

The following code checks whether the logged-in user is a follower of the user whose profile they are visiting:

```
if userFollower.followers.filter
(username=request.user.username).exists():
```

Adding or removing the follower

Let's create a `post()` method for the profile to add or remove followers based on parameters:

```
def post(self, request, username):
  follow = request.POST['follow']
  user = User.objects.get(username= request.user.username)))
  userProfile === User.objects.get(username=username)
  userFollower, status = UserFollower.objects.get_or_create
  (user=userProfile)
  if follow=='true':
    #follow user
    userFollower.followers.add(user)
  else:
    #unfollow user
    userFollower.followers.remove(user)
  return HttpResponse(json.dumps(""),
  content_type="application/json")
```

This is a simple function that checks the parameters to add or remove users to or from the followers list.

The follow button part of the `profile.html` file should be updated with the class names so that we can trigger the JavaScript event functionalism, as follows:

```html
<p class="navbar-text navbar-left">
  <span class="glyphicon glyphicon-user"> </span>
  {{ profile.username }}'s Profile Page
    {% if profile.username != user.username %}
    <span class="btn btn-xs btn-default follow-btn" title="Click
    to follow {{ profile.username }}" value="{{ following }}"
    username="{{ profile.username }}">
      <span class="glyphicon glyphicon-plus"></span><span
      class="follow-text">
      {{ following|yesno:"Unfollow,Follow" }}
    </span>
  </span>
  {% endif %}
</p>
```

Finally, let us create the `profile.js` file which has the `post()` method whenever the follow/unfollow button is clicked:

Create a JavaScript file named as `profile.js` and add the following code:

```javascript
$(".follow-btn").click(function () {
  var username = $(this).attr('username');
  var follow = $(this).attr('value') != "True";
  $.ajax({
    type: "POST",
    url:  "/user/"+username+"/",
    data: { username: username , follow : follow  },
    success: function () {
      window.location.reload();
    },
    error: function () {
      alert("ERROR !!");
    }
  })
});
```

Don't forget to add this JavaScript file in the `profile.html` file at the bottom of the page, as shown in the following code:

```
{% block js %}
<script src="{% static 'js/profile.js' %}"></script>
{% endblock %}
```

Displaying the most followed user

After we have implemented the feature for following users, we can move ahead with a new page design where we will list the most followed user. The logic of this page can be reused to design the page that has the highest number of comments.

The basic components for this page design are:

- **View**: The users.html file
- **Controller**: The most followed user
- URL mapping

Add the following content in the view.html file:

```
{% extends "base.html" %}
{% load staticfiles %}
{% block navbar %}
<p class="navbar-text navbar-right">
  <span class="glyphicon glyphicon-user"></span>
  {{ user.username }}
</p>
{% endblock %}
{% block content %}
<div class="row clearfix">
  <div class="col-md-12 column">
    {% for userFollower in userFollowers %}
    <div class="well">
      <span class="username">{{ userFollower.user.username
      }}</span>
      <span class="count text-muted"> ({{ userFollower.count
      }} followers)</span>
    </div>
    {% endfor %}
  </div>
</div>
{% endblock %}
```

Add the following class in the controller:

```
class MostFollowedUsers(View):
  def get(self, request):
    userFollowers = UserFollower.objects.order_by('-count')
    params = dict()
    params['userFollowers'] = userFollowers
    return render(request, 'users.html', params)
```

This following line orders the followers in the order of who has the most followers:

```
userFollowers = UserFollower.objects.order_by('-count')
```

We need to update the URL mapping as well, as follows:

```
url(r'^mostFollowed/$', MostFollowedUsers.as_view()),
```

That's all! We are done with a page where all the users are listed by follower count. If the count gets too high, you can also limit it using this basic Python list syntax:

```
userFollowers = UserFollower.objects.order_by('-count')[:10]
```

This will list only the top 10 users.

Summary

In this chapter, we have learned to create login, logout, and registration page templates. We also learned how to allow the following of another user and displaying the most followed users.

The next chapter switches to new topics. Sooner or later, you will need an administration interface for your application to manage your data models. Fortunately, Django comes with a full-fledged administration interface ready to be used. We will learn how to enable and customize this interface in the next chapter, so keep reading!

8

Creating an Administration Interface

In this chapter, we will learn the features of the administrator interface using Django's inbuilt features. We will also cover how to show tweets in a customized way, with sidebar or pagination enabled. We will deal with the following topics in this chapter:

- Customizing the administration interface
- Customizing listing pages
- Overriding administration templates
- Users, groups, and permissions
    - ○ User permissions
    - ○ Group permissions
    - ○ Using permissions in views
- Organizing content into pages (pagination)

Customizing the administration interface

The administration interface provided by Django is very powerful and flexible, and from the version 1.6, it comes activated by default. This will give you a fully featured administration kit for your site. Although the administration application should be sufficient for most needs, Django offers several ways to customize and enhance it. In addition to specifying which models are available in the administration interface, you can also specify how listing pages are presented and even override the templates used to render the administration pages. So, let's learn about these features.

Customizing listing pages

As we saw in the previous chapter, we registered our model classes to the administration interface using the following methods:

- admin.site.register (Tweet)
- admin.site.register (Hashtag)
- admin.site.register (UserFollower)

We can also customize several aspects of the administration pages. Let's learn about this by example. The tweet listing page displays the string representation of each tweet, as we can see in the following screenshot:

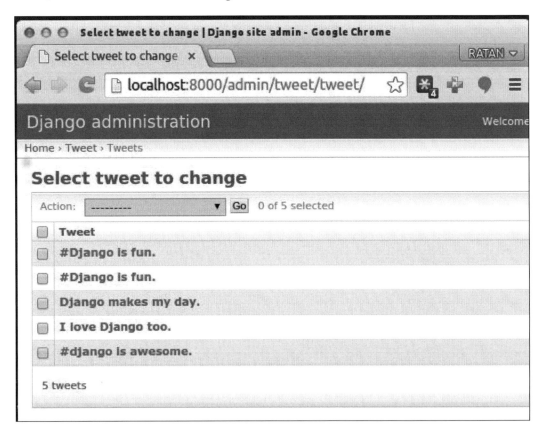

Wouldn't this page be more useful if it were to display the name of the user who has posted the tweet, as well as the time of posting, in separate columns? It turns out that implementing this functionality only requires adding a few lines of code.

Edit the tweet model in `tweet/admin.py` file as follows:

```
from django.contrib import admin
from models import Tweet, HashTag
from user_profile.models import UserFollower
# Register your models here.
admin.site.register(Tweet)
admin.site.register(HashTag)
admin.site.register(UserFollower)
```

Add new lines of code above `#Register your models here` and the updated code will look like this:

```
from django.contrib import admin
from models import Tweet, HashTag
from user_profile.models import UserFollower
class TweetAdmin(admin.ModelAdmin):
  list_display = ('user', 'text', 'created_date')
# Register your models here.
admin.site.register(Tweet, TweetAdmin)))
admin.site.register(HashTag)
admin.site.register(UserFollower)
```

This code adds the extra column in the administrator view for the `TweetAdmin()` class:

```
class TweetAdmin(admin.ModelAdmin):
  list_display = ('user', 'text', 'created_date')
```

Moreover, we have passed an extra parameter to register calls for the administrator tweet; that is, `admin.site.register(Tweet)` becomes `admin.site.register(Tweet, TweetAdmin)` now. Refresh the same page and note the changes, as shown in the following screenshot:

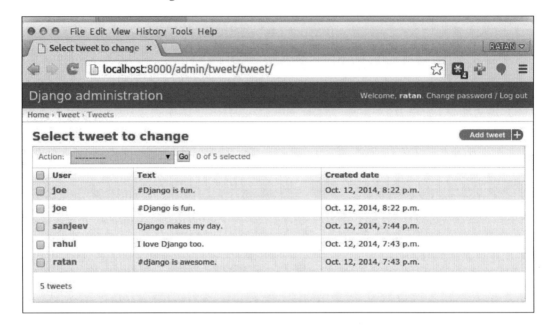

The table is now better organized! We simply defined a tuple attribute called `list_display` in the `TweetAdmin()` class of the `Tweet` model. This tuple contains the names of the fields to be used in the listing page.

There are other attributes that we can define in the Admin class; each one should be defined as a tuple of one or more field names.

- `list_filter`: If defined, this creates a sidebar with links that can be used to filter objects according to one or more fields in the model.
- `ordering`: The fields that are used to order objects in the listing page.
- `search_fields`: If defined, it creates a search field that can be used to search. The field name is preceded by a minus sign, and descending order is used instead of ascending order for the available objects in the data model according to one or more fields.

Let's utilize each of the preceding attributes in the tweet listing page. Again, edit the Tweet model in the `tweet/admin.py` file and append the following highlighted lines:

```
from django.contrib import admin
from models import Tweet, HashTag
from user_profile.models import UserFollower

class TweetAdmin(admin.ModelAdmin):
    list_display = ('user', 'text', 'created_date')
    list_filter = ('user', )
    ordering = ('-created_date', )
    search_fields = ('text', )

# Register your models here.
admin.site.register(Tweet, TweetAdmin)
admin.site.register(HashTag)
admin.site.register(UserFollower)
```

This is how it looks after using these attributes:

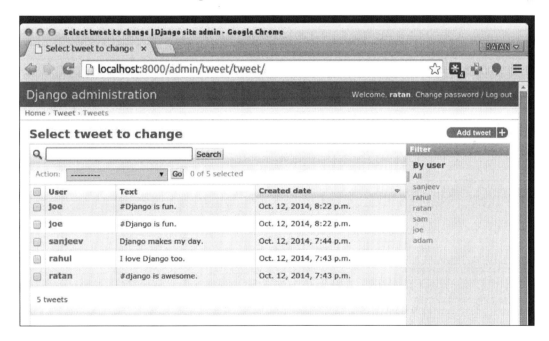

As you can see, we were able to customize and enhance the tweet listing page with only a few lines of code. Next, we will learn about customizing the templates used to render administration pages, which will give us even greater control over the administration interface.

Overriding administration templates

There are times when you want to change the look and feel of the administration interface or to move the elements on the various administration pages and rearrange them. Fortunately, the administration interface is flexible enough to do all of this and more by allowing us to override its templates. The process of customizing an administration template is simple. First, you copy the template from the administration application folder to your project's templates folder, and then you edit this template and customize it to your liking. The location of the administration templates depends on where Django is installed. Here is a list of the default installation paths of Django under the major operating systems:

- **Windows**: `C:\PythonXX\Lib\site-packages\django`
- **UNIX and Linux**: `/usr/lib/pythonX.X/site-packages/django`
- **Mac OS X**: `/Library/Python/X.X/site-packages/django`

(Here, **X.X** is the version of Python on your system. The `site-packages` folder can also be found as `dist-packages`.)

If you cannot find Django in the default installation path for your operating system, perform a file system search for `django-admin.py`. You will get multiple hits, but the one that you want will be under the Django installation path, inside a folder called `bin`.

After locating the Django installation path, open `django/contrib/admin/templates/` and you will find the templates used by the administration application.

There are many files in this directory, but the most important ones are these:

- `admin/base_site.html`: This is the base template for the administration. This template generates the interface. All pages inherit from this template in the following model.
- `admin/change_list.html`: This template generates a list of available objects.
- `admin/change_form.html`: This template generates a form for adding or editing an object.
- `admin/delete_confirmation.html`: This template generates the confirmation page when an object is deleted.

Let's try to customize one of these templates. Suppose that we want to change the string **Django administration** located at the top of all admin pages. To do so, create a folder called `admin` inside the `templates` folder of our project, and copy the `admin/base_site.html` file to it. After that, edit the file to change all instances of `Django` to `Django Tweet`:

```
{% extends "admin/base.html" %}
{% load i18n %}
{% block title %}{{ title|escape }} |
{% trans 'Django Tweet site admin' %}{% endblock %}
{% block branding %}
<h1 id="site-name">{% trans 'Django Tweet administration'
%}</h1>
{% endblock %}
{% block nav-global %}{% endblock %}
```

The result will look like this:

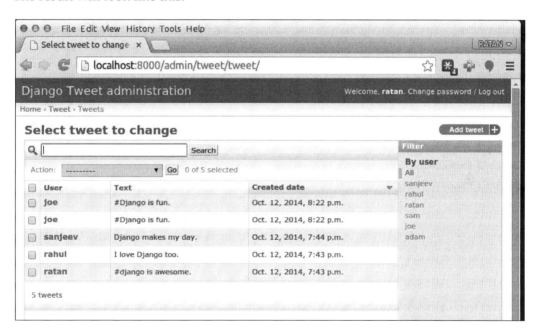

Because of the modular design of the admin templates, it is usually neither necessary nor advisable to replace an entire template. It is almost always better to override only the section of the template that you need to change.

The process was pretty simple, wasn't it? Feel free to experiment with other templates. For example, you may want to add a help message to a listing or edit pages.

The administration templates make use of many advanced features of the Django template system, so if you see a template tag that you are not familiar with, you can refer to the Django documentation.

Users, groups, and permissions

So far, we have been logged in to the administration interface using the superuser account that we created with the `manage.py syncdb` command. In reality, however, you may have other trusted users who need access to the administration page. In this section, we will see how to allow other users to use the administration interface, and we will learn more about the Django permissions system in the process.

However, before we continue, I want to emphasize this: only trusted users should be given access to the administration pages. The administration interface is a very powerful tool, so only those whom you know well should be granted access to it.

User permissions

If you don't have users in the database other than the superuser, create a new user account using the registration form that we built in *Chapter 7, Following and Commenting*. Alternatively, you could use the administration interface itself by clicking on **Users** and then **Add User**.

Next, return to the users list and click on the name of the newly created user. You will get a form that can be used to edit various aspects of the user account, such as name and e-mail information. Under the **Permissions** section of the edit form, you will find a checkbox labelled **Staff status**. Enabling this checkbox will let the new user enter the administration interface. However, they won't be able to do much after they log in because this checkbox only grants access to the administration area; it does not give the ability to see or change data.

To give the new user enough permissions to change data models, you can enable the **Superuser status** checkbox, which will grant the new user full permission to perform any function that they want. This option makes the account as powerful as the superuser account created by the `manage.py syncdb` command.

On the whole, however, it's not desirable to grant a user full access to everything. Therefore, Django gives you the ability to have fine control over what users can do through the permissions system. Below the **Superuser status** checkbox, you will find a list of permissions that you can grant to the user. If you examine this list, you will find that each data model has three types of permissions:

- Adding an object to the data model
- Changing an object in the data model
- Deleting an object from the data model

These permissions are automatically generated by Django for data models that contain an Admin class. Use the arrow button to grant some permissions to the account that we are editing. For example, give the account the ability to add, edit, and delete tweets and hashtags. Next, log out and then log in to the administration interface again using the new account. You will notice that you will only be able to manage the tweets and hashtags data models.

The permissions section of the user edit page also contains a checkbox called **Active**. This checkbox can be used as a global switch to enable and disable the account. When unchecked, the user won't be able to log in to the main site or the administration area.

Group permissions

If you have a considerable number of users who share the same permissions, it would be a tedious and error-prone task to edit each user's account and assign the same permissions to them. Therefore, Django provides another user management facility: groups. To put it simply, groups are a way of categorizing users who share the same permissions. You can create a group and assign permissions to it. When you add a user to the group, this user is granted all of the group's permissions.

Creating a group is not very different from other data models. Click on **Groups** on the main page of the administration interface, and then click on **Add Group**. Next, enter a group name and assign some permissions to the group; finally, click on **Save**.

To add a user to a group, edit the user account, scroll to the **Groups** section in the edit form, and select whichever group you want to add the user to.

Using permissions in views

Although we have only used permissions in the administration interface so far, Django also lets us utilize the permission system while writing views. It is possible to use permissions while programming a view to grant a group of users access to a particular feature or page, such as private content. We will learn about the methods that can be used to do so in this section. We won't actually make changes to the code of our application, but feel free to do so if you want to experiment with the methods explained.

If you wanted to check whether a user has a particular permission, you could use the `has_perm()` method on the `User` object. This method takes a string that represents the permission in the following format:

```
app.operation_model
```

The `app` parameter specifies the name of the application where the model is located; the `operation` parameter could be `add`, `change` or `delete`; the `model` parameter specifies the name of the model.

For example, to check whether the user can add tweets, use this:

```
user.has_perm('tweets.add_tweet')
```

To check if the user can change tweets, use this:

```
user.has_perm('tweets.change_tweet')
```

Furthermore, Django provides a function named `decorator` that can be used to restrict a view to users who have a particular permission. The decorator is called `permission_required`, and it is located in the `django.contrib.auth.decorators` package.

Using this decorator is similar to how we used the `login_required` function. The decorator function is to restrict pages to logged in users. Let's say we want to restrict the `tweet_save_page` view (in the `tweets/views.py` file) to users who have the `tweet.add_tweet` permission. To do so, we can use the following code:

```
from django.contrib.auth.decorators import permission_required
@permission_required('tweets.add_tweet', login_url="/login/")
def tweet_save_page(request):
    # [...]
```

This decorator takes two parameters: the permission to check for and where to redirect the user if they don't have the required permission.

The question of whether to use the `has_perm` method or the `permission_required` decorator depends on the level of control that you want. If you need to control access to a view as a whole, use the `permission_required` decorator. However, if you need finer control over permissions inside a view, use the `has_perm` method. These two approaches should be sufficient for any permission-related needs.

Organizing content into pages – pagination

In previous chapters, we have covered things such as listing down the tweets of users and listing down most followed users, but consider a use case when these small numbers scale up and we start getting a large number of results for each type of query. To cover such a situation, we should manipulate our code so as to make it support pagination.

The page would increase in size, and finding an item within the page would become difficult. Fortunately, there is a simple and intuitive solution to this: pagination. **Pagination** is the process of breaking content into pages. And, as always, Django already has a component that implements this functionality, ready for us to use!

If we have a large set of tweets, we split the set into pages with ten (or so) items on each page, present the first page to the user, and provide links to browse other pages.

The Django pagination functionality is encapsulated in a class called `Paginator`, which is located in the `django.core.paginator` package. Let's learn the interface of this class using the interactive console:

```
from tweet.models import *
from django.core.paginator import Paginator
query_set = Tweet.objects.all()
paginator = Paginator(query_set, 10)
```

 Open the Django shell with the `python manage.py shell` command.

Here we import some classes, build a query set containing all bookmarks, and instantiate an object called `Paginator`. The constructor of this class takes the query set to be paginated, and the number of items on each page is set.

Let's see how to retrieve information from the `Paginator` object (of course, the results will vary depending on the amount of bookmarks that you have):

```
>>> paginator.num_pages # Number of pages
1
>>> paginator.count # Total number of items
5
# Items in first page (index is zero-based)
>>> paginator.object_list
[<Tweet: #django is awesome.>, <Tweet: I love Django too.>, <Tweet:
Django makes my day.>, <Tweet: #Django is fun.>, <Tweet: #Django is
fun.>]


# Does the first page have a previous page?
>>> page1 = paginator.page(1)
# Stores the first page object to page1
>>> page1.has_previous()
False
# Does the first page have a next page?
>>> page1.has_next()
True
```

As you can see, `Paginator` does the heavy lifting for us. It takes a query set, breaks it into pages, and enables us to render the query set into multiple pages.

Let's implement pagination into one of our views, the tweet page for example. Open `tweet/views.py` and modify the `user_page` view as follows:

We have our user profile page listing with the following class:

```
class Profile(LoginRequiredMixin, View):
    """User Profile page reachable from /user/<username> URL"""
    def get(self, request, username):
        params = dict()
        userProfile = User.objects.get(username=username)
        userFollower = UserFollower.objects.get(user=userProfile)
        if userFollower.followers.filter
        (username=request.user.username).exists():
            params["following"] = True
        else:
            params["following"] = False
            form = TweetForm(initial={'country': 'Global'})
            search_form = SearchForm()
            tweets = Tweet.objects.filter(user=userProfile).
            order_by('-created_date')
```

```
params["tweets"] = tweets
params["profile"] = userProfile
params["form"] = form
params["search"] = search_form
return render(request, 'profile.html', params)
```

We need to modify the preceding code to use pagination:

```
class Profile(LoginRequiredMixin, View):
    """User Profile page reachable from /user/<username> URL"""
    def get(self, request, username):
        params = dict()
        userProfile = User.objects.get(username=username)
        userFollower = UserFollower.objects.get(user=userProfile)
        if userFollower.followers.filter
        (username=request.user.username).exists():
            params["following"] = True
        else:
            params["following"] = False
            form = TweetForm(initial={'country': 'Global'})
            search_form = SearchForm()
            tweets = Tweet.objects.filter(user=userProfile).
            order_by('-created_date')
            paginator = Paginator(tweets, TWEET_PER_PAGE)
            page = request.GET.get('page')
        try:
            tweets = paginator.page(page)
            except PageNotAnInteger:
                # If page is not an integer, deliver first page.
                tweets = paginator.page(1)
        except EmptyPage:
            # If page is out of range (e.g. 9999), deliver last page
            of results.
            tweets = paginator.page(paginator.num_pages)
            params["tweets"] = tweets
            params["profile"] = userProfile
            params["form"] = form
            params["search"] = search_form
            return render(request, 'profile.html', params)
```

The following code snippet mainly works the pagination magic in the preceding code:

```
tweets = Tweet.objects.filter(user=userProfile).
order_by('-created_date')
paginator = Paginator(tweets, TWEET_PER_PAGE)
page = request.GET.get('page')
try:
    tweets = paginator.page(page)
except PageNotAnInteger:
```

```
            # If page is not an integer, deliver first page.
            tweets = paginator.page(1)
        except EmptyPage:
            # If page is out of range (e.g. 9999), deliver last page
            of results.
            tweets = paginator.page(paginator.num_pages)
```

To make this code work, add the TWEET_PER_PAGE = 5 parameter in the settings.
py file, and, in the preceding code, just add the import settings.py statement at
the top of the code.

We read a get variable called page from the request, which tells Django which page
has been requested. We also set the TWEET_PER_PAGE parameter in the settings.py
file to show the number of tweets on a single page. For this specific case, we choose it
to be 5.

The paginator = Paginator(tweets, TWEET_PER_PAGE) method creates a
pagination object that holds all the information about the query.

Now, just with a URL user/<username>/?page=<page_numer>, the page will look
as shown in the following screenshot. The first image shows the user's tweet with the
page number in the URL.

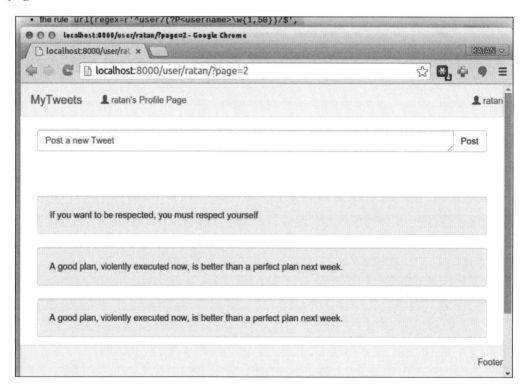

The following screenshot shows the tweet list of a user on their homepage:

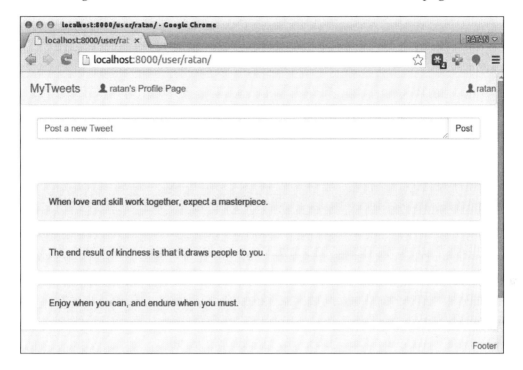

Summary

Although this chapter is relatively short, we learned how to implement a lot of things. This emphasizes the fact that Django lets you do a lot with only a few lines of code. You learned how to utilize Django's powerful administration interface, how to customize it, and how to take advantage of the comprehensive permission system offered by Django.

In the next chapter, you will learn about several exciting features found in almost every Web 2.0 application nowadays.

Extending and Deploying

9

In this chapter, we will prepare our application for deployment in production by utilizing various Django framework features. We will add support for multiple languages, improve performance by caching and automated testing, and configure the project for a production environment. There is a lot of interesting and useful information in this chapter, so make sure you go through it before publishing your application online!

In this chapter, you will learn about the following topics:

- Sending invitation e-mails to friends
- Internationalization (i18n) — offering the site in multiple languages
- Caching — improving the performance of your site during high traffic
- Unit testing — automating the process of testing your application

Sending invitation e-mails to friends

Enabling our users to invite their friends carries many benefits. People are more likely to join our site if their friends already use it. After they join, they will also invite their friends, and so on, which means more and more users for our application. Therefore, it is a good idea to include an "invite a friend" feature in our app.

Building this feature requires the following components:

- An invitation data model to store invitations in the database
- A form in which users can type the e-mail IDs of their friends and send invitations
- An invitation e-mail with an activation link
- A mechanism to process activation links sent in e-mails

Throughout this section, we will implement each of these components. However, because this section involves sending e-mails, we first need to configure Django to send e-mails by adding some options to the settings.py file. So, open the settings.py file and add the following lines:

```
SITE_HOST = '127.0.0.1:8000'
DEFAULT_FROM_EMAIL = 'MyTwitter <noreply@mytwitter.com>'
EMAIL_HOST = 'mail.yourisp.com'
EMAIL_PORT = ''
EMAIL_HOST_USER = 'username+mail.yourisp.com'
EMAIL_HOST_PASSWORD = ''
```

Let's see what each variable in the preceding code does:

- SITE_HOST: This is the hostname of your server. Leave it as 127.0.0.1:8000 for now. When we deploy our server in the next chapter, we will change this.

- DEFAULT_FROM_EMAIL: This is the e-mail address that appears in the **From** field of the outgoing e-mail server. For the host username, input your username plus your e-mail server, as shown in the preceding code snippet. Leave the fields empty if your ISP does not require them.

- EMAIL_HOST: This is the hostname of your e-mail server.

- EMAIL_PORT: This is the port number of the outgoing e-mail server. If you leave it empty, the default value (25) will be used. You also need to obtain this from your ISP.

- EMAIL_HOST_USER and EMAIL_HOST_PASSWORD: This is the username and password for e-mails sent by Django.

If your development machine doesn't run a mail server, most likely this is the case, then you need to enter your ISP's outgoing e-mail server. Contact your ISP for more information.

To verify that your settings are correct, launch the interactive shell and enter the following:

```
>>> from django.core.mail import EmailMessage
>>> email = EmailMessage('Hello', 'World', to=['your_email@example.com'])
>>> email.send()
```

Replace the your_email@example.com parameter with your actual e-mail address. If the preceding call to send mail does not raise an exception and you receive the e-mail, then all is set. Otherwise, you need to verify your settings with your ISP and try again.

But wait, what if you don't get any information from the ISP? We then try the alternate way: using Gmail to send a mail (of course, not as `noreply@mytweet.com`, but from your real e-mail ID). Let's look at the changes you will have to make in the `settings.py` file of `MyTweeets` project for the same.

Remove the previous `settings.py` file entries entirely and add the following:

```
EMAIL_USE_TLS = True
EMAIL_HOST = 'smtp.gmail.com'
EMAIL_HOST_USER = 'your-gmail-email-id'
EMAIL_HOST_PASSWORD = 'your-gmail-application-password'
EMAIL_PORT = 587
SITE_HOST = '127.0.0.1:8000'
```

If you are getting an error such as:

```
(534, '5.7.9 Application-specific password required. Learn more at\
n5.7.9 http://support.google.com/accounts/bin/answer.py?answer=185833
zr2sm8629305pbb.83 - gsmtp')
```

This means that the `EMAIL_HOST_PASSWORD` parameter needs a application authorization password that is not your e-mail password. Follow the link mentioned in the host section to get more details on how to create one.

After setting the things up, try sending the mail again from the shell using the following commands:

```
>>> from django.core.mail import EmailMessage
>>> email = EmailMessage('Hello', 'World', to=['your_email@example.com'])
>>> email.send()
```

Here, the `your_email@example.com` parameter is any e-mail address that you want to send a mail to. The from address of the mail will be the Gmail e-mail address that we passed to the following variable:

```
EMAIL_HOST_USER = 'your-gmail-email-id'
```

Now, once the settings are correct, sending an e-mail in Django is a piece of cake! We will use the `EmailMessage` function to send the invitation e-mail, but first, let's create a data model to store invitations.

The invitation data model

An invitation consists of the following information:

- The recipient name
- The recipient e-mail
- The user object of the sender

We also need to store an activation code for the invitation. This code will be sent in the invitation e-mail. The code will serve two purposes:

- Before accepting the invitation, we can use the code to verify that the invitation actually exists in the database
- After accepting the invitation, we can use the code to retrieve the invitation information from the database and to follow relationships between the sender and recipient

With the preceding information in mind, let's create the invitation data model. Open the user_profile/models.py file and append the following code to it:

```
class Invitation(models.Model):
    name = models.CharField(maxlength=50)
    email = models.EmailField()
    code = models.CharField(maxlength=20)
    sender = models.ForeignKey(User)
    def __unicode__(self):
        return u'%s, %s' % (self.sender.username, self.email)
```

There shouldn't be anything new or difficult to understand in this model. We have simply defined fields for the recipient name, recipient e-mail, activation code, and the sender of the invitation. We also created a __unicode__ method for debugging and enabled the model in the administration interface. Do not forget to run the python manage.py syncdb command to create the new model's table in the database.

We will also create the invitation form for this. Create a file called forms.py in the user_profile directory and update it with the following code:

```
from django import forms

class InvitationForm(forms.Form):
    email = forms.CharField(widget=forms.TextInput(attrs={'size':
    32, 'placeholder': 'Email Address of Friend to invite.',
    'class':'form-control search-query'}))
```

Creating the view page from where the invitations will be sent is similar to creating the other pages that we created for search and tweets forms that we made by creating a new file called `template/invite.html`:

```
{% extends "base.html" %}
{% load staticfiles %}
{% block content %}
<div class="row clearfix">
  <div class="col-md-6 col-md-offset-3 column">
    {% if success == "1" %}
      <div class="alert alert-success" role="alert">Invitation
      Email was successfully sent to {{ email }}</div>
    {% endif %}
    {% if success == "0" %}
      <div class="alert alert-danger" role="alert">Failed to
      send Invitation Email to {{ email }}</div>
    {% endif %}
    <form id="search-form" action="" method="post">{%
    csrf_token %}
      <div class="input-group input-group-sm">
      {{ invite.email.errors }}
      {{ invite.email }}
        <span class="input-group-btn">
          <button class="btn btn-search"
          type="submit">Invite</button>
        </span>
      </div>
    </form>
  </div>
</div>
{% endblock %}
```

The URL entry for this is as follows:

```
url(r'^invite/$', Invite.as_view()),
```

Now, we need to create `get` and `post` methods to send an invitation mail with this form.

As sending an e-mail is more specific to a user than a tweet, we will create this method in `user_profile` views, contrary to the tweet view that we used before.

Update the `user_profile/views.py` file with the following code:

```
from django.views.generic import View
from django.conf import settings
from django.shortcuts import render
from django.template import Context
```

```
from django.template.loader import render_to_string
from user_profile.forms import InvitationForm
from django.core.mail import EmailMultiAlternatives
from user_profile.models import Invitation, User
from django.http import HttpResponseRedirect
import hashlib

class Invite(View):
  def get(self, request):
    params = dict()
    success = request.GET.get('success')
    email = request.GET.get('email')
    invite = InvitationForm()
    params["invite"] = invite
    params["success"] = success
    params["email"] = email
    return render(request, 'invite.html', params)


  def post(self, request):
    form = InvitationForm(self.request.POST)
    if form.is_valid():
      email = form.cleaned_data['email']
      subject = 'Invitation to join MyTweet App'
      sender_name = request.user.username
      sender_email = request.user.email
      invite_code = Invite.generate_invite_code(email)
      link = 'http://%s/invite/accept/%s/' % (settings.SITE_HOST,
      invite_code)
      context = Context({"sender_name": sender_name,
      "sender_email": sender_email, "email": email, "link": link})
      invite_email_template =
      render_to_string('partials/_invite_email_template.html',
      context)
      msg = EmailMultiAlternatives(subject, invite_email_template,
      settings.EMAIL_HOST_USER, [email],
      cc=[settings.EMAIL_HOST_USER])
      user = User.objects.get(username=request.user.username)
      invitation = Invitation()
      invitation.email = email
      invitation.code = invite_code
      invitation.sender = user
      invitation.save()
      success = msg.send()
      return HttpResponseRedirect('/invite?success='+str(success)
      +'&email='+email)

  @staticmethod
```

```
def generate_invite_code(email):
  secret = settings.SECRET_KEY
  if isinstance(email, unicode):
    email = email.encode('utf-8')
    activation_key = hashlib.sha1(secret+email).hexdigest()
    return activation_key
```

Here, the `get()` method is as simple as rendering the `invite.html` file with the invite form as a parameter and a flag called the `success` and `email` variable is initially unset.

The `post()` method uses the usual form check and variable extraction concept; the code you will see for the first time is as follows:

```
invite_code = Invite.generate_invite_code(email)
```

This is actually a static function call that generated the activation token with a unique key for every invited user. The `render_to_string()` method works when you load a template called `_invite_email_template.html` and pass the following variables to it:

- `sender_name`: This is the name of the person who has invited or is the sender of the e-mail

- `sender_email`: This is the e-mail address of the sender

- `email`: This is the e-mail address of the person who has been invited

- `link`: This is the invitation acceptance link

The template is then used to render the body of the invitation e-mail. After that, we use the `EmailMultiAlternatives()` method to send the e-mail, as we did during the interactive session in the previous section.

There are several observations to be made here:

- The format of the activation link is `http://SITE_HOST/invite/accept/CODE/`. We will write a view to handle such URLs later in this section.

- This is the first time we used a template to render something other than a web page. As you can see, the template system is quite flexible and allows us to build e-mails, as well as web pages, or any other text for that matter.

- We used the `render_to_string()` and `render()` methods to build the message body as opposed to the usual `render_to_response` call. If you remember, this is how we rendered templates earlier in this book. We are doing this here because we are not rendering a web page.

Since the `send` method loads a template called `_invite_email_template.html`, create a file with this name in the templates folder and insert the following content:

```
Hi,
   {{ sender_name }}({{ sender_email }}) has invited you to join
   Mytweet.
   Please click {{ link }} to join.
This email was sent to {{ email }}. If you think this is a mistake
Please ignore.
```

We are halfway through the implementation of the "invite a friend" feature. At the moment, clicking on the activation link produces a 404 page not found error, so, next, we will write a view to handle it.

Handling activation links

We have made good progress; users are now able to send invitations to their friends via e-mail. The next step is to build a mechanism that handles activation links in invitations. Here is an outline of what we are going to do.

We will build a view that handles activation links. This view verifies that the invitation code actually exists in the database, and that the user who registers automatically follows the user who sent the link and gets redirected to the registration page.

Let's start by writing a URL entry for the view. Open the `urls.py` file and add the highlighted line to it:

```
url(r'^invite/accept/(\w+)/$', InviteAccept.as_view()),
```

Create a class in the `user_profile/view.py` file with thename of the class as `InviteAccept()`.

Logically, InviteAccept will work as the users will be asked to register for the application, and if they have already registered, they will be asked to follow the user who invited them.

For the sake of simplicity, we will redirect the user to the registration page with the activation code so that when they register, they automatically become followers. Let's take a look at the following code:

```
class InviteAccept(View):
  def get(self, request, code):
    return HttpResponseRedirect('/register?code='+code)
```

Then, we will write the registration page with the following code:

```
class Register(View):
  def get(self, request):
    params = dict()
    registration_form = RegisterForm()
    code = request.GET.get('code')
    params['code'] = code
    params['register'] = registration_form
    return render(request, 'registration/register.html', params)

  def post(self, request):
    form = RegisterForm(request.POST)
    if form.is_valid():
      username = form.cleaned_data['username']
      email = form.cleaned_data['email']
      password = form.cleaned_data['password']
      try:
        user = User.objects.get(username=username)
      except:
        user = User()
        user.username = username
        user.email = email
        commit = True
        user = super(user, self).save(commit=False)
        user.set_password(password)
        if commit:
          user.save()
        return HttpResponseRedirect('/login')
```

As you can see, the view follows the URL format sent in invitation e-mails. The activation code is captured from the URL using a regular expression and is, then, passed to the view as a parameter.

This was a bit time-consuming, but we were able to put our Django knowledge to good use while implementing it. You can now click on the invitation link that you received via e-mail to see what happens. You will be redirected to the registration page; you can create a new account there, log in, and note how the new account, and your original one, became followers of the sender.

Internationalization (i18n) – offering the site in multiple languages

People won't use our application if they cannot read its pages. So far, we have been concerned with English-speaking users only. However, there are people all over the world who do not know English or prefer to use their native language. To appeal to those people, it would be a good idea to offer the interface of our application in multiple languages. This would overcome the language barrier and open new frontiers for our application, especially in regions where English is not common.

As you may have guessed, Django provides all the components needed to translate a project into multiple languages. The system that is responsible for providing this feature is called the **internationalization system (i18n)**. The process of translating a Django project is quite simple.

You follow these three steps:

1. Specify which strings should be translated in your application—for example, status and error messages are translatable, whereas usernames are not.

2. Create a translation file for each language you want to support.

3. Enable and configure the i18n system.

We will go through each step in detail in the following subsections. By the end of this section of the chapter, our application will support multiple languages and you will be able to translate any other Django project with ease.

Marking strings as translatable

The first step in translating an application is telling Django which strings should be translated. Generally speaking, strings that are part of views and templates need to be translated, while strings that are entered by the user do not need to be. Marking a string as translatable is done with a function call. The name of the function and how it is called depends on where the string is located: in a view, template, model, or form.

This step is much easier than it initially looks. Let's learn about it with an example. We will translate the "invite follower" functionality in our application. The process of translating the rest of the application will be exactly the same. Open the `user_profile/views.py` file and make the highlighted changes to the invite view:

```
from django.utils.translation import ugettext as _
from django.views.generic import View
from django.conf import settings
from django.shortcuts import render
from django.template import Context
```

```
from django.template.loader import render_to_string
from user_profile.forms import InvitationForm
from django.core.mail import EmailMultiAlternatives
from user_profile.models import Invitation, User
from django.http import HttpResponseRedirect
import hashlib

class Invite(View):
  def get(self, request):
    params = dict()
    success = request.GET.get('success')
    email = request.GET.get('email')
    invite = InvitationForm()
    params["invite"] = invite
    params["success"] = success
    params["email"] = email
    return render(request, 'invite.html', params)


  def post(self, request):
    form = InvitationForm(self.request.POST)
    if form.is_valid():
      email = form.cleaned_data['email']
      subject = _('Invitation to join MyTweet App')
      sender_name = request.user.username
      sender_email = request.user.email
      invite_code = Invite.generate_invite_code(email)
      link = 'http://%s/invite/accept/%s/' % (settings.SITE_HOST,
      invite_code)
      context = Context({"sender_name": sender_name,
      "sender_email": sender_email, "email": email, "link": link})
      invite_email_template =
      render_to_string('partials/_invite_email_template.html',
      context)
      msg = EmailMultiAlternatives(subject, invite_email_template,
      settings.EMAIL_HOST_USER, [email],
      cc=[settings.EMAIL_HOST_USER])
      user = User.objects.get(username=request.user.username)
      invitation = Invitation()
      invitation.email = email
      invitation.code = invite_code
      invitation.sender = user
      invitation.save()
      success = msg.send()
    return HttpResponseRedirect('/invite?success='+str(success)
    +'&email='+email)

  @staticmethod
```

```
def generate_invite_code(email):
  secret = settings.SECRET_KEY
  if isinstance(email, unicode):
    email = email.encode('utf-8')
    activation_key = hashlib.sha1(secret+email).hexdigest()
  return activation_key
```

Note that the subject string starts with a "_"; alternatively, you can also write it as:

```
from django.utils.translation import ugettext
  subject = ugettext('Invitation to join MyTweet App')
```

Either way, it works well.

As you can see, the changes are minimal:

- We imported a function called `ugettext` from `django.utils.translation`.

- We used as a keyword to assign a shorter name to the function (the underscore character). We did so because this function will be used to mark strings as translatable in views, and since this is a very common task, it's a good idea to give the function a shorter name.

- We marked a string as translatable simply by passing it to the _ function.

That was pretty simple, wasn't it? However, there is one little observation that we need to make here. The first message uses string formatting, and we applied the % operator after calling the _() function. This is necessary to avoid translating the e-mail address. It's also preferable to use named formats, which give you greater control while doing the actual translation later. So, you may want to define the following code:

```
message= \
 _('An invitation was sent to %(email)s.') % {
 'email': invitation.email}
```

Now that we know how to mark strings as translatable in views, let's move to templates. Open the `invite.html` file in the templates folder and modify it as follows:

```
{% extends "base.html" %}
{% load staticfiles %}
{% load i18n %}
{% block content %}
<div class="row clearfix">
  <div class="col-md-6 col-md-offset-3 column">
    {% if success == "1" %}
    <div class="alert alert-success" role="alert">
      {% trans Invitation Email was successfully sent to  %}{{
      email }}
```

```
    </div>
    {% endif %}
    {% if success == "0" %}
    <div class="alert alert-danger" role="alert">Failed to send
    Invitation Email to {{ email }}</div>
    {% endif %}
      <form id="search-form" action="" method="post">{%
      csrf_token %}
        <div class="input-group input-group-sm">
        {{ invite.email.errors }}
        {{ invite.email }}
          <span class="input-group-btn">
            <button class="btn btn-search"
            type="submit">Invite</button>
          </span>
        </div>
      </form>
    </div>
  </div>
  {% endblock %}
```

Here, we placed the `{% load i18n %}` parameter at the beginning of the template to give it access to translation tags. The `<load>` tag is generally used to enable additional template tags that are not available by default. You need to place it at the top of every template that uses translation tags. i18n is shorthand for internationalization, which is the name of the Django framework that provides translation features.

Next, we used a template tag called `trans` to mark strings as translatable. This template tag works exactly the same as the `gettext` function in views. It's worth noting that the `trans` tag does not work if the string contains a template variable. In this case, you would need to use the `blocktrans` tag like:

```
{% blocktrans %}
```

You can pass a variable block, that is, `{{ variable }}` also inside `{% endblocktrans %}` block to make it more meaningful for the readers.

Now you know how to deal with translatable strings in templates too. So, let's move to forms and models. Marking a string as translatable in a form or model is slightly different from views. To learn how it is done, open the `user_profile/forms.py` file and modify the invite form, as follows:

```
from django.utils.translation import gettext_lazy as _
class InvitationForm(forms.Form):
    email = forms.CharField(widget=forms.TextInput(attrs={'size':
    32, 'placeholder': _('Email Address of Friend to invite.'),
    'class':'form-control'}))
```

The only difference here is that we imported the `gettext_lazy` function instead of `gettext` . `gettext_lazy`, which delays translating the string until its return value is accessed. This is needed here because the attributes of the form are created only once: when the application is started. If we use the normal `gettext` function, the translated labels will be stored in the form attributes using the default language (usually English) and will never be translated again. However, if we use the `gettext_lazy` function, the function will return a special object that will translate the string every time it is accessed and, hence, the translation will be done correctly. This feature makes the `gettext_lazy` function ideal for form and model attributes.

With this, we finish marking the strings of the "invite friend" view for translation. To help you remember what's covered in this subsection, here is a quick summary of the techniques used to mark the translatable strings:

- In views, mark the translatable strings using the `gettext` function (usually imported as _)

- In templates, mark the translatable strings using the `trans` template tag for strings that do not contain variables and the `blocktrans` tag for the strings that do

- In forms and models, mark the translatable strings using the `gettext_lazy` function (usually imported as _)

Of course, there are special cases that may need to be handled separately. For example, you may want to translate default parameter values in views using the `gettext_lazy` function instead of the `gettext` function. As long as you understand the difference between these two functions, you should be able to decide when you need to do so.

Creating translation files

Now that we have finished marking strings for translation, the next step is to create a translation file for each language that we want to support. This file contains all the translatable strings along with their translations and is created using a utility provided by Django.

Let's create a translation file. First, you need to locate a file named `make-messages.py` in the `bin` directory inside your Django installation folder. The easiest way to find it is by using the search functionality in your operating system. Once you find it, copy it to your system path (`/usr/bin/` in Linux and Mac OS X and. `c:\windows\` in Windows).

Also, make sure that it is executable by running the following command in Linux and Mac OS X (this step is not needed for Windows users):

```
$ sudo chmod +x /usr/bin/make-messages.py
```

The `make-messages.py` utility uses a software package called GNU gettext to extract the translatable strings from the source code. So, you need to install this package. For Linux, search for the package in your package manager and install it. Windows users will find an installer for the package at `http://gnuwin32.sourceforge.net/packages/gettext.htm`.

Finally, Mac OS X users will find a version of the package for their operating system along with the installation instructions at `http://gettext.darwinports.com/`.

Once you have the GNU gettext package installed, open a terminal, go to your project folder, create a folder called `locale` there, and then run the following command:

```
$ make-messages.py -l de
```

This command creates a translation file for the German language. The `de` variable is the language code for German. If you want to target another language, put its language code instead of `de` and continue to do so for the rest of the chapter. In addition to this, if you want to support more than one language, run the previous command for each language and apply the instructions to the rest of this section to all languages.

Once you run the preceding command, it will create a file called `django.po` at `locale/de/LC_MESSAGES/`. This is the translation file for the German language. Open it in a text editor to see what it looks like. The file starts with some metadata, such as the creation date and a character set. After that, you will find an entry for each translatable string. Each entry consists of the filename and line number of the string, the string itself, and an empty string below it where the translation should go. Here is a sample entry from the file:

```
#: user_profile/forms.py
msgid "Friend's Name"
msgstr ""
```

To translate the string, simply use your text editor to type the translation in the empty string on the third line. You can also use a specialized translation editor, such as `Poedit` (available for all major operating systems at `http://www.poedit.net/`), but for our simple file, a regular text editor should suffice. Make sure that you set a valid character in the metadata section of the file. I recommend that you use **UTF-8**:

```
"Content-Type: text/plain; charset=UTF-8\n"
```

You may note that the translation file contains some strings from the admin interface. This is because the `admin/base_site.html` admin template uses the `trans` template tag to mark its strings as translatable. There is no need to translate these strings; Django already comes with translation files for them.

Once you're done translating, you need to compile the translation file into a format that Django can use. This is done using another utility provided by Django called the `compile-messages.py` command. Locate and move this file to your system path and make sure that it is executable by following the same procedure as we did with the `make-messages.py` command.

Next, run the following command from within your project folder:

```
$ compile-messages.py
```

If the utility complains about an error in the file (such as a missing quotation mark), correct the error and try again. Once it is successful, the utility will create a compiled translation file called `django.mo` in the same folder and everything will be set for the next step in this section.

Enabling and configuring the i18n system

Django comes with the i18n system enabled by default. You can verify this by searching for the following line in the `settings.py` file:

```
USE_I18N = True
```

There are two ways to configure the i18n system. You can either set the language globally for all users or let users specify their preferred languages individually. We will see how to do both in this subsection.

To set the active language globally, find the variable called LANGUAGE_CODE in the `settings.py` file and assign your preferred language code to it. For example, if you want to set German as the default language for our project, change the language code as follows:

```
LANGUAGE_CODE = 'de'
```

Now, start the development server if it's not already running, and navigate to the "invite friend" page. There, you will find that the strings have changed according to what you entered in the German translation file. Now, change the value of the LANGUAGE_CODE variable to 'en' and note how the page reverts back to English.

The second configuration method is to let users choose the language. To do so, we should enable a class called `LocaleMiddleware`. To put it simply, a middleware is a class that processes a request or response object. Many components of Django make use of middleware classes to implement features. To see this, open the `settings.py` file and search for the `MIDDLEWARE_CLASSES` variable. You will find a list of strings there, and one of them will be `django.contrib.sessions.middleware.SessionMiddleware`, which attaches session data to the request object. We don't need to learn how middleware classes are implemented before using them. To enable `LocaleMiddleware`, simply add its classpath to the `MIDDLEWARE_CLASSES` list. Make sure that you put `LocaleMiddleware` after `SessionMiddleware` because the locale middleware utilizes the session API, as we will see next. Open the `settings.py` file and modify the file as highlighted in the following code snippet:

```
MIDDLEWARE_CLASSES = (
'django.middleware.common.CommonMiddleware',
'django.contrib.sessions.middleware.SessionMiddleware',
'django.contrib.auth.middleware.AuthenticationMiddleware',
'django.middleware.doc.XViewMiddleware',
'django.middleware.locale.LocaleMiddleware',
)
```

The locale middleware determines the active language for the user by following these steps:

1. It looks for a key named `django_language` in the session data.
2. If the key does not exist, it looks for a cookie called `django_language`.
3. If the cookie does not exist, it looks at the language code in the Accept-Language HTTP header. This header is sent by the browser to the web server indicating which languages you would prefer to receive content in.
4. If all else fails, the `LANGUAGE_CODE` variable in the `settings.py` file is used.

In all the preceding steps, Django looks for a language code that matches one of the available translation files. To effectively utilize the locale middleware, we need a view that enables the user to choose a language and updates the session data accordingly. Fortunately, Django already comes with such a view for us to use. The view is called **setlanguage**, and it expects a language code in a GET variable called language. It updates the session data using this variable and redirects the user to the originating page. To enable this view, edit the `urls.py` file and add the following highlighted lines to it:

```
urlpatterns = patterns('',
# i18n
(r'^i18n/', include('django.conf.urls.i18n')),
)
```

Adding the preceding lines is similar to how we added URL entries for the admin interface. If you recall from a previous chapter, the `include()` function can be used to include URL entries from another application under a specific path. Now, we can let the user change the language to German by providing a link, such as `/i18n/setlang/language=de`. We will modify the base template to add such links to all pages. Open the `templates/base.html` file and add the following highlighted lines to it:

```
<!DOCTYPE html PUBLIC "-//W3C//DTD XHTML 1.0 Transitional//EN"
"http://www.w3.org/TR/xhtml1/DTD/xhtml1-transitional.dtd">
<html>
  <head>
    [...]
  </head>
  <body>
    [...]
    <div id="footer">
    Django Mytweets <br />
    Languages:
      <a href="/i18n/setlang/?language=en">en</a>
      <a href="/i18n/setlang/?language=de">de</a>
      [ 218 ]Chapter 11
    </div>
  </body>
</html>
```

Additionally, we will style the new footer by appending the following CSS code to the `site_media/style.css` file:

```
#footer {
margin-top: 2em;
text-align: center;
}
```

Now, the i18n functionality of our application is ready. Point your browser to the "invite friend" page and try the new language links at the bottom of the page. The language should change according to which link is clicked.

Before we conclude this section, there are a few observations to be made here:

- You can access the currently active language in views using the request `LANGUAGE_CODE` attribute.

- Django itself is translated in a number of languages. You can see this by triggering a form error while a language other than English is active. Error messages will appear in the selected language even though you didn't translate them yourself.

- In templates, when the `RequestContext` variable is used, the currently active language is accessible using the `LANGUAGE_CODE` template variable.

This section was a bit long, but you learned a very important feature from it. By offering our application in multiple languages, we make it accessible to a broader audience, which gives it greater potential to attract more and more users. This actually applies to any web application, and, now, we will be able to translate any Django project in multiple languages with ease.

In the next section, we will shift to a different topic. When the user base of your application grows, the load on your server will increase and you will start to look for ways to improve the performance of your application. This is where caching comes to rescue.

So, please read on to learn about this very useful technique!

Caching – improving the performance of your site during high traffic

Pages of web applications are dynamically generated. Code is executed to process user input and generate output every time a page is requested. There are a lot of overheads involved in generating dynamic pages, especially when compared to serving static HTML files. The code may connect to a database, perform expensive calculations, process files, and so on. At the same time, being able to generate pages with code is exactly what makes a website dynamic and interactive.

Wouldn't it be great if we could get the best of both worlds? This is what caching does, and it's a feature that is implemented on most the sites with medium to high traffic. When a page is requested, caching stores the generated HTML of the page and reuses it later when the same page is requested again. This cuts a lot of overheads by avoiding the generation of the same page over and over again. Of course, cached pages are not stored forever. When a page is cached, an expiration period is set for the cache. When the cached page expires, it is deleted and the page is generated and cached again. The expiration period is usually between a few seconds and a few minutes, depending on the traffic of the site. The expiration period ensures that the cache is updated periodically and that users receive content updates, while, at the same time, reducing the overhead of generating pages.

Although caching is particularly useful for medium to high traffic sites, sites with low traffic can also benefit from it. If the site happens to receive a surge of high traffic suddenly, perhaps because it was featured on a major news site, you can enable caching to reduce the server load and help your website survive the surge of high traffic. Later, when the traffic calms down, you can turn off caching. So, caching is also useful for small websites. You never know when you may need it, so you'd better have this information ready.

Enabling caching

We will start this section by enabling the caching system. To use caching, you first need to choose a caching backend and specify your choice in a variable called CACHE_BACKEND in the settings.py file. The contents of this variable depend on the caching backend you choose. Some of the available options are:

- **Simple Caching**: For this, the cache data is stored in process memory. This is only useful to test the caching system during development and must not be used in production. To enable it, add the following to the settings.py file:

  CACHE_BACKEND = 'simple:///'

- **Database Caching**: For this, the cache data is stored in a database table. To create the cache table, run the following command:

  ```
  $ python manage.py createcachetable cache_table
  ```

  Then, add the following to the settings.py file:

  CACHE_BACKEND = 'db://cache_table'

  Here, the cache table was called cache_table. You can call it whatever you want as long as it doesn't conflict with an existing table.

- **Filesystem Caching**: Here, the cache data is stored in the local filesystem. To use it, add the following to the settings.py file:

  CACHE_BACKEND = 'file:///tmp/django_cache'

  Here, the /tmp/django_cache variable is used to store cache files. You can specify another path if you like.

- **Memcached**: Memcached is an advanced, highly efficient, and fast caching framework. Installing and configuring it is beyond the scope of this book, but if you already have a Memcached server available, you can specify its IP and port in the settings.py file, as follows:

  CACHE_BACKEND = 'memcached://ip:port/'

If you are not sure which backend to choose for this section, go with simple caching. In reality, however, if you are caught in a sudden surge of traffic and want to improve server performance, go with Memcached or database caching, depending on what's available to you on the server. On the other hand, if you have a website with medium to high traffic, I highly recommend you to use Memcached, as it is definitely the fastest caching solution available for Django. The information presented in this section works the same regardless of which caching backend you choose.

So, decide on a caching backend and insert the corresponding `CACHE_BACKEND` variable in the `settings.py` file. Next, you should specify the expiration duration of cached pages in seconds. Add the following to the `settings.py` file to cache pages for five minutes:

```
CACHE_MIDDLEWARE_SECONDS = 60 * 5
```

Now, we are done with enabling the caching system. Continue reading to learn how to utilize caching to improve the performance of your application.

Configuring caching

You can configure Django to cache your whole site or specific views. We will learn how to do both in this subsection.

Caching the whole site

To cache your whole site, add the `CacheMiddleware` class to your `MIDDLEWARE_CLASSES` class in the `settings.py` file:

```
MIDDLEWARE_CLASSES = (
'django.middleware.common.CommonMiddleware',
'django.contrib.sessions.middleware.SessionMiddleware',
'django.contrib.auth.middleware.AuthenticationMiddleware',
'django.middleware.cache.CacheMiddleware',
'django.middleware.doc.XViewMiddleware',
'django.middleware.locale.LocaleMiddleware',
)
```

Order matters here as it did when we added the locale middleware. The caching middleware class should be added after the session and authentication middleware classes and before the locale middleware class.

This is all that you need to cache your Django site. From now on, whenever a page is requested, Django will store the generated HTML and reuse it later. It's important to realize that the caching system only caches pages that do not have GET and POST variables. So, our users will still be able to post tweets and follow friends because the views of these pages expect GET or POST variables. On the other hand, pages such as tweets and hashtag listings will be cached.

Caching specific views

Sometimes, you will want to cache only specific pages of your website—perhaps a high-traffic site linked to a page of yours, so that most of the traffic will be directed to this particular page. In this case, it would make sense to cache this page only. Another good candidate for caching is a page that is expensive to generate, so you would only want it to be generated once every five minutes or so. The tag cloud page in our application fits the latter case. Every time the page is requested, Django iterates through all the tags in the database and counts the number of tweets for each tag. This is an expensive operation because it requires a large number of database queries. Therefore, caching this view is a good idea.

To cache the view based on the hashtag class, you simply apply a method called `cache_page` and the caching parameter with it. Try this by editing the `mytweets/urls.py` file as highlighted in the following code:

```
from django.views.decorators.cache import cache_page
...
...
url(r'^search/hashTag$',  cache_page(60 * 15)(SearchHashTag.as_
view())),
...
...
```

Using the `cache_page()` method is straightforward. It lets you specify which views to cache. The rules mentioned in site caching also apply to view caching. If the view receives GET or POST parameters, Django won't cache it.

With this information, we finish this section. Caching won't be necessary when you first release your website to the public. However, when your website grows, or if you suddenly receive a surge of high traffic, the caching system will certainly become handy. So, keep it in mind while monitoring the performance of your application.

Next, we are going to learn about the Django testing framework. Testing can sometimes be a tedious task. Wouldn't it be great if you could run a single command and it took care of testing your site? Django lets you do this, and we will learn about it in the next section.

Template fragments can be cached in the following manner:

```
% load cache %}
{% cache 500 sidebar %}
    .. sidebar ..
{% endcache %}
```

Unit testing – automating the process of testing your application

During the course of this book, we sometimes modified a view that we wrote previously. This actually happens quite often while developing software. One may modify or even rewrite a function to change the implementation details, because the requirements have changed, or simply to refactor the code and make it more readable.

When you modify a function, you have to test it again to make sure that your changes didn't introduce bugs. However, testing will become a boring task if you have to repeat the same tests over and over every time you modify a function. You may also forget to test all aspects of the function if they are not well documented. Clearly, this is not an ideal situation; we definitely need a better mechanism to handle testing.

Fortunately, a solution already exists for this. It is called unit testing. The idea is that you write code to test your code. The testing code calls your functions and verifies that they behave as expected and then prints a report of the results. You only have to write the testing code once. Later, whenever you want to test, you can simply run the testing code and examine the resulting report.

Python comes with a framework for unit testing. It is located in the unit test module. Django extends this framework to add support for view testing. We will learn how to use the Django unit testing framework in this section.

The test client

In order to interact with views, Django provides a class that emulates browser functionality. You can use it to send requests to your application and receive the responses. Let's learn about it using the interactive console. Launch the console using this command:

```
$ python manage.py shell
```

Import the Client() class, create a Client object, and retrieve the homepage of the application using a GET request:

```
>>>from django.test.client import Client
client = Client()
>>> response = client.get('/')
>>> print response
```

```
X-Frame-Options: SAMEORIGIN
Content-Type: text/html; charset=utf-8


<html>
  <head>
    <link href="/static/css/bootstrap.min.css"
    rel="stylesheet" media="screen">
  </head>
  <body>
    <nav class="navbar navbar-default" role="navigation">
      <a class="navbar-brand" href="#">MyTweets</a>
    </nav>
  <div class="container">
  </div>
  <nav class="navbar navbar-default navbar-fixed-bottom"
  role="navigation">
    <p class="navbar-text navbar-right">Footer </p>
  </nav>
  <script src="/static/js/jquery-2.1.1.min.js"></script>
  <script src="/static/js/bootstrap.min.js"></script>
  <script src="/static/js/base.js"></script>
  </body>
</html>
>>>
```

Try to send a POST request to the login view. The output will vary depending on whether you provide correct credentials or not:

```
>>> print client.post('/login/',{'username': 'your_username',
'password': 'your_password'})
```

Finally, if there is a view that is restricted only to the users that are logged in, you can send a request to it like this:

```
>>> print client.login('/friend/invite/', 'your_username',
'your_password')
```

As you can see from the interactive session, the `Client()` class provides three methods:

- `get`: This method sends a GET request to a view. It takes the URL of the view as a parameter. You can pass an optional dictionary of GET variables to this method.

- `post`: This method sends sends a POST request to a view. It takes the URL of the view and a dictionary of POST variables as parameters.

- `login`: This method sends a GET request to a view that is restricted to logged in users only. It takes the URL of the view, a username, and password as parameters.

The `Client()` class is stateful, which means that it retains its state across requests. Once you log in, later requests will be handled while you are logged in. The response object returned by the `Client()` class's methods contains the following attributes:

- `status_code`: This is the HTTP status of the response

- `content`: This is the body of the response page

- `template`: This is the `Template` instance used to render the page; if multiple templates were used, this attribute would be a list of Template objects

- `context` : This is the `Context` object used to render the template

These fields are useful to check whether the test succeeded or failed, as we will see next. Feel free to experiment more with the `Client()` class. It's important to understand how it works before you continue to the next subsection, where we will create the first unit test.

Testing the registration view

Now that you are comfortable with the `Client()` class, let's write our first test. Unit tests should reside in a module named `tests.py` inside the application folder. Each test should be a method in a class derived from the `django.test.TestCase` module. The name of the method must start with the word test. With this in mind, we will write a test method that tries to register a new user account. So, create a file named `tests.py` inside the `bookmarks` folder and type the following content in it:

```python
from django.test import TestCase
from django.test.client import Client
class ViewTest(TestCase):
def setUp(self):
self.client = Client()
def test_register_page(self):
data = {
'username': 'test_user',
'email': 'test_user@example.com',
'password1': 'pass123',
'password2': 'pass123'
}
response = self.client.post('/register/', data)
self.assertEqual(response.status_code, 302)
```

Let's go through the code line by line:

- First, we imported the `TestCase` and `Client` classes.
- Next, we defined a class called `ViewTest()`, which is derived from the `TestCase` class. As I said earlier, all test classes must be derived from this base class.
- After that, we defined a method called `setUp()`. This method is called when the testing process starts. Here, we created a `Client` object.
- Finally, we defined a method called `test_register_page`. The name of the method starts with the word test, indicating that it is a test method. The method sends a POST request to the registration view and checks the status code for equality with the number `302`. This number is the HTTP status for a redirect.

If you recall from a previous chapter, the registration view redirects the user if the request succeeds.

We checked the response object using a method called `assertEqual()`. This method is inherited from the `TestCase` class. It raises an exception if the two passed arguments are not equal. If an exception is raised, the testing framework knows that the test failed; otherwise, if no exception is raised, it assumes that the test succeeded.

The `TestCase` class provides a set of methods to be used in testing. Here is a list of the important ones:

- `assertEqual`: This expects two values to be equal
- `assertNotEquals`: This expects two values to be unequal
- `assertTrue`: This expects a value to be `True`
- `assertFalse`: This expects a value to be `False`

Now that you understand the test class, let's run the actual test by issuing the command:

```
$ python manage.py test
```

The output will be similar to the following:

```
Creating test database...
Creating table auth_message
Creating table auth_group
Creating table auth_user
Creating table auth_permission
[...]
Loading 'initial_data' fixtures...
```

```
No fixtures found.
.
-------------------------------------------------------------
Ran 1 test in 0.170s
OK
Destroying test database...
```

So, what has happened here? The testing framework starts by creating a test database with tables similar to those in the real database. Next, it runs the tests found in the tests module. Finally, it prints a report of the results and destroys the test database.

Here, our single test succeeded. To see what the output would be like if the test fails, modify the `test_register_page` view in the `tests.py` file by removing a required form field:

```
def test_register_page(self):
data = {
'username': 'test_user',
'email': 'test_user@example.com',
'password1': '1',
# 'password2': '1'
}
response = self.client.post('/register/', data)
self.assertEqual(response.status_code, 302)
```

Now, run the `python manage.py test` command again to see the results:

```
==============================================================
FAIL: test_register_page (mytweets.user_profile.tests.ViewTest)
-------------------------------------------------------------
Traceback (most recent call last):
File "mytweets/user_profile/tests.py", line 19, in test_
register_page
self.assertEqual(response.status_code, 302)
AssertionError: 200 != 302

-------------------------------------------------------------
Ran 1 test in 0.170s
FAILED (failures=1)
```

Our test is working! Django detected an error and gave us the exact details of what happened. Don't forget to return the test to its original form once you're done. Now, let's write another test, a slightly more advanced one, to understand the testing framework better.

There are many other scenarios for which you can write unit tests:

- Checking whether registration fails if the two password fields do not match
- Testing the "add friend" and "invite friend" views
- Testing the "edit bookmark" functionality
- Testing that a search returns correct results

The preceding list shows just examples. Writing unit tests to cover as many use cases as possible is important to maintain a healthy application and to minimize bugs and regressions. The more unit tests you write, the more confident you can be when your application passes all the tests. Django makes it extremely easy to unit test your application, so make use of this fact.

At some point in the application's life, it will move from the development mode to production. The next section explains how to prepare your Django project for a production environment.

Deploying Django

So, you have done a lot of work on your web application, and now it is the time to go live. To make sure that the transition from development to production goes smoothly, there are a number of changes that must be made to the application before it goes live. This section covers these changes to help make the launch of your web application successful.

The production web server

We have been using the development web server that comes with Django throughout this book. While this server is perfect for the development process, it's definitely not intended to be a production web server, as it wasn't developed with security or performance in mind. Therefore, it is certainly not suitable for production.

There are several options to choose from when it comes to a web server, but **Apache** is by far the most popular choice, and the Django development team actually recommends it. The details of how to set up Django with Apache depends on your hosting solution. Some hosting plans offer preconfigured Django hosting, where you only have to copy your project files to the server, whereas other hosting plans give you the freedom to configure everything yourself.

The details of setting up Apache can vary depending on a number of factors and are beyond the scope of this book. If you end up having to configure Apache yourself, consult the Django documentation at `http://www.djangoproject.com/documentation/apache_auth/` for detailed instructions.

Summary

This chapter covered a variety of interesting topics. We developed an important set of features for our project in this chapter. A follower's networks are very important to help users socialize and share interests together. We learned about several Django frameworks that are useful while deploying Django. We also learned how to move a Django project from a development to a production environment. Notably, the frameworks that we learned about are all very easy to use, so you will be able to effectively utilize them in your future projects. These features are common in web 2.0 applications, and, now, you will be able to incorporate them in any Django website.

In the next chapter, we will learn about improving various aspects of our application, mainly performance and localization. We will also learn how to deploy our project on a production server. The next chapter comes with a lot of useful information, so read on!

10
Extending Django

It's been a long journey so far, and we've dealt with lots of code and basic concepts related to Django's functionalities. In this chapter, we will discuss Django a little more, but we will discuss, in brief, different parameters, such as custom tags, filters, sub-frameworks, message system, and so on. The following are the topics that we will deal with in this chapter:

- Custom template tags and filters
- Class-based generic views
- Contributed sub-frameworks
- A message system
- The subscription system
- User scores

Custom template tags and filters

The Django template system comes with many template tags and filters that make writing templates an easy and flexible job. Sometimes, however, you may wish to extend the template system with your own tags and filters. This usually happens when you find yourself repeating the same tag structure many times, when you wish to wrap the structure in a single tag, or even when there is a filter that you want to add to the template system.

Guess what? Django already allows you to do this, and it is quite easy too! You basically add a new package to your application called **templatetags** and put modules that contain tags and filters in it. Let's learn about this by adding a filter that capitalizes a string. Add a `templatetags` folder to the `mytweets` parent folder and put an empty file called `__init__.py` in it, so that Python treats the folder as a package. Now, create a module called `mytweet_filters` in it. We are going to write our filter in this module. Here is an illustration of the directory structure:

```
templatetags/
    |-- __init__.py
    -- mytweet_filters.py
```

Now, add the following code to the `mytweet_filters.py` file:

```
from django import template
register = template.Library()

@register.filter
def capitalize(value):
    return value.capitalize()
```

The `register` variable is an object that can be used to introduce new tags and filters to the template system. Here, we used the `register.filter` decorator to add the capitalize function as a filter.

To use the new filter from within a template, put the following line at the beginning of your template file:

```
{% load mytweet_filters %}
```

Then, you can use the new filter just like any other filter offered by Django:

```
Hi {{ name|capitalize }}!
```

Adding custom template tags works in a similar way with filters. Basically, you define methods to process the tag and then register the tag to make it available for templates. The process is slightly more involved because tags can be more complicated than filters. Further information about custom template tags is available in the Django online documentation.

While writing a custom filter, you have to take care of Django's auto-escaping behavior with the filter. There are three type of strings that can be passed to the filter:

- **Raw string**: This string is prepared either by the `str` command or is formed with the unicode. They are automatically escaped if auto-escaping is enabled.

- **Safe strings**: These strings are the strings that are marked safe from further escaping. They don't need any further escaping. To mark the output as a safe string, use the `django.utils.safestring.mark_safe()` module.

- **Strings marked as "needing escaping"**: As the name suggests, they always need to escape.

Class-based generic views

While working with Django, you will note that there are certain types of views that are always needed regardless of the project that you are working on. For this reason, Django comes with a set of views that can be used in any project. These views are called **generic views**.

Django offers generic views for the following purposes:

- To create simple views for tasks, such as redirecting to another URL or rendering a template

- Listing and forming detail views to display objects from a data model - these views are similar to how the admin page displays lists and detail pages for data models

- To generate date-based archive pages; these can be particularly useful for blogs

- To create, edit, and delete objects in data models

Django's class-based view can be configured by defining subclasses, or by passing arguments directly in the URL conf.

The subclasses are full of conventions that remove the hassle to rewrite templates of common situations. When you use the subclass, you can actually override the attribute or methods of the main class by providing a new value:

```
# app_name/views.py
from django.views.generic import TemplateView

class ContactView(TemplateView):
  template_name = "contact.html"
```

We will also add its entry to the `urls.py` file to get it redirected:

```
# project/urls.py
from django.conf.urls.defaults import *
from some_app.views import ContactView

urlpatterns = patterns('',
   (r'^connect/', ContactView.as_view()),
)
```

Interestingly, we can achieve the same with the on file change, and in a few lines, by adding the following to the `urls.py` file:

```
from django.conf.urls.defaults import *
from django.views.generic import TemplateView

urlpatterns = patterns('',
   (r'^contact/', TemplateView.as_view
   (template_name="contact.html")),
)
```

Contributed sub-frameworks

The `django.contrib` package contains Django's standard library. We used the following sub-frameworks from this package in the earlier chapters in this book:

- `admin`: This is the Django admin interface
- `auth`: This is the user authentication system
- `sessions`: This is the Django session framework
- `syndication`: This is the feed generation framework

These sub-frameworks greatly simplify our work irrespective of whether we create registration and authentication facilities, build an administration page, or provide feeds for our content. The `django.contrib` package is a very important part of Django. Knowing its subpackages and how to use them will save you a lot of time and effort.

This section will provide you a brief introduction of other frameworks in this package. You won't get into the details of how to use each framework, but you will learn enough to know when to use the framework. Once you want to use a framework in a project, you can read the online documentation to learn more about it.

Flatpages

Web applications may contain pages that are static in nature. For example, your website may include a set of help pages that rarely change. Django provides an application called **flatpages** to serve static pages. The application is pretty simple; it provides you a data model to store various bits of information about each page, including the following:

- The URL
- The title
- The content
- The template name
- Whether registration is required to view the page

To use the application, you can simply enable it in the INSTALLED_APPS variable in the settings.py file and add its middleware to the MIDDLEWARE_CLASSES variable. After that, you can store and manage your static pages using a data model provided by the flatpages application.

Humanize

The **humanize** application offers a set of filters to add a human touch to your pages.

Here is a list of the available filters:

- **apnumber**: For numbers 1-9, this returns the number spelled out. Otherwise, it returns the number. In other words, 1 becomes 'one', 9 becomes 'nine', and so on, whereas 10 remains 10.

- **intcomma**: This takes an integer and converts it into a string with a comma, for example:

  ```
  4500 becomes 4,500.
  45000 becomes 45,000.
  450000 becomes 450,000.
  4500000 becomes 4,500,000.
  ```

- **intword**: This converts an integer into an easy-to-read form, for example:

  1000000 becomes 1.0 million.

  ```
  1200000 becomes 1.2 million.
  1200000000 becomes 1.2 billion.
  ```

- **naturalday**: Based on the range the date is in, if a given date is in the *(+1,0,-1)* range, this shows the date as "tomorrow", "today", and "yesterday" respectively, for example, (if today is January 26, 2007):

  ```
  25 Jan 2007 becomes yesterday.

  26 Jan 2007 becomes today.

  27 Jan 2007 becomes tomorrow.
  ```

- **naturaltime**: This returns a string representing how many seconds, minutes, or hours ago the date event occurred, for example, (If now is January 26, 2007 16:30:00):

  ```
  26 Jan 2007 16:30:00 becomes now.

  26 Jan 2007 16:29:31 becomes 29 seconds ago.
  26 Jan 2007 16:29:00 becomes a minute ago.
  26 Jan 2007 16:25:35 becomes 4 minutes ago.
  26 Jan 2007 15:30:29 becomes 59 minutes ago.
  26 Jan 2007 15:30:01 becomes 59 minutes ago.
  26 Jan 2007 15:30:00 becomes an hour ago.
  26 Jan 2007 13:31:29 becomes 2 hours ago.
  25 Jan 2007 13:31:29 becomes 1 day, 2 hours ago.
  25 Jan 2007 13:30:01 becomes 1 day, 2 hours ago.
  25 Jan 2007 13:30:00 becomes 1 day, 3 hours ago.
  26 Jan 2007 16:30:30 becomes 30 seconds from now.
  26 Jan 2007 16:30:29 becomes 29 seconds from now.
  26 Jan 2007 16:31:00 becomes a minute from now.
  26 Jan 2007 16:34:35 becomes 4 minutes from now.
  26 Jan 2007 17:30:29 becomes an hour from now.
  26 Jan 2007 18:31:29 becomes 2 hours from now.
  27 Jan 2007 16:31:29 becomes 1 day from now.
  ```

- **ordinal**: This converts an integer to its ordinal form. Here, 1 becomes '1st', and so on between every three digits.

Sitemap

Sitemap is a framework to generate sitemaps, which are XML files that help search engine indexers to find dynamic pages on your site. It tells the indexer how important a page is and how often it changes. This information makes the indexing process more accurate and efficient.

The sitemaps framework lets you express the preceding information in Python code and then generates an XML document that represents the sitemap of your site. This covers the most commonly used sub-frameworks from the `django.contrib` package. The package contains additional applications that are not as important as the preceding ones and it is updated from time to time with new applications. To learn about any application from the `django.contrib` package, you can always read its documentation, which is available online.

Cross-site request forgery protection

We discussed how to prevent two types of web attacks in *Chapter 5, Introducing Hashtags*, namely, SQL injection and cross-site scripting. Django provides protection against another type of attack called cross-site request forgery. In this attack, a malicious site tries to manipulate your application by tricking a user who is logged in on your website to open a specially crafted page. This page usually contains JavaScript code that tries to submit a form to your website. CSRF protection works by embedding a token (that is a secret code) into all forms and verifies the token when the form is submitted. This effectively makes CSRF attacks infeasible.

To activate CSRF protection, you just need to add the `'django.contrib.csrf.middleware.CsrfMiddleware'` parameter to the `MIDDLEWARE_CLASSES` variable, and this will work, transparently, to prevent CSRF attacks.

The message system

Our application allows users to add each other as friends and monitor friend bookmarks. Although these two forms of communication are related to the nature of our bookmarking application, sometimes users want the flexibility of sending private messages to each other. This feature is especially useful for enhancing the social aspect of our website.

The message system can be implemented in a variety of ways. It can be as simple as providing each user a contact form, which works by sending its content to the user's e-mail when it is submitted. You already have all of the information needed to build the components of this functionality:

- A message form with a text field for the subject and a text area for the body of the message
- A view that displays the message form of a user and sends the contents of the form to the user via the `send_mail()` function

When allowing users to send e-mails via your site, you need to be careful in order to prevent abuse of the feature. Here, you can restrict the contact forms only to the logged-in users or friends only.

Another approach to implement the message system is by storing and managing messages in the database. This way, users can send and view messages using our application itself instead of using e-mail. While this approach is more bound to our application, and therefore keeps users on our website, it involves more work to get implement. However, as in the previous approach, you already have all of the information needed to implement this approach too. The components needed here are as follows:

- A data model to store messages. It should contain fields for the sender, recipient, subject, and body. You can also add fields for the date, read status, and so on.
- A form to create messages. The fields for the subject and body are needed.
- A view to list the available messages.
- A view to display a message.

The preceding list is just one way that is used to implement the message system. You can, for example, join the list and message views into a single view, or provide a view to display the sent messages in addition to the received ones. The possibilities are numerous and depend on how advanced you want the feature to be.

The subscription system

We offer several web feeds that enable users to monitor updates on our website. However, some users may still prefer the old way of monitoring updates via e-mail. For those users, you may want to implement an e-mail subscription system to the application. For example, you can let users receive notifications when a bookmark is posted by a friend, or when a bookmark is posted under a certain tag.

Furthermore, you can group such notifications and send them in batches to avoid sending a large number of e-mails. The implementation details of this feature greatly depends on how you want it to work. It can be as simple as a data model that stores the tags that each user is subscribed to. It would have a loop that goes through all users who are subscribed to a particular tag and sends notifications to them when a bookmark is posted under this tag. This approach, however, is too basic and generates a lot of e-mails. A more sophisticated approach may involve storing notifications in a data model and sending them in one e-mail on a daily basis.

User scores

Some websites (such as `Slashdot.org` and `reddit.com`) track the activity of users by assigning a score to each user. This score is incremented whenever the user contributes to the website in some way. Users' scores can be utilized in a variety of ways. For example, you can release new features to your most active users first, or provide other advantages to active users, which will motivate other users to contribute more to your website.

Implementing user scores is pretty simple. You need a data model to maintain scores in the database. After that, you can use the Django model API to access and manipulate scores from within views.

Summary

The purpose of this chapter is to prepare you for tasks that are not covered in this book. It introduced you to a number of topics. When a need arises for a certain feature, you now know where to look in order to find a framework that helps you to implement the feature quickly and cleanly.

This chapter also gave you some ideas that you may want to implement into our bookmarking application. Working on these features will give you more opportunities to experiment with Django and extend your knowledge of its frameworks and inner workings.

In the next chapter, we are going to cover various ways of database connectivity, such as MySQL, NoSQL, PostgreSQL and so on, which is required for any database-based application.

11
Database Connectivity

Django is a database-agnostic framework, which means that the database fields provided by Django are designed to work across different databases, such as **SQLite**, **Oracle**, **MySQL**, and **PostgreSQL**. In fact, they also work on several third-party database backends. PostgreSQL is a great database for Django in production, whereas SQLite is used for a development environment, and you will end up doing a lot of work if you don't want to use RDBMS for your project. This chapter will give you the detailed difference between the two types and will show you which is a better fit for Django, and, also, how we can actually implement them in our Django project.

The following are the topics that we will deal with in this chapter:

- SQL versus NoSQL
- Django with relational databases
- Django with NoSQL
- Setting up a database system
- The single-page application project—URL shortener

First of all, let's see the difference between SQL and NoSQL.

SQL versus NoSQL

SQL databases, or relational databases, have been around for a very long time; in fact, the databases were roughly assumed as SQL databases until the new term was coined—which is NoSQL.

Well, we are talking about the high-level differences between SQL and NoSQL. The following are the differences between them:

SQL database (RDBMS)	NoSQL database
SQL databases are relational databases (RDBMS)	NoSQL databases are nonrelational or distributed databases
SQL databases are based on tables and its relationship with other tables	NoSQL are document based, key-value pairs, graph database, or wide column stores
A SQL database stores its data in rows of a table	NoSQL is a collection of key-value pairs, documents, graph database, or wide column stores
SQL databases have a predefined schema	NoSQL has a dynamic schema
SQL databases are vertically scalable	NoSQL databases are horizontally scalable
SQL database examples are MySQL, Oracle, SQLite, PostgreSQL, and MS SQL	NoSQL database examples are MongoDB, BigTable, Redis, RavenDB, Cassandra, HBase, Neo4j, and CouchDB

Let's try to understand the basic features of some of the famous SQL and NoSQL databases.

SQL databases

The following sections deal with different SQL databases and their usage.

MySQL – open source

Being one of the most popular databases in the world, MySQL has some benefits that make it suitable for all kinds of business problems. The following are a few important benefits of MySQL:

- **Replication**: MySQL supports replication, that is, by replicating a MySQL database, the work load can be significantly reduced from one machine, and an application can be easily scaled
- **Sharding**: When the number of write operations are very high, sharding helps by partitioning the application server that divides the database into small chunks

PostgreSQL

As mentioned before, PostgreSQL is the most popular database within the Django community. It also has the widest feature set of the core-supported databases.

Evolved PostgresSQL's advanced queries and features have made it possible to achieve the complex line of conventional SQL query into much simpler lines to write query. However, the implementation of arrays, hstore, JSON, and so on is kind of tricky with the conventional SQL databases.

NoSQL databases

This concept was introduced when horizontal scaling was tough and RDBMS-based databases were not able to scale as much as they were expected to. It is often termed as Not only SQL. It provides a mechanism to store and retrieve data other than the traditional SQL methods.

MongoDB

MongoDB is one of the most popular document-based NoSQL databases, as it stores data in JSON-like documents. It is a nonrelational database with a dynamic schema. It was developed by the founders of **DoubleClick**. It is written in **C++** and is currently used by some big companies, such as The New York Times, Craigslist, and MTV Networks. The following are some of the benefits and strengths of MongoDB:

- **Speed**: For simple queries, it gives good performance, as all the related data is in a single document that eliminates join operations
- **Scalability**: It is horizontally scalable, that is, you can reduce the workload by increasing the number of servers in your resource pool instead of relying on a standalone resource
- **Manageable**: It is easy to use for both developers and administrators. This also gives MondoDB the ability to share databases
- **Dynamic schema**: It gives you the flexibility to evolve your data schema without modifying the existing data

CouchDB

CouchDB is also a document-based NoSQL database. It stores data in the form of JSON documents. The following are some of the benefits and strengths of CouchDB:

- **Schema less**: As a member of the NoSQL family, it also has a schema-less property that makes it more flexible, as it has the form of JSON documents to store data

- **HTTP query**: You can access your database documents using your web browser
- **Conflict resolution**: It has automatic conflict, which is useful when you are going to use a distributed database
- **Easy replication**: Replicating is fairly straightforward

Redis

Redis is another open source NoSQL database that is mainly used because of its lightening speed. It is written in the ANSI C language. The following are some of the benefits and strengths of Redis:

- **Data structures**: Redis provides efficient data structures to such an extent that it is sometimes called as a data structure server. The keys stored in a database can be hashes, lists, and strings, and can be sorted or unsorted sets.
- **Redis as cache**: You can use Redis as a cache by implementing keys with limited time to improve the performance.
- **Very fast**: It is considered as one of the fastest NoSQL servers, as it works with the in-memory dataset.

Setting up a database system

Django supports several database engines. Interestingly, however, you only need to learn one API in order to use any of these database systems.

This is possibly because of Django's database layer that abstracts access to the database system.

You will learn about this later, but, for now, you only need to know that regardless of which database system you choose, you will be able to run the Django applications developed in this book (or elsewhere) without modification.

Unlike client-server database systems, SQLite does not require a resident process in memory, and it stores the database in a single file, making it ideal for our development environment. That is why we have used this database throughout this project, until now. Of course, you are free to use your preferred database management system. We can tell Django which database system to use by editing a configuration file. It is also worth noting that if you want to use MySQL, you will need to install MySQL, which is the MySQL driver for Python.

Installing a database system in Django is really simple; all your need to do is install the database you want to configure first, then add a few configuration lines in the `settings.py` file, and you are done with the database setup.

Setting up MySQL

We will install and configure MySQL and its related plugins step by step in the following sections.

Installing MySQL in Linux – Debian

Execute the following command to install MySQL in Linux (Debian here):

```
sudo apt-get install mysql-server
```

After executing this command, you will be asked to set up MySQL and configure the database with a username and password.

Installing the MySQL plugin for Python

To install the MySQL-related plugins that you require, use the following command:

```
pip install MySQL-python
```

Now, open the `settings.py` file and add the following lines for Django to connect with MySQL:

```
DATABASES = {
    'default': {
    'ENGINE': 'django.db.backends.mysql',
    'NAME': 'django_db',
    'USER': 'your_username',
    'PASSWORD': 'your_password',
    }
}
```

That's it, all you need to do now is to recreate all the tables in the new database that you just configured and run the following command:

```
python manage.py syncdb
```

 You will get the `django.db.utils.ConnectionDoesNotExist` exception if you have not defined the database that you are trying to access.

The advantage of Django is that you can use it with multiple databases at once.

However, you may think, what is the need of multiple databases in the same project?

Until the NoSQL database came into existence, in most of the cases, the same database was often used to keep the records of all types of data, from critical data, such as user details, to dump data, such as logs; all were kept in the same database and the system faced challenges while scaling up the system.

For a multiple database system, an ideal solution could be to store the relational information, such as users, their role, and other account information, in an SQL database, such as MySQL. The application data, which is independent, can be stored in a NoSQL database, such as MongoDB.

We need to define multiple databases through a configuration file. Django needs to be told when you want to use more than one database with the database servers you use. So, in the `settings.py` file, you need to change the `DATABASES` setting with the database aliases map.

An appropriate example of the multiple database configuration can be written as follows:

```
DATABASES = {
  'default': {
    'NAME': 'app_data',
    'ENGINE': 'django.db.backends.postgresql_psycopg2',
    'USER': 'postgres_user',
    'PASSWORD': 's3krit'
  },
  'users': {
    'NAME': 'user_data',
    'ENGINE': 'django.db.backends.mysql',
    'USER': 'mysql_user',
    'PASSWORD': 'priv4te'
  }
}
```

The preceding example uses two databases, which are PostgreSQL and MySQL with the required credentials.

Migration and the need for migration

Migration allows you to update, change, and delete models by creating migration files that represent the model changes and which can be run on any development, staging, or production database.

Schema migration with Django has had a long and complex history; for the last few years, the third-party application **South** was the only go-to choice. If you think about the importance of migration, Django 1.7 was released with an inbuilt support of migration.

We need to know about South versus Django migrations as well. For those who are familiar with South, this should feel pretty familiar and probably a little bit cleaner. For easy reference, the following table compares the old South workflow to the new Django migrations workflow:

Steps	South	Django migration
Initial migration	Run `syncdb` and then `./manage.py schemamigration <appname> --initial`	`./manage.py makemigrations <appname>`
Apply migration	`./manage.py migrate <appname>`	`./manage.py migrate <appname>`
Non-first migration	`./manage.py schemamigration <appname> --auto`	`./manage.py makemigration <appname>`

So, from the table, we can see that Django migrations basically follow the same process as South, at least for the standard migration process—this just simplifies things a bit.

The new features in Django migration

The new migration code will be in the improved version of South, but will be based on the same concepts, which are as follows:

- Migration per application
- Auto detection of the changes
- Data migration alongside schema migration

Let's take a look at the following term list to understand the advantages of Django migration:

- **Improved migration format**: The much improved migration format is readable, and can thus be optimized or examined without actual execution
- **Rebasing**: In this, there is no need to keep or execute the whole history of migration every time, as it will now be possible to create new first migrations as the project grows
- **Improved auto detection**: New and custom field changes will be detected more easily, as migration will be built in with the improved field API
- **Better merge detection**: The new migration format will automatically resolve the merging between different VCS branches, which will no longer need any work if we are able to merge the changes

Once you set up your project and start the application, that is, your application has generated the necessary tables in your database, you are not supposed to make complex changes to your Django models, that is, you should not delete your attributes from a class. However, practically, that is not possible, as you might need to change your model classes accordingly. In such cases, we have a solution to fix these kind of problems. The process is called **migration**, and, in Django, these migrations are done with a module called South.

Until the 1.7 version of Django, which is the latest one, you have to separately install the south module. However, since Django's 1.7 migration, the south module is a built-in module. You might have always been doing it, for example, when you changed (changes such as adding new attributes) your model classes using the following command:

```
$python manage.py syncdb
```

With the newer version, `manage.py syncdb` has been deprecated for migration, but if you still like the old way, this works for now.

Backend support

This is very important for any Django application that is used in production to get migration support. Thus, choosing a database that is primarily supported by the migration module will always be a better decision.

A few of the most compatible databases are as follows:

- **PostgreSQL**: In terms of migration or schema support, PostgresSQL is the most compatible database out there.

> You can initialize your new column with `null=True`, as this will be added much faster.

- **MySQL**: MySQL is a widely used database, as Django supports it seamlessly. The catch here is that there is no support for transaction when schema alteration operations are done, that is, if an operation fails, you will have to manually revert the changes. Also, for every schema update, all the tables are rewritten, and this could take a lot of time, and getting your application up again can take a lot of time.

- **SQLite**: This is the default database that comes with Django and is mainly used for development purposes. Thus, it has little schema alteration support that is limited to the following cases:
  - ° Creation of a new table
  - ° Data copying
  - ° Dropping an old table
  - ° Renaming a table

How to do migrations?

Migration is done mainly with the first three commands, which are as follows:

- `makemigrations`: This is based on the changes you made to the models that prepare the migration query
- `migrate`: This applies the changes prepared by the `makemigrations` query and lists their status
- `sqlmigrate`: This displays the SQL query that the `makemigrations` query prepared

Thus, the flow for Django's schema migration can be stated as follows:

```
$python manage.py makemigrations 'app_name'
```

This will prepare the migration file, which will look similar to the following:

```
Migrations for 'app_name':
  0003_auto.py:
    - Alter field name on app_name
```

Then, after the file has been created, you can check the directory structure. You will see a file named `0003_auto.py` under the `migration` folder; you can apply the changes with the following command:

```
$ python manage.py migrate app_name
```

The following are the operations that you need to perform:

```
Synchronize non migrated apps: sessions, admin, messages, auth,
staticfiles, contenttypes
Apply all migrations: app_name
Synchronizing apps without migrations:
Creating tables...
Installing custom SQL...
Installing indexes...
```

```
Installed 0 object(s) from 0 fixture(s)
Running migrations:
Applying app_name.0003_auto... OK
```

The OK message says that the migration has been applied successfully.

To make it more understandable, the migration can be explained with the following diagram:

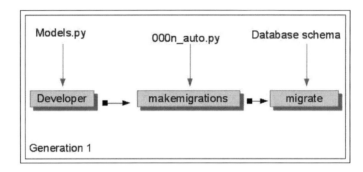

There are three separate entities:

- Source code
- Migration files
- Database

A developer makes changes in the source code, mainly in the models.py file, and alters the previously defined schema. For example, when they create a new field as per the business requirements, or update max_length from 50 to 100.

We will complete a proper migration of our project to see how this migration actually works.

First, we have to create an initial migration of the application:

```
$ python manage.py makemigrations tweet
```

The output of which is as follows:

```
Migrations for 'tweet':
0001_initial.py:
- Create model HashTag
- Create model Tweet
- Add field tweet to hashtag
```

This shows that the initial migration has been created.

Now, let's change our tweet modal, which is now as follows:

```
text = models.CharField(max_length=160, null=False, blank=False)
```

We will change the preceding tweet modal to:

```
text = models.CharField(max_length=140, null=False, blank=False)
```

As we have changed our schema, we now have to do the migration to run the application properly.

From the migration flow, we understood that, now, we have to run the `makemigrations` command, which is as follows:

```
$python manage.py makemigrations tweet
```

The output of which is as follows:

```
Migrations for 'tweet':
0002_auto_20141215_0808.py:
- Alter field text on tweet
```

As you can see, it has detected the change in our field.

Just for verification, we will open our SQL database and check the current schema of our tweet table.

Login to MySQL as:

```
$mysql -u mysql_username -pmysql_password mytweets
```

In the MySQL console, write:

```
$mysql> desc tweet_tweet;
```

This will show you the schema of the tweet table, as follows:

```
+---------------------+--------------+------+-----+---------+--------------
--+
| Field | Type | Null | Key | Default | Extra |
+--------------+--------------+------+-----+---------+----------------+
| id | int(11) | NO | PRI | NULL | auto_increment |
| user_id | int(11) | NO | MUL | NULL | |
| text | varchar(160) | NO | | NULL | |
| created_date | datetime | NO | | NULL | |
| country | varchar(30) | NO | | NULL | |
| is_active | tinyint(1) | NO | | NULL | |
+--------------+--------------+------+-----+---------+----------------+
6 rows in set (0.00 sec)
```

As we have not applied our migration yet, the database clearly displays the text as 160 in the character field:

```
text | varchar(160) | NO | | NULL
```

We will do the exact same thing after we apply our migration:

```
$python manage.py migrate tweet
```

The following are the operations that we need to perform:

```
Apply all migrations: tweet
Running migrations:
Applying tweet.0002_auto_20141215_0808... OK
```

Our migration has been successfully applied; let's verify the same from the database.

To run the same MySQL `desc` command on the `tweet_tweet` table, use the following:

```
mysql> desc tweet_tweet;
+--------------+--------------+------+-----+---------+----------------+
| Field        | Type         | Null | Key | Default | Extra          |
+--------------+--------------+------+-----+---------+----------------+
| id           | int(11)      | NO   | PRI | NULL    | auto_increment |
| user_id      | int(11)      | NO   | MUL | NULL    |                |
| text         | varchar(140) | YES  |     | NULL    |                |
| created_date | datetime     | NO   |     | NULL    |                |
| country      | varchar(30)  | NO   |     | NULL    |                |
| is_active    | tinyint(1)   | NO   |     | NULL    |                |
+--------------+--------------+------+-----+---------+----------------+
6 rows in set (0.00 sec)
```

Indeed! Our migration was successfully applied:

```
| text | varchar(140) | YES | | NULL | |
```

How migrations know what to migrate

Django will never run a migration more than once on the same database, which means that it persists this information. This information is managed by a table called `django_migrations`, which is created the very first time the Django application is started, and for every migration thereafter, a new row is inserted.

For example, here is what the table might look like after running our migration:

```
mysql> select * from django_migrations;

+----+-------+-------------------------+---------------------+
| id | app   | name                    | applied             |
+----+-------+-------------------------+---------------------+
| 1  | tweet | 0001_initial            | 2014-12-15 08:02:34 |
| 2  | tweet | 0002_auto_20141215_0808 | 2014-12-15 08:13:19 |
+----+-------+-------------------------+---------------------+
```

The preceding table shows that there are two migrations with tagged information, and that every time you migrate, it will skip these changes, as there is already an entry in this table corresponding to that migration file.

This means that even if you change the migration file manually, it will be skipped.

This makes sense, as you generally don't want to run migrations twice.

However, if for some reason you really want to apply the migration twice, you can simply delete the table entry *"THIS IS NOT A OFFICIALLY RECOMMENDED WAY"* and it will work fine.

Conversely, if you want to undo all the migrations for a particular application, you can migrate to a special migration called zero.

For example, if you type, all the migrations for the tweet application will be reversed:

```
$python manage.py migrate tweet zero
```

In addition to using zero, you can also use any arbitrary migration, and if that migration is in the past, then the database will be rolled back to the state of that migration, or will be rolled forward if the migration hasn't yet been run.

The migration file

So, what does the migration file contain and what exactly happens when we run the following command?

```
$python manage.py migrate tweet
```

After you run this, you can see a directory called `migrations`, where all the migration files are stored. Let's have a look at them. As they are Python files, they might be easy to understand.

Open the `tweet/migrations/0001_initial.py` file, as this is the file where the initial migration code is created. It should look similar to the following:

```python
# -*- coding: utf-8 -*-
from __future__ import unicode_literals
from django.db import models, migrations

class Migration(migrations.Migration):
dependencies = [
  ('user_profile', '__first__'),
]

operations = [
  migrations.CreateModel(
  name='HashTag',
  fields=[
    ('id', models.AutoField(verbose_name='ID', serialize=False,
    auto_created=True, primary_key=True)),
    ('name', models.CharField(unique=True, max_length=64)),
  ],
  options = {
  },
  bases=(models.Model,),
  ),
  migrations.CreateModel(
  name='Tweet',
  fields=[
    ('id', models.AutoField(verbose_name='ID', serialize=False,
    auto_created=True, primary_key=True)),
    ('text', models.CharField(max_length=160)),
    ('created_date', models.DateTimeField(auto_now_add=True)),
    ('country', models.CharField(default=b'Global',
    max_length=30)),
    ('is_active', models.BooleanField(default=True)),
    ('user', models.ForeignKey(to='user_profile.User')),
  ],
  options = {
  },
  bases=(models.Model,),
  ),
  migrations.AddField(
    model_name='hashtag',
    name='tweet',
    field=models.ManyToManyField(to='tweet.Tweet'),
    preserve_default=True,
  ),
]
```

For migration to actually work, there must be a class called `Migration()` that inherits from the `django.db.migrations.Migration` module. This is the main class that is used for a migration framework, and this migration class contains two main lists, which are as follows:

- **Dependencies**: This is the list of other migrations that must run before the migration starts. In cases where there is a dependency, such as in the case of a foreign key relationship, the foreign key model must exist before its key is added here. In the preceding case, we have such a dependency on the `user_profile` parameter.

- **Operations**: This list contains the list of migrations to be applied, and the whole migration operation can be of the following categories:

    - `CreateModel`: From the name itself, it's very clear that this will create a new model. From the preceding model file, you can see lines such as:

```
migrations.CreateModel(
name='HashTag',....
migrations.CreateModel(
name='Tweet',..
```

    These migration lines create the new model with the defined attributes.

    - `DeleteModel`: This will contain the statement to delete the model from the database. These are the opposite to the `CreateModel` method.

    - `RenameModel`: This renames the model with the given new name from the old name.

    - `AlterModelTable`: This will change the name of the associated table with the model.

    - `AlterUniqueTogether`: This is the unique constraints of the table that is changed.

    - `AlteIndexTogether`: This changes the custom index set of the model.

    - `AddField`: This simply adds a new field to the existing model.

    - `RemoveField`: This drops the field from the model.

    - `RenameField`: This renames the field name from the old name to the new name for a model.

The migration of a schema is not the only thing that needs to be migrated while updating the application; there is another important thing called **data migration**. This is the data that is already stored in the database by previous operations and, thus, also needs to be migrated.

Data migration can be used in many situations. Among them, the most logical situations are:

- Loading an external data to the application
- When there is a change in the model schema and the dataset needs to be updated as well

Let's play with our project by loading a tweet from the `username.txt` file. Create an empty migration for our project using the following command:

$python manage.py makemigrations --empty tweet

This will generate a migration file named `mytweets/migrations/003_auto<date_time_stamp>.py`.

Open this file; it will look something like the following:

```
# -*- coding: utf-8 -*-
from __future__ import unicode_literals

from django.db import models, migrations

class Migration(migrations.Migration):

dependencies = [
  ('tweet', '0002_auto_20141215_0808'),
]

operations = [
]
```

This is nothing but the basic structure of the Django migration tool, and to do data migration, we have to add the `RunPython()` function in the operations, as follows:

```
# -*- coding: utf-8 -*-
from __future__ import unicode_literals

from django.db import models, migrations

def load_data(apps, schema_editor):
  Tweet(text='This is sample Tweet',
    created_date=date(2013,11,29),
    country='India',
    is_active=True,
  ).save()
```

```
class Migration(migrations.Migration):

    dependencies = [
        ('tweet', '0002_auto_20141215_0808'),
    ]

    operations = [
        migrations.RunPython(load_data)
    ]
```

That is all. Now, run the migrate command:

`$python manage.py migrate`

These are the operations that you need to perform as follows:

```
Synchronize unmigrated apps: user_profile
Apply all migrations: admin, contenttypes, tweet, auth, sessions
Synchronizing apps without migrations:
Creating tables...
Installing custom SQL...
Installing indexes...
Running migrations:
Applying contenttypes.0001_initial... FAKED
Applying auth.0001_initial... FAKED
Applying admin.0001_initial... FAKED
Applying sessions.0001_initial... FAKED
Applying tweet.0003_auto_20141215_1349... OK
```

After executing the preceding command, the command migrated all the applications and finally applied our migration in which we created the new tweet from the loaded data:

```
mysql> select * from tweet_tweet;
+----+---------+------------------------------------------------+-----------
----------+---------+-----------+
| id | user_id | text | created_date | country | is_active |
+----+---------+------------------------------------------------+-----------
----------+---------+-----------+
| 1 | 1 | This Tweet was uploaded from the file. | 2014-12-15 14:17:42 |
India | 1 |
+----+---------+------------------------------------------------+-----------
----------+---------+-----------+
2 rows in set (0.00 sec)
```

That's awesome, right?

This kind of a solution is much needed when you have external data in the form of a JSON or XML file.

The ideal solution will be to use the command-line argument to get the file path and to load the data as:

```
$python load data tweet/initial_data.json
```

Don't forget to add your migration folders to Git, as they are as important as your source code.

Django with NoSQL

Django does not officially support the NoSQL database, but with such a great community of developers, Django does have a fork that has **MongoDB** as a backend database.

For the purpose of illustration, we will use the Django-Norel project to configure Django with the MongoDB database.

You can find the detailed information regarding this at http://django-nonrel.org/.

MongoDB can be installed by following the steps mentioned at http://docs. mongodb.org/manual/installation/ as per the configuration you have.

Here, we will set up MongoDB for the Debian version of Linux (specifically, Ubuntu).

Import the MongoDB public GPG Key:

```
sudo apt-key adv --keyserver hkp://keyserver.ubuntu.com:80 --recv
7F0CEB10
```

Create a list file for MongoDB:

```
echo 'deb http://downloads-distro.mongodb.org/repo/ubuntu-upstart dist
10gen' | sudo tee /etc/apt/sources.list.d/mongodb.list
```

Reload the local package database:

```
sudo apt-get update
```

Install the MongoDB packages:

```
sudo apt-get install -y mongodb-org
```

Start MongoDB:

```
sudo service mongod start
```

The single-page application project – URL shortener

There are two ways in which MongoDB can be used with Django, which are as follows:

- **MongoEngine**: This is a **Document-object Mapper** (think of ORM, but for document databases) that is used to work with MongoDB from Python

- **Django non-rel**: This is a project to support Django on nonrelational (NoSQL) databases; currently it supports MongoDB

MongoEngine

Installation of MongoEngine is required before we move further and show you how to configure MongoEngine with Django. Install MongoEngine by typing the following command:

```
sudo pip install mongoengine
```

In order to protect the previous project we created, and to better understand, we will create a separate new project for MongoDB configuration, and we will use our existing project to configure MySQL:

```
$django-admin.py startproject url_shortner
$cd url_shortner
$python manage.py startapp url
```

This will create the basic structure of the project, as we very well know.

Connecting MongoDB with Django

We will have to modify the `settings.py` file, and if we are only using MognoDB for the project, which is true in this case, then we can ignore the standard database setting. All we have to do is to call the `connect()` method on the `settings.py` file.

We will place a dummy backend for MongoDB. Just replace the following code in the `settings.py` file, which is as follows:

```
DATABASES = {
  'default': {
  'ENGINE': 'django.db.backends.sqlite3',
  'NAME': os.path.join(BASE_DIR, 'db.sqlite3'),
  }
}
```

Replace the preceding code with the following:

```
DATABASES = {
  'default': {
  'ENGINE': 'django.db.backends.dummy'
  }
}
```

Authentication in Django

The advantage of MongoEngine is that it includes a Django authentication backend.

A user model becomes a MongoDB document and implements most of the methods and attributes that a normal Django user model does, which makes MongoEngine compatible with Django. We can also use the authentication infrastructure and decorators, such as the login_required() and authentication() methods. The auth module also contains the get_user() method, which takes a user ID as an argument and returns the user object.

To enable this backend for MognoEngine, add the following in the settings.py file:

```
AUTHENTICATION_BACKENDS = (
   'mongoengine.django.auth.MongoEngineBackend',
)
```

Storing sessions

In Django, you can use different databases to store a session for an application. To enable the MongoEngine session that is stored in MongoDB, there must be an entry of the django.contrib.sessions.middleware.SessionMiddleware parameter in MIDDLEWARE_CLASSES in the settings.py file. There must also be an entry of django.contrib.sessions in INSTALLED_APPS, which are there as we started the project from Django's basic structure.

Now, all you need to do is add the following line in the settings.py file:

```
SESSION_ENGINE = 'mongoengine.django.sessions'
SESSION_SERIALIZER = 'mongoengine.django.sessions.BSONSerializer'
```

We are now all set up to get started with a small demo project, where we will implement the URL short project in MongoDB.

Let's create a URL modal first, which is where we will store all the long URLs and their corresponding short URLs.

Go to the following `url/models.py` file:

```
from django.db import models
from mongoengine import *
connect('urlShortener')
```

You are already familiar with the first two lines of the preceding code, which imports the modules.

The third line, that is, `connect('urlShortener')`, connects Django with the MongoDB database named `urlShortener`.

MongoDB gives many connection mechanisms that you can choose from, which are as follows:

```
from mongoengine import connect
connect('project1')
```

The method that we are using takes MongoDB from its default port, which is 27017; if you are running MongoDB on an other port, use the `connect()` method to connect it:

```
connect('project1', host='192.168.1.35', port=12345)
```

If you configured a password to MongoDB, you can pass the parameters as:

```
connect('project1', username='webapp', password='pwd123')
```

Like Django's default model fields, MongoDB also gives you different fields, which are:

- `BinaryField`: This field is used to store raw binary data.
- `BooleanField`: This is a Boolean field type.
- `DateTimeField`: This is a datetime field.
- `ComplexDateTimeField`: This handles microseconds exactly the way they are instead of rounding them up like `DateTimeField` does.
- `DecimalField`: This is a fixed point decimal number field.
- `DictField`: This is a dictionary field that wraps a standard Python dictionary. This is similar to an embedded document, but the structure is not defined.
- `DynamicField`: This is a truly dynamic field type capable of handling different and varying types of data.
- `EmailField`: This is a field that validates input as an e-mail address.
- `FileField`: This is a GridFS storage field.
- `FloatField`: This is a floating point number field.

- `GeoPointField`: This is a list that stores the longitude and latitude coordinates.
- `ImageField`: This is the image file storage field.
- `IntField`: This is a 32-bit integer field.
- `ListField`: This is a list field that wraps a standard field, allowing multiple instances of the field to be used as a list in the database.
- `MapField`: This is a field that maps a name to a specified field type. This is similar to `DictField`, except that the 'value' of each item must match the specified field type.
- `ObjectIdField`: This is a field wrapper around MongoDB's object IDs.
- `StringField`: This is a unicode string field.
- `URLField`: This is a field that validates input as a URL and more.

 By default, fields are not required. To make a field mandatory, set the required keyword argument of a field to `True`. Fields also may have validation constraints available (such as, max_length in the preceding example). Fields may also take default values, which will be used if a value is not provided. Default values may optionally be a callable, which will be called to retrieve the value (as in the preceding example).

The full list of different fields can be seen at `http://docs.mongoengine.org/en/latest/apireference.html`.

Now, we will create our `Url()` class, which will be similar to other models that we created so far, such as tweets and so on:

```
class Url(Document):
full_url = URLField(required=True)
short_url = StringField(max_length=50, primary_key=True,
unique=True)
date = models.DateTimeField(auto_now_add=True)
```

Let's take a look at the following term list:

- `full_url`: This is a URL field that will store the full URL, and the same URL where the request will be redirected when its short URL is trigged
- `short_url`: This is the short URL for the corresponding long URL
- `date`: This will store the date when the `Url` object was created

Now, we will move to view and create two classes:

- **Index**: Here, a user can generate short URLs. This will also have a `post()` method that saves every long URL.
- **Link**: This is the short URL redirection controller. When a short URL is queried, this controller redirects the request to a long URL, such as shown in the following code snippet:

```
class Index(View):
def get(self, request):
return render(request, 'base.html')

def post(self, request):
long_url = request.POST['longurl']
short_id = str(Url.objects.count() + 1)
url = Url()
url.full_url = long_url
url.short_url = short_id
url.save()
params = dict()
params["short_url"] = short_id
params['path'] = request.META['HTTP_REFERER']
return render(request, 'base.html', params)
```

Let's take a look at the following term list:

- The `get()` method is simple: it forwards the request to the `base.html` file (which we will create soon)
- The `post()` method takes the long URL from the request's POST variable and sets the object count, just as the short URL saves the `Url` object to the database:

```
params['path'] = request.META['HTTP_REFERER']
```

This is used to pass the current path to the view so that the short URL can be made clickable with the anchor tag.

This is how this URL object is saved in DB:

```
{ "_id" : ObjectId("548d6ec8e389a24f5ea44258"), "full_url" :
"http://sample_long_url", "short_url" : "short_url" }
```

Now, we will move on to the `Link()` class, which will take the short URL request and redirect to the long URL:

```
class Link(View):
def get(self, request, short_url):
url = Url.objects(short_url=short_url)
result = url[0]
return HttpResponseRedirect(result.full_url)
```

The `short_url` parameter is the `short_url` code from the requested URL:

```
url = Url.objects(short_url=short_url)
```

The preceding line queries the database to check whether the matching long URL exists for the given short URL:

```
return HttpResponseRedirect(result.full_url)
```

This redirects the request to find the long URL from the database.

For the view, all we need to create is the `base.html` file.

As the aim of this project is not to teach you user interface, we will not include any library and will make the page with as little HTML as possible.

The code for the `base.html` file is as follows:

```html
<!DOCTYPE html>
  <html>
    <head lang="en">
      <meta charset="UTF-8">
      <title>URL Shortner</title>
    </head>
    <body>
      <form action="" method="post">
        {% csrf_token %}
        Long Url:<br>
        <textarea rows="3" cols="80" name="longurl"></textarea>
        <br>
        <input type="submit" value="Get short Url">
      </form>

      <div id="short_url">
      {% if short_url %}
        <span>
          <a href="{{ path }}link/{{ short_url }}"
          target="_blank">{{ path }}link/{{ short_url }}</a>
        </span>
        {% endif %}
      </div>
    </body>
  </html>
```

This shows a text area with the form, and after submitting the form, it shows the short link beneath the long URL.

This is how the minimalistic URL shortner home page looks:

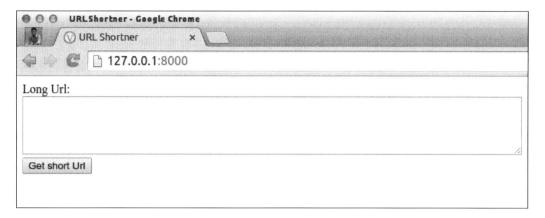

To make this work, all we need to do now is to create the required URL mapping, which is as follows:

```
url_shortner/urlmapping.py

from django.conf.urls import patterns, url
from url.views import Index, Link
from django.contrib import admin
admin.autodiscover()

urlpatterns = patterns('',
url(r'^$', Index.as_view()),
url(r'^link/(\w+)/$', Link.as_view()),
)
```

Summary

The purpose of this chapter is to prepare you to create your project with different databases, and also to give you a basic idea about database migration and how these migrations work. This will not only help you to debug your migration, but also you can create your own data migration scripts to load the data from a JSON file, or any other file format, directly to the Django application to initialize it.

The chapter also gave you a basic idea of how to set up Django with MongoDB, and we also saw a small project demonstration followed by the real-world application of scaling the Django system with MongoDB here.

12
Using Third-party Packages

It's time to combine all the theories and principles that we learned so far and try to understand how we can utilize third-party packages to achieve lots of possible projects, such as the Twitter API, the use of Social Auth, and so on.

You will learn the following topics in this chapter:

- Diving into the world of open source
- Using Social Auth in Django projects
- Building REST APIs in Django

Apart from the core modules required to build a website using Django and Python, we need some third-party packages as well. There are many third-party packages freely available over the Internet; you can find many useful packages at `https://www.djangopackages.com/`. We will try to use open source third-party packages for our project(s).

Diving into the world of open source

When we see the word open source, the first question that comes to our mind is what does open source actually mean?

Well, open source is a term that refers to something whose design is publicly accessible and can be modified by anyone as per their need, without requiring any prior permission.

Okay then, let's move on, and dive deep into the aspects of the open source world.

What is an open source software?

Open source software means that the software's source code is publicly accessible, thus it can be modified in any possible way. Also, anyone can contribute to the source code, which often leads to enhancement of the software.

Now, most software users don't ever see source code, which programmers can modify to get the result as per their need; this basically means that having the source code in the programmer's hand gives them total control over the software.

A programmer can then move forward with the software either by fixing any bugs or by adding any new feature to it.

What's the difference between open source and other software?

If the source code is not released for public access, or the code is accessible only to the particular group of people who created it, this type of software is called **proprietary software** or **closed source software**. Examples of closed source software are Microsoft products, such as Microsoft Windows, Word, Excel, PowerPoint, Adobe Photoshop, and so on.

To use proprietary software, users must agree (usually by signing a license that is displayed the first time they run this software) that they will not do anything with the software that the software's authors have not expressly permitted.

Whereas open source software is different. Authors of open source software make its code available to others who would like to view that code, copy it, learn from it, alter it, or share it. Python and Django programs are examples of open source software.

Just as there are licenses for proprietary software, open source software also has a license, but a much different one. These licenses promote open source development; they allow modification and bug fixes to their own source code.

Doesn't open source just mean that something is free of charge?

"Open source doesn't just mean getting access to the source code." As explained by **Open Source Initiative**, it means that anyone should be able to modify the source code to suit a programmer's need.

There can be a misconception about what an open source ecosystem can be thought of as. Programmers can charge the open source software they create, but that will not make any sense, as the person buying it has the full right to modify it and distribute it free of cost. Instead of charging for the open source software, programmers charge for the services they build around it, such as support, or other secondary components that add much value to the original software. Companies such as **Red Hat** charge by giving support to their open source Red Hat operating system. **Elasticsearch** charges for a component called marvel that monitors Elasticsearch, which helps a lot when Elasticsearch runs in production.

A lot of people think that only Internet-famous rock star programmers can contribute to open source projects, but, in fact, open source communities thrive on contributions from beginners to experts, and even nonprogrammers.

Using SocialAuth in Django projects

Every website needs to store user data to give them a better and exclusive experience, but to do this, the website needs you to register by filling out the user details form, where they ask you to enter your basic information. Filling these can be boring and tedious. One practical solution to such a problem is **Social Auth**, where you get registered to a site by a single click that fills up your basic information automatically from the social site that you are already registered on.

For example, you might have seen many sites while browsing the Web that give you the option of a couple of social buttons, such as, Google, Facebook, Twitter, and so on, to login or register on their website. If you login or register using any of these social buttons, they will pull up your basic details, such as e-mail, gender, and so on, from that social site where the information is already updated, so that you don't need to fill out the form manually.

Building the complete end-to-end implementation of this alone could be a project in Django, and if you want your site to have the same functionality, you don't need to reinvent the wheel. We can just import a third-party library, which, with minimal configuration changes in the `settings.py` file, will make users log in or register with the help of their existing social account.

How OAuth works

To understand how **OAuth** works, let's consider the following example.

OAuth is like a valet key for the Web. Most luxury cars come with a valet key, which the owner hands down to the parking attendant. With that key, the car is not allowed to travel longer distance, and other features, such as trunk on board luxury features, are disabled.

In the same way, the login button you see on a website does not give the site full access to your social account; it will simply pass on the details that you grant, or the default information, such as an e-mail, gender, and so on.

In order to access this information, sites used to ask for a user's username and password, which increased the risk of getting your personal information exposed or account hacked. The possibility of people having the same username and password for their banking account makes it more dangerous.

Thus, the aim of OAuth is to provide a method for users to grant third-party access to their information without sharing the passwords. By following this method, limited access can also be granted (such as, e-mail, permission to create a post, and so on).

For example, for a login register site, it will be very weird if they ask for access to your personal photos. So, at the time of giving permission to the application using OAuth, permission can actually be reviewed.

The following diagram gives you the overview of the OAuth mechanism:

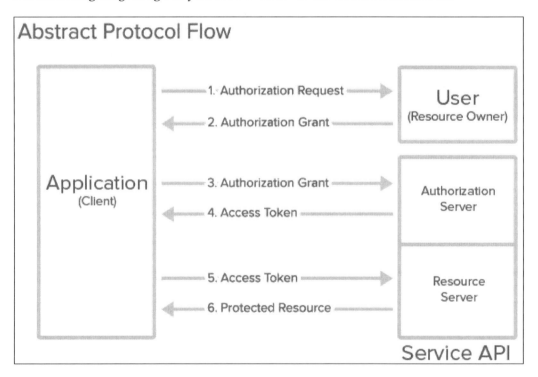

In the preceding figure, you can see the client application that needs your credentials asking you to either login or register using any of the social accounts. This is shown in the first part of the figure, where the client asks the user for social account authorization.

Once you decide to login via a social account and you grant the client application permission to access your social account, the client application that is already registered with the same social site with an API key of its own, asks the social site for your user details with its API request. At this stage, you might have seen the list of the records that the client application will access. Some sites may also let you edit these access rights. After the server grants authorization to the client application, the client gets an access token for your social account access.

Client application may store this access token for future use or, as it is popularly called, **offline access**.

The difference between registering and logging in with this social OAuth method is that when you are already registered, chances are that the client application will store your access token, so that the next time you try to log in, you don't have to go through the same social site authorization page, as you have already given them your authorization credentials.

Implementing social OAuth

In this section, we will learn to implement social OAuth in our existing project. To implement social authentication for our application, we will use a third-party library called `python-social-auth`. We will use Twitter social Auth to authenticate our users. Let's take a look at the following steps:

1. First, we will install the third-party app called **Python-Social-Auth**. The installation of `python-social-auth` can be done simply using the following command:

    ```
    $pip install python-social-auth
    ```

2. Once we have completed the installation of this third-party library, we will move to our mytweet application and make the configuration changes in the `settings.py` file.

    We are including this third-party library as an application in our application, so we have to create the entry of this application in the `INSTALLED_APPS` variable.

    So, add the `'social.apps.django_app.default'` parameter to the `INSTALLED_APPS` variable, as follows:

    ```
    INSTALLED_APPS = (
    'django.contrib.admin',
    'django.contrib.auth',
    'django.contrib.contenttypes',
    'django.contrib.sessions',
    'django.contrib.messages',
    ```

```
'django.contrib.staticfiles',
'user_profile',
'tweet',
'social.apps.django_app.default',
)
```

3. Next, we need to add the AUTHENTICATION_BACKEND variable in the
    settings.py file, which enlists all social login sites that we want to support.
    For this demonstration, we will add only Twitter social Auth, but as per
    the use case, you can add any or as many Twitter social Auth as you want.
    The AUTHENTICATION_BACKENDS parameter is the list of the Python class
    paths, which knows how to authenticate the user. The default points to the
    'django.contrib.auth.backends.ModelBackend' parameter. We will
    add the 'social.backends.twitter.TwitterOAuth' parameter to the
    AUTHENTICATION_BACKENDS variable:

```
AUTHENTICATION_BACKENDS = (
    'social.backends.twitter.TwitterOAuth',
    'django.contrib.auth.backends.ModelBackend',
)
```

4. We need to add the TEMPLATE_CONTEXT_PROCESSORS parameter, which will
    add backends and associated data in the template's context, which will in
    turn load the backend key with three entries, as follows:

    ○   **Associated**: If the user is logged in, this will be a list of
        UserSocialAuth instances; otherwise, it will be empty.

    ○   **Not_associated**: If the user is logged in, this will be a list of
        nonassociated backends; otherwise, it will contain a list of all the
        available backends.

    ○   **Backends**: This is a list of all the available backend names. Let's take
        a look at the following code snippet:

```
TEMPLATE_CONTEXT_PROCESSORS = (
'django.contrib.auth.context_processors.auth',
'django.core.context_processors.debug',
'django.core.context_processors.i18n',
'django.core.context_processors.media',
'django.contrib.messages.context_processors.messages',
'social.apps.django_app.context_processors.backends',
)
```

5. Our mytweet application already has a user model through which users are able to log in and post tweets. We will use the same model class to create a user from social Auth. For this, we need to add this line that tells `python-social-auth` to use the existing `user_profile` parameter:

```
SOCIAL_AUTH_USER_MODEL = 'user_profile.User'
```

6. Now, we will add custom URLs that will be used for social Auth:

```
SOCIAL_AUTH_LOGIN_REDIRECT_URL = '/profile/'
SOCIAL_AUTH_LOGIN_ERROR_URL = '/login-error/'
SOCIAL_AUTH_LOGIN_URL = '/login/'
SOCIAL_AUTH_DISCONNECT_REDIRECT_URL = '/logout/'
```

Adding these to the `settings.py` file tells social Auth to fall for the corresponding URLs in the following situation:

- `SOCIAL_AUTH_LOGIN_REDIRECT_URL`: This URL will be triggered when the social authentication is successful. We will use this URL to send the logged-in user his profile page.

- `SOCIAL_AUTH_LOGIN_ERROR_URL`: This URL will be triggered when there is an error during social authentication.

- `SOCIAL_AUTH_LOGIN_URL`: This is the URL from where social Auth will be done.

- `SOCIAL_AUTH_DISCONNECT_REDIRECT_URL`: After the user has logged out, he/she will be redirected to this URL.

7. As we have added a new application to our existing project, we need to create the corresponding tables in our database, which we have already learned in the previous chapters.

Now, we need to migrate our database:

```
$ python manage.py makemigrations
Migrations for 'default':
0002_auto_XXXX_XXXX.py:
- Alter field user on user_profile
$ python manage.py migrate
Operations to perform:
Apply all migrations: admin, default, contenttypes, auth, sessions
Running migrations:
Applying default.0001_initial... OK
Applying default.0002_auto_XXXX_XXXX... OK
```

8. For the last configuration change, we need to add an entry to the social Auth URLs:

```
url('', include('social.apps.django_app.urls',
namespace='social'))
```

The updated URL patterns will look like this:

```
urlpatterns = patterns('',
....
url('', include('social.apps.django_app.urls',
namespace='social'))
)
```

Creating a Twitter application

Now, we will move ahead and create a Twitter application that will give us the API keys to make this social Auth work:

1. Log into your Twitter account and open `https://apps.twitter.com/app/new`.

   The page will look somewhat like this:

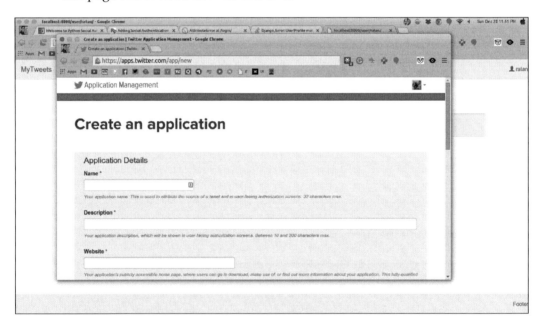

2. Fill up the details and create your Twitter application.

   As we are locally testing our app, place `http://127.0.0.1:8000/complete/twitter` as the callback URL, and also check the **Allow this application to be used to Sign in with Twitter** checkbox.

When it is successfully created, your application will look like this:

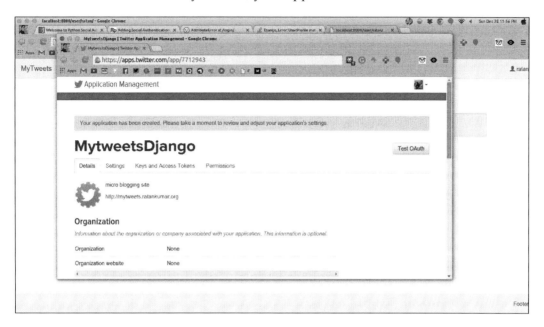

3. Move ahead with the **Keys and Access Tokens** tab and copy the **Consumer Key** (API key) and **Consumer Secret** (API secret) keys, as shown in the following screenshot:

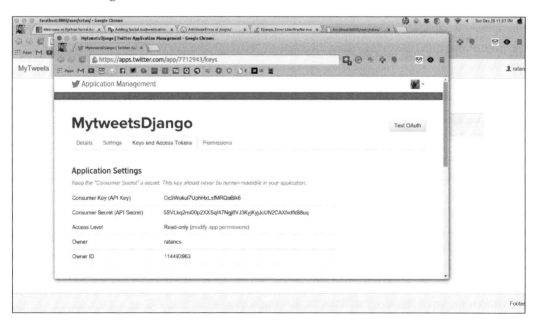

4. Add the following lines to the `settings.py` file:

```
SOCIAL_AUTH_TWITTER_KEY = 'your_key'
SOCIAL_AUTH_TWITTER_SECRET = 'your_secret'
```

5. Update our user class to use the Auth appropriately:

```
class User(AbstractBaseUser, PermissionsMixin):
"""
Custom user class.
"""
    username = models.CharField('username', max_length=10,
    unique=True, db_index=True)
    email = models.EmailField('email address', unique=True)
    date_joined = models.DateTimeField(auto_now_add=True)
    is_active = models.BooleanField(default=True)
    is_admin = models.BooleanField(default=False)
    is_staff = models.BooleanField(default=False)

    USERNAME_FIELD = 'username'
    objects = UserManager()
    REQUIRED_FIELDS = ['email']
    class Meta:
      db_table = u'user'
      def __unicode__(self):
    return self.username

    importing the PermissionsMixin as from
    |django.contrib.auth.models import AbstractBaseUser,
    PermissionsMixin
```

6. Now, start the server or open `http://127.0.0.1:8000/login/twitter/`.

   This will take you to the following authorization page:

7. Click on the **Sign In** button as we will use this Twitter application to sign into our app.

   After this, it will redirect the request back to the mytweet app with your basic information, as shown in the following screenshot:

If the username does not exist in our database, it will create the user profile with the Twitter username.

8. Let's create two tweets and save them.

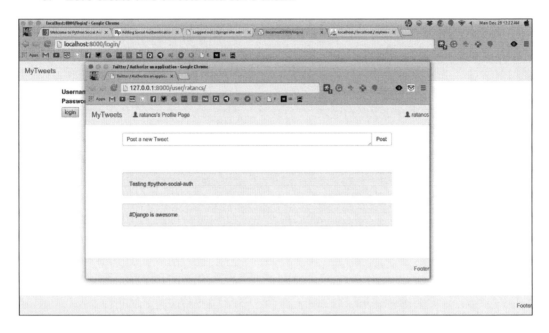

Now, just to check whether social Auth works, we will log out and try to open the URL again. You will get redirected to the same preceding profile page after redirection.

So, we learned how to create a Twitter API step by step by registering your application with Twitter to set your keys in your program. Then, we saw how our application sends you to the Twitter site for authentication, and how it redirects you to our site after the authentication done from the Twitter website.

Building REST APIs in Django

Representational State Transfer (**REST**) is the underlying architectural principle of the Web. Any API that follows REST principles is designed so that the client who is the browser here does not need to know anything about the structure of the API. The API server only needs to respond to the request made by clients.

HTTP works on the verbs that get applied to the resources. Some of the verbs that are very popular are GET and POST, but there exists other important verbs, such as PUT, DELETE, and so on.

For example, we will use our Twitter database, which is managed by a web service as the REST API. For all REST communication, the media type is the main thing that an API server has to care about, and the format in which it has to respond to the client's request. Our API service uses a custom hypermedia based on JSON, for which we will assign the /json+tweetdb MIME type application.

A request for the base resource will return something as follows:

```
Request
GET /
Accept: application/json+tweetdb
Response
200 OK
Content-Type: application/json+tweetdb
{
  "version": "1.0",
  "links": [
    {
      "href": "/tweets",
      "rel": "list",
      "method": "GET"
    },
    {
      "href": "/tweet",
      "rel": "create",
      "method": "POST"
    }
  ]
}
```

We can observe the output by referring to the href links through which we are trying to send or retrieve the information, which are nothing but Hypermedia controls. We can get the user list by sending another request through the /user command with the GET request:

```
Request
GET /user
Accept: application/json+tweetdb
  Response
  200 OK
  Content-Type: application/json+tweetdb

  {
    "users": [
    {
      "id": 1,
      "name": "Ratan",
      "country: "India",
```

```
        "links": [
          {
            "href": "/user/1",
            "rel": "self",
            "method": "GET"
          },
          {
            "href": "/user/1",
            "rel": "edit",
            "method": "PUT"
          },
          {
            "href": "/user/1",
            "rel": "delete",
            "method": "DELETE"
          }
        ]
      },
      {
        "id": 2,
        "name": "Sanjeev",
        "country: "India",
        "links": [
          {
            "href": "/user/2",
            "rel": "self",
            "method": "GET"
          },
          {
            "href": "/user/2",
            "rel": "edit",
            "method": "PUT"
          },
          {
            "href": "/user/2",
            "rel": "delete",
            "method": "DELETE"
          }
        ]
      }
    ],
    "links": [
      {
        "href": "/user",
        "rel": "create",
        "method": "POST"
      }
    ]
  }
```

Seeing the preceding generated output, we can guess who all the users are, and which are the requests that we can send, such as the DELETE or PUT request. In the same way, we can even create a new user by sending a POST request to /user, as shown in the following code snippet:

```
Request
POST /user
Accept: application/json+tweetdb
  Content-Type: application/json+tweetdb
  {
    "name": "Zuke",
    "country": "United States"
  }
Response
201 Created
Content-Type: application/json+tweetdb
{
  "user": {
    "id": 3,
    "name": "Zuke",
    "country": "United States",
    "links": [
      {
        "href": "/user/3",
        "rel": "self",
        "method": "GET"
      },
      {
        "href": "/user/3",
        "rel": "edit",
        "method": "PUT"
      },
      {
        "href": "/user/3",
        "rel": "delete",
        "method": "DELETE"
      }
    ]
  },
  "links": {
    "href": "/user",
    "rel": "list",
    "method": "GET"
  }
}
```

We can also update the existing data:

```
Request
PUT /user/1
Accept: application/json+tweetdb
  Content-Type: application/json+tweetdb
  {
    "name": "Ratan Kumar",
    "country": "United States"
  }
  Response
  200 OK
  Content-Type: application/json+tweetdb
  {
    "user": {
      "id": 1,
      "name": "Ratan Kumar",
      "country": "United States",
      "links": [
        {
          "href": "/user/1",
          "rel": "self",
          "method": "GET"
        },
        {
          "href": "/user/1",
          "rel": "edit",
          "method": "PUT"
        },
        {
          "href": "/user/1",
          "rel": "delete",
          "method": "DELETE"
        }
      ]
    },
    "links": {
      "href": "/user",
      "rel": "list",
      "method": "GET"
    }
  }
```

As you can easily note, we are using different HTTP verbs (GET, PUT, POST, DELETE, and so on) to manipulate these resources.

Now, you have the basic idea of how REST works, so we will move ahead and use a third-party library called **Tastypie** to play with our mytweets application.

Using Django Tastypie

Django Tastypie makes developing RESTful APIs for web applications easier.

To install Tastypie, run the following command:

```
$pip install django-tastypie
```

Add the `tastypie` parameter to the `INSTALLED_APPS` variable in the `settings.py` file.

There are many other configurable settings that an API needs, such as a limit on API calls and so on, but by default, they are set to default initially. You can either change this, or leave it like that.

Some of the API settings that you should know about, and can modify as per your need, are as follows:

- `API_LIMIT_PER_PAGE` (optional): This option controls the default number of records that Tastypie will return in the `view.applies` list when a user does not specify a limit to the GET parameter. The number of results to be returned are not overridden by the `resource` subclass.

  For example:
  ```
  API_LIMIT_PER_PAGE = 15
  ```

  The default limit here is 20 though.

- `TASTYPIE_FULL_DEBUG` (optional): When an exception occurs, this controls the behavior of whether to show the REST response or the 500 error page.

  If set to `True` and `settings.DEBUG = True`, the **500 Error** page is displayed.

  If it is not set or set to `False`, Tastypie returns a serialized response.

  If `settings.DEBUG` is `True`, you'll get the actual exception message plus a trace back.

  If `settings.DEBUG` is `False`, Tastypie will call the `mail_admins()` function and provide a canned error message (which you can override with `TASTYPIE_CANNED_ERROR`) in the response.

  For example:
  ```
  TASTYPIE_FULL_DEBUG = True
  ```

  The default is `False` though.

- `TASTYPIE_CANNED_ERROR` (optional): You can write your customized error messages when an unhandled exception is raised and `settings.DEBUG` is `False`.

For example:

```
TASTYPIE_CANNED_ERROR = "it's not your fault, it's our we
will fix it soon."
```

The default here is *"Sorry, this request could not be processed. Please try again later."*

- `TASTYPIE_ALLOW_MISSING_SLASH` (optional): You can call the REST API without giving the final slashes, which are mainly used to iterate the API with other systems.

  You must also have `settings.APPEND_SLASH = False`, so that Django does not emit HTTP 302 redirects.

  For example:

  ```
  TASTYPIE_ALLOW_MISSING_SLASH = True
  ```

  The default here is `False`.

- `TASTYPIE_DATETIME_FORMATTING` (optional): This setting configures the global datetime/date/time data for the API.

  The valid options for this are:

  - iso-8601
  - DateTime::ISO8601
  - ISO-8601 (example: 2015-02-15T18:37:01+0000)
  - iso-8601-strict, which is the same as iso-8601 but trips the microseconds
  - rfc-2822
  - DateTime::RFC2822
  - RFC 2822 (for example, Sun, 15 Feb 2015 18:37:01 +0000)

  Take the following code as an example:

  ```
  TASTYPIE_DATETIME_FORMATTING = 'rfc-2822'
  ```

  The default here is iso-8601.

- `TASTYPIE_DEFAULT_FORMATS` (optional): This globally configures the list of serialization formats for your entire site.

  For example:

  ```
  TASTYPIE_DEFAULT_FORMATS = [json, xml]
  ```

  This defaults to [`json, xml, yaml, html, plist`].

Implementing a simple JSON API

To make REST-style architecture, we need to define the resource class for our tweets, so let's create a `api.py` file in the `tweets` folder with the following content:

```
from tastypie.resources import ModelResource
from tweet.models import Tweet

class TweetResource(ModelResource):
class Meta:
queryset = Tweet.objects.all()
resource_name = 'tweet'
```

We also need a URL where all the API requests will be made for this Tweet resource, so let's add an entry for this in the `urls.py` file:

```
from tastypie.api import Api
from tweet.api import TweetResource

v1_api = Api(api_name='v1')
v1_api.register(TweetResource())

urlpatterns = patterns('',
...
url(r'^api/', include(v1_api.urls)),
)
```

That's all that we need to create a basic REST API for tweets.

Now, we will see the various outputs based on the variations of the REST URL. In a browser, open the URLs, as follows, and observe the output in the `.json` format.

The first URL will display the Tweet API details in the `.json` format:

```
http://127.0.0.1:8000/api/v1/?format=json

{
  "tweet": {
    "list_endpoint": "/api/v1/tweet/",
    "schema": "/api/v1/tweet/schema/"
  }
}
```

Based on the first output, we will call our tweet API, which would give us details of the tweet info and other details, shown as follows:

```
http://127.0.0.1:8000/api/v1/tweet/?format=json

    {
      "meta": {
        "limit": 20,
        "next": null,
        "offset": 0,
        "previous": null,
        "total_count": 1
      },
      "objects": [
        {
          "country": "Global",
          "created_date": "2014-12-28T20:54:27",
          "id": 1,
          "is_active": true,
          "resource_uri": "/api/v1/tweet/1/",
          "text": "#Django is awesome"
        }
      ]
    }
```

Our basic REST API is ready, which lists all tweets. If you look at the schema, it gives us many details about the API, such as which HTTP methods are allowed, which format the output will be in, and other different fields. This actually helps us to understand what we can do using our API:

```
http://127.0.0.1:8000/api/v1/tweet/schema/?format=json

    {
      "allowed_detail_http_methods": [
        "get",
        "post",
        "put",
        "delete",
        "patch"
      ],
      "allowed_list_http_methods": [
        "get",
        "post",
        "put",
        "delete",
        "patch"
      ],
      "default_format": "application/json",
      "default_limit": 20,
```

```
"fields": {
  "country": {
    "blank": false,
    "default": "Global",
    "help_text": "Unicode string data. Ex: \"Hello World\"",
    "nullable": false,
    "readonly": false,
    "type": "string",
    "unique": false
  },
  "created_date": {
    "blank": true,
    "default": true,
    "help_text": "A date & time as a string. Ex: \"2010-11-
    10T03:07:43\"",
    "nullable": false,
    "readonly": false,
    "type": "datetime",
    "unique": false
  },
  "id": {
    "blank": true,
    "default": "",
    "help_text": "Integer data. Ex: 2673",
    "nullable": false,
    "readonly": false,
    "type": "integer",
    "unique": true
  },
  "is_active": {
    "blank": true,
    "default": true,
    "help_text": "Boolean data. Ex: True",
    "nullable": false,
    "readonly": false,
    "type": "boolean",
    "unique": false
  },
  "resource_uri": {
    "blank": false,
    "default": "No default provided.",
    "help_text": "Unicode string data. Ex: \"Hello World\"",
    "nullable": false,
    "readonly": true,
    "type": "string",
    "unique": false
  },
```

```
      "text": {
        "blank": false,
        "default": "No default provided.",
        "help_text": "Unicode string data. Ex: \"Hello World\"",
        "nullable": false,
        "readonly": false,
        "type": "string",
        "unique": false
      }
    }
  }
}
```

Some APIs might need authorized access, such as a user profile, account details, and so on. Basic HTTP authorization can be added to the Tastypie API by just adding a basic authorization line:

```
authentication = BasicAuthentication()
```

Basic HTTP authorization can be added with a header file as:

```
from tastypie.authentication import BasicAuthentication
```

This will ask for authentication via a basic HTTP request, which looks like the following screenshot. Once this is successful, all requests in the current session are authenticated.

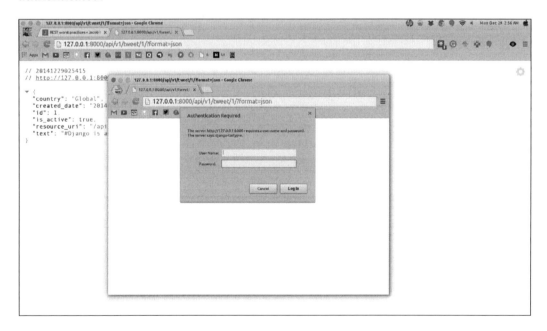

This, followed by a demonstration, shows the real-world application of how to scale the Django system with MongoDB.

Summary

In this chapter, you learned about open source and how to use and implement open source third-party packages in our project. Now, you will be comfortable to implement social Auth from Twitter. You can try the same for Facebook and Google+ by yourself as well.

In the next chapter, you will learn more about the debugging techniques that we need to use when we face any errors or warnings in our code, or some configuration issues. You will also learn the tools for product development, such as Git, the Sublime Text editor, and so on.

13

The Art of Debugging

In this chapter, you will learn three important things about Django's web development, which every programmer should know about. These are the concepts and techniques that you would need when your code goes wrong:

- Logging
- Debugging
- IPDB – interactive way of busting bugs

Logging

Every application that runs on production must have some logging enabled; if not, then it will be very difficult to figure out what and where something went wrong.

Django uses Python's basic logging, thus we will go through the Python logging in detail in the following section and see how we can use the logging service to log in Django.

The formal definition of logging is the tracking of events in a software. Developers call the logging service to state that an event has occurred, or is going to occur. Logging can consist of some description or value of any important variable that needs to be tracked.

The `logging` module of Python comes with five logging functions that are categorized based on the severity of an event. These are `debug()`, `info()`, `warning()`, `error()`, and `critical()`.

These are categorized in a tabular form in order of their severity (starting from the least severe to the most severe):

- `debug()`: This is used while fixing bugs and generally has detailed information of the data.

- `info()`: This makes a log when things work as they are supposed to. This basically tells whether an execution was successful or not.

- `warning()`: This is raised when some unexpected event occurs. This does not actually halt the execution, but it might stop the execution in future. For example, 'low disk space'.

- `error()`: This is the next level of warning, which states that the execution of some function might have halted.

- `critical()`: This is the highest level of any logging function. This is raised when a very serious error occurs, which might stop the execution of an entire program.

The `logging` module is divided into the following four categories:

- **Loggers**: Logger is the entry point for the log message of a system. Programs write logging information to loggers, which then process whether it has to be given to a console for output or should be written to file.

  Every logger comprises of the preceding five logging functions. Every message that is written to the logger is called a log record. A log record contains the severity of the log as well as the important log variable or details, such as an error code or a complete stack trace.

  Loggers themselves have a log level, which works as: if the log level of the log message is greater than or equal to the log level of the logger, then the message will be further processed for logging; otherwise, it will be ignored by the logger.

  When a logger's preprocessing for a log's evaluation is done and the resulting log has to be processed, then the message is passed to the handler.

- **Handlers**: Handlers actually decide what to do with the log message. They are responsible for taking actions for the log record, such as writing to the console or to a file, or sending it over the network.

  The same as loggers, handlers also have a log level. Log messages are ignored by the handler if the log level of a log record is not greater than or equal to the level of handler.

  Multiple handlers can be binned to a logger, for example, there can be a handler for a logger that sends ERROR and CRITICAL messages over an e-mail, whereas another handler can write the same log to a file for a later debug analysis.

- **Filters**: A filter adds an extra evaluation when a log record is passed from a logger to handler. The default behavior is that it will start processing the mails when a log message level has met the level of a handler.

  This process can be interrupted further for extra evaluation by applying filter.

  For example, a filter allows only one source to log the ERROR message to a handler.

  A filter can also be used to alter the priority of the log record, so that the logger and handler are triggered accordingly.

- **Formatters**: The final step before the log message actually gets logged, which will be in a text format, is that the formatter actually formats the log record that consists of the Python formatting string.

  To enable logging in our application, we will create a logger first. We need to create the LOGGING dictionary in the settings.py file, which describes loggers, handlers, filters, and formatters.

  The full documentation about the logging setup can be found at https://docs.python.org/2/library/logging.config.html.

The following is an example of a simple logging setup:

```
# settings.py
LOGGING = {
  'version': 1,
  'disable_existing_loggers': False,
  'formatters': {
    'simple': {
      'format': '%(levelname)s %(message)s'
    },
  },
  'handlers': {
    'file':{
      'level':'DEBUG',
      'class': 'logging.FileHandler',
      'formatter': 'simple',
      'filename': 'debug.log',
    }
  },
  'loggers': {
    'django': {
      'handlers':['file'],
      'propagate': True,
      'level':'INFO',
    },
  }
}
```

This logger setup defines one logger (Django) that is for Django request, and a handler (file) that writes to the log file with a formatter.

We will use the same to test the logging for our `mytweet` project.

Now, we need to make the logger's entry to the view, where we want to track the event.

To test the project, we will update our user profile redirection class to make a log whenever an unauthorized user tries to access it, and, also, when a registered user tries to open the URL.

Open the `tweet/view.py` file and change the `UserRedirect` class to the following:

```
class UserRedirect(View):
  def get(self, request):
    if request.user.is_authenticated():
      logger.info('authorized user')
      return HttpResponseRedirect('/user/'+request.user.username)
    else:
      logger.info('unauthorized user')
      return HttpResponseRedirect('/login/')
```

Also, initialize the logger with an `import` statement and add the following code to the preceding code:

```
import logging
logger = logging.getLogger('django')
```

That is it. Now, open the browser and click on the URL `http://localhost:8000/profile`.

You will be redirected to the login page if you're not already logged in.

Now, open the `debug.log` file. It contains `INFO` of an unauthorized user, which means that our logger is working perfectly fine:

```
INFO unauthorized user
```

Debugging

Debugging is the process of finding and removing bugs (error). When we develop the web application with Django, we often need a case where we need to know the variables submitted in an Ajax request.

The tools for debugging are:

- The Django debug toolbar
- IPDB (interactive debugger)

The Django debug toolbar

This is a set of panels that is used to display various information about the current page's request/response, and in more detail when the panel is clicked on.

Rather than simply displaying the debug information in HTML comments, the **Django debug tool** displays it in a more advanced way.

Installing the Django debug toolbar

To install the Django debug toolbar, run the following command:

```
$ pip install django-debug-toolbar
```

After the installation, we need to do basic configuration changes to see the Django debug toolbar.

Add the debug_toolbar parameter to the INSTALLED_APPS variable in the settings.py file:

```
# Application definition
INSTALLED_APPS = (
    'django.contrib.admin',
    'django.contrib.auth',
    'django.contrib.contenttypes',
    'django.contrib.sessions',
    'django.contrib.messages',
    'django.contrib.staticfiles',
    'user_profile',
    'tweet',
    'social.apps.django_app.default',
    'tastypie',
    'debug_toolbar',
)
```

This is more than enough for a simple Django project. The Django debug toolbar will automatically adjust itself when a server runs in development mode.

Restart the server to see the Django debug toolbar, as shown in the following screenshot:

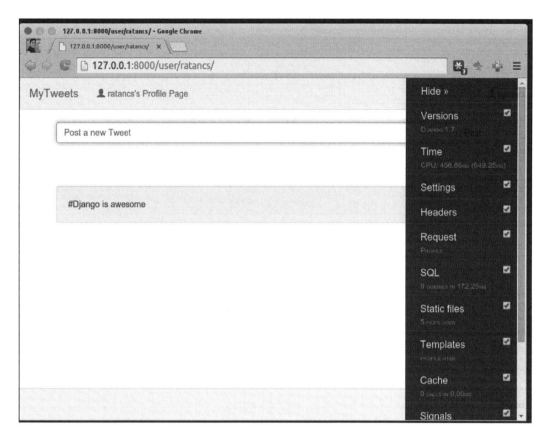

As you can see, there is a toolbar on the right-hand side of the profile page. The Django debug toolbar has many panels, of which a few are installed as default, which you can see in the preceding screenshot, and other third-party panels can also be installed here as well.

Now, we will discuss the panels that are enabled by default:

- **VersionPath**: `debug_toolbar.panels.versions.VersionsPanel`. This panel shows the basic information, such as the versions of Python, Django, and of other installed applications, if the information is available:

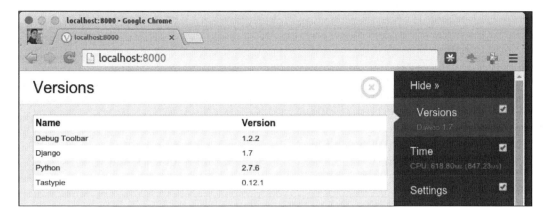

- **TimerPath**: `debug_toolbar.panels.timer.TimerPanel`

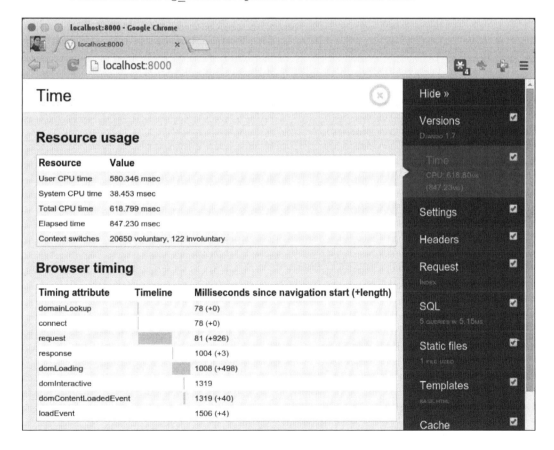

This panel contains some very important stats for the Django development. It shows two tables, as you can see in the preceding screenshot, which are **Resource usage** and **Browser timing**.

- ° **Resource usage**: This shows the Django resource consumption on the server machine.

- ° **Browser timing**: This shows the details on the client-side. The request and response times are vital for knowing whether a piece of code can be optimized, and domLoading can be looked up if too much of rendering slows the page from getting loaded.

- **SettingsPath**: `debug_toolbar.panels.settings.SettingsPanel`. A list of settings that are defined in the `settings.py` file are **headers**

- **Path**: `debug_toolbar.panels.headers.HeadersPanel`

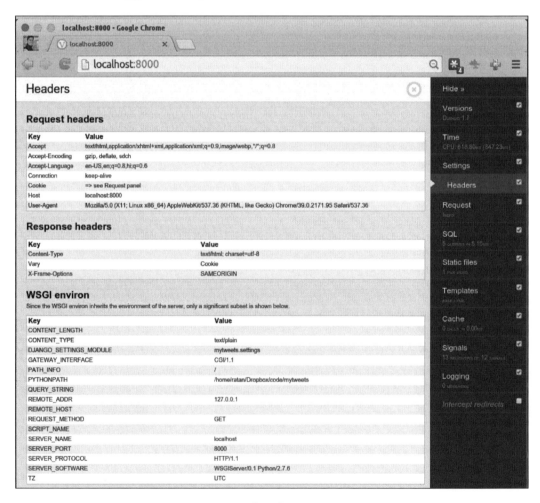

This panel shows the HTTP request and response headers and variables from the WSGI environment.

- **Request Path**: `debug_toolbar.panels.request.RequestPanel`

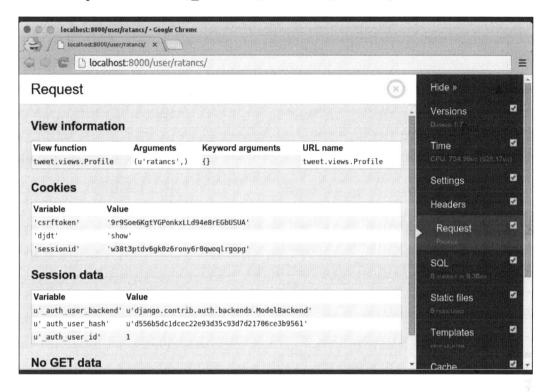

This panel shows the variables from the framework, starting from the view variables, which also has the **ratancs** argument variable; then, the **Cookies**, **Session**, and GET, and POST variables, as these are very helpful to debug the form submission.

- **SQL Path**: `debug_toolbar.panels.sql.SQLPanel`

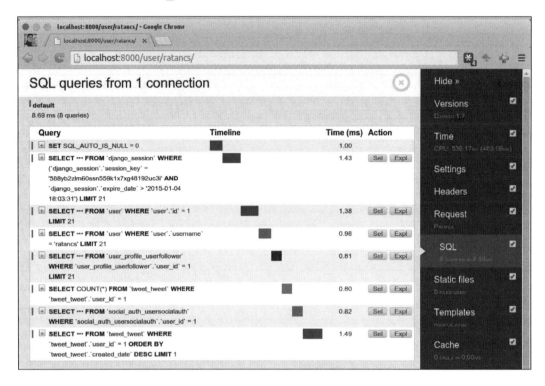

This panel is also very important as it shows the SQL queries made to the database for the page's response. This helps a lot at the time of scaling the application, as queries can be thoroughly examined and combined together to reduce database hits and improve the page response performance.

This also shows the code snippet that makes that SQL call, which is also very helpful while debugging the application.

- **Static files Path**: `debug_toolbar.panels.staticfiles.StaticFilesPanel`

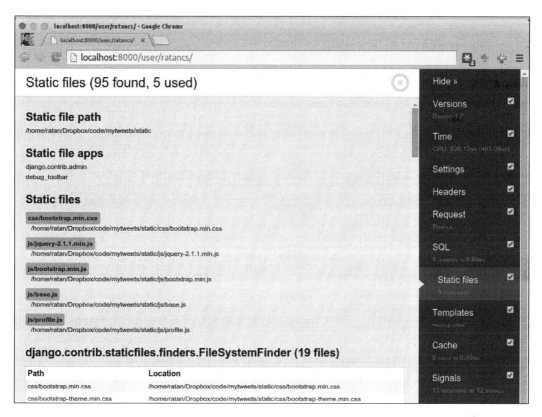

This will list all the static files used from the static files location that we had set in the `settings.py` file.

- **Template Path**: `debug_toolbar.panels.templates.TemplatesPanel`

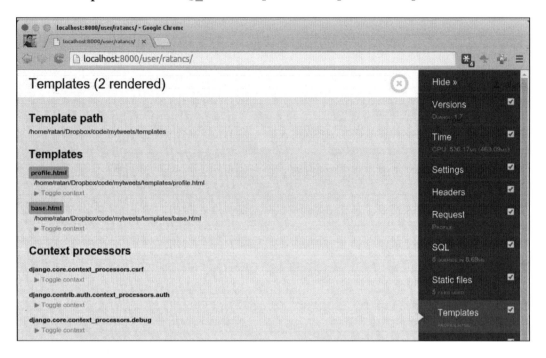

This will list down the templates and context used for the current request.

- **Cache Path**: `debug_toolbar.panels.cache.CachePanel`

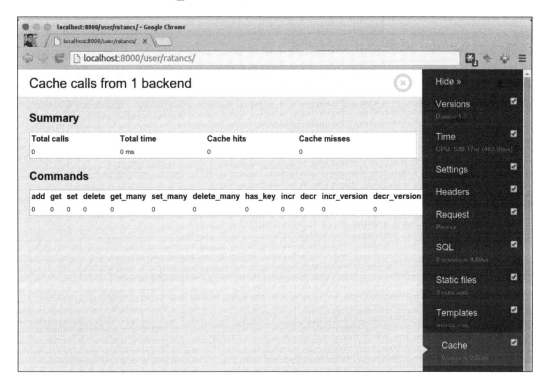

If we enable the cache, then this will show the details of the cache hit for the given URL.

- **Signal Path**: `debug_toolbar.panels.signals.SignalsPanel`

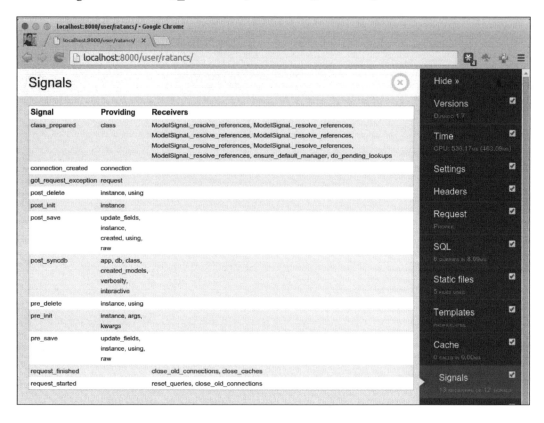

This panel shows the list of signals and their args and receivers.

- **Logging Path**: `debug_toolbar.panels.logging.LoggingPanel`

  If you have enabled logging, then this panel will show the log's messages, as shown in the following screenshot:

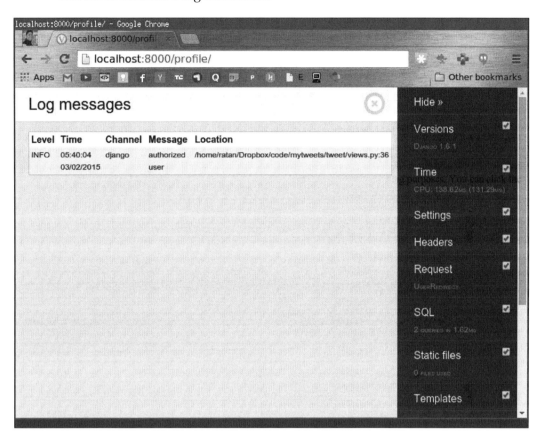

- **Redirects Path**: `debug_toolbar.panels.redirects.RedirectsPanel`

  When there is a page redirection on a URL, enable this to debug the intermediate page. Generally, you don't debug the redirect URL, so, by default, this is disabled.

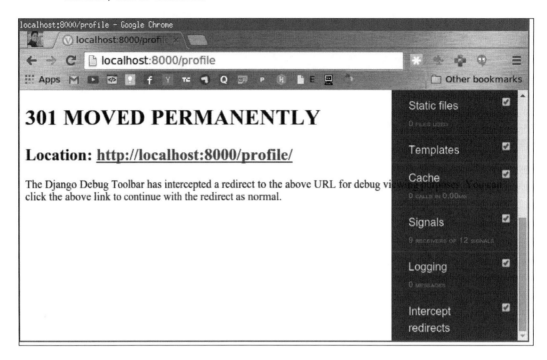

IPDB – interactive way of busting bugs

Ipdb is an interactive source code debugger for Python programs.

Run the following command to install Ipdb:

```
$pip install ipdb
```

Ipdb is the interactive way of debugging Python application. After installing Ipdb, to use it in any function, just write the following code:

```
import ipdb;ipdb.set_trace()
```

This magical line will halt the whole Django execution at the point where this code is present, and will give you an active console, where you can find out the bugs or check the variable's value in real time.

The shortcuts for ipdb (when you are in the active console) are:

- `n`: This refers to next
- `ENTER`: This refers to repeat previous
- `q`: This refers to quit
- `p <variable>`: This is the print value
- `c`: This refers to continue
- `l`: This is the list where you are
- `s`: This is to step into a subroutine
- `r`: This means to continue till the end of the subroutine
- `! <python command>`: To run Python command inside the active console

Summary

There is more to do than what is covered in this chapter. These were just the basics of debugging that we are going to use in our Django projects. You learned how to log and debug our code for a better and more efficient coding practice. We also saw how to use Ipdb for more debugging.

In the next chapter, you will learn the various ways to deploy our Django projects.

14
Deploying Django Projects

So, you have done a lot of work on your web application and now it is time to make it live. To make sure that the transition from development to production goes smoothly, there are a number of changes that must be made to the application before it goes live. This chapter covers the changes to be made to the following topics to help make the launch of your web application successful:

- The production web server
- The production database
- Turning off the debug mode
- Changing configuration variables
- Setting error pages
- Django on cloud

The production web server

We have been using the development web server that comes with Django throughout this book. While this server is perfect for the development process, it's definitely not intended to be a production web server, as it wasn't developed with security or performance in mind. Therefore, it is certainly not suitable for production.

There are several options to choose from when it comes to the web server, but **Apache** is by far, the most popular choice and the Django development team actually recommends it. The details of how to set up Django with Apache depends on your hosting solution. Some hosting plans offer a preconfigured Django hosting solution, where you only have to copy your project files to the server, whereas other hosting plans give you the freedom to configure everything yourself.

The details of how to set up Apache varies depending on a number of factors that are beyond the scope of this book. If you want to configure Apache yourself, consult the Django documentation online at `https://docs.djangoproject.com/en/1.8/howto/deployment/wsgi/apache-auth/` for detailed instructions.

In this section, we are going to deploy our Django application on Apache and the `mod_wsgi` module. So, let's install these two first.

Run the following command to install Apache:

```
$sudo apt-get install apache2
```

The `mod_wsgi` parameter is an Apache HTTP server module that provides a **Web Server Gateway Interface (WSGI)** compliant interface to host web applications based on Python 2.3+ under Apache.

Run the following command to install the `mod_wsgi` module:

```
$sudo aptitude install libapache2-mod-wsgi
```

Django with Apache and the `mod_wsgi` module is the most popular way of deploying Django in production.

In most of the cases, the development machine and the deployment machine are different. Thus, it is advised that you copy the project folder to the `/var/www/html/` folder, so that your deployment files have limited permission and access.

As you have installed the Apache server, try visiting `localhost` in your browser, that is, `127.0.0.1`. By doing this, you should see the default Apache page, as shown in the following screenshot:

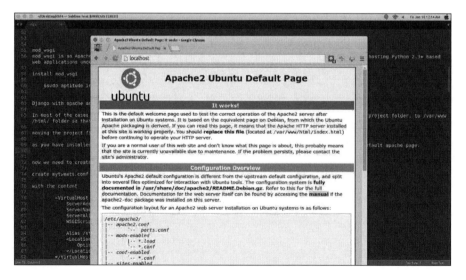

We have to make the Apache server our Django project. For that, we need to create the configuration file for Apache.

To do so, create a mytweets.conf file in the sites-available folder that you can find by navigating to /etc/apache2/sites-available with the following content:

```
<VirtualHost *:80>
  ServerAdmin mail@ratankumar.org
  ServerName mytweets.com
  ServerAlias www.mytweets.com
  WSGIScriptAlias / /var/www/html/mytweets/mytweets/wsgi.py
  Alias /static/ /var/www/html/mytweets/static/
  <Location "/static/">
    Options -Indexes
  </Location>
</VirtualHost>
```

Let's take a look at the following term list that describes the various parameters used in the preceding code snippet:

- ServerAdmin: This e-mail address will be shown if you have not configured your custom error page, which will tell users to contact this e-mail address.

- ServerName: This is the name of the server you would like to run your project on.

- ServerAlias: This is the name of the site you want to run the project on.

- WSGIScriptAlias: This is the location of the wsgi.py file of the project, which was already there when we ran the first command to create the Django project.

- Alias: This is the path alias, the actual location of the folder on the disk is mapped like a project directory.

Now, we need to enable this site configuration with the a2ensite command, and to disable an existing site configuration, you can use the a2dissite command.

Let's enable the mytweets.conf file for Apache by using the following command:

$a2ensite mytweets.conf

This will enable our mytweets.conf file. You can also disable the default 000-default.conf configuration by using the following command:

$a2dissite 000-default.conf

 Verify the file permission of the static files of the project. Don't forget to write an entry in allowed host in the settings.py file.

Now, restart the server:

```
$sudo service apache2 restart
```

That's all, Django now runs on the deployment mode, that is, it is now production ready.

The production database

So far, we have been using SQLite as our database engine. It is simple and does not require a resident server in memory. SQLite will perform fine in the production mode for small websites. However, it is highly recommended that you switch to a database engine that uses the client-server model in production. As we saw in an earlier chapter, Django supports several database engines, including all the popular ones. The Django team recommends you to use PostgreSQL, but MySQL should be fine as well. Regardless of your choice, you only have to change the database options in the settings.py file to switch to a different database engine.

If you want to use MySQL, create a database, username, and password for Django. Then, change the DATABASE_* variables accordingly. Everything else should remain the same. This is the whole point of the Django database layer.

Turning off the debug mode

Whenever an error occurs during development, Django presents a detailed error page with a lot of useful information. However, when the application goes into production, you don't want your users to see such information. Apart from confusing your users, you risk exposing your website to security problems if you let strangers see such information.

In the beginning when we used the django-admin.py mytweets command, which created all the basic configuration for the project for which we used the debug=True parameter in the settings.py file when this mode was True. The following extra work is done by Django to help you debug the problem faster. The memory usage of Django is more, as all the queries are stored as django.db.connection.queries in the database.

For every error message, a proper stack trace of the message gets displayed, which is not recommended when you run in the production mode, as this may contain sensitive information and may weaken the security of the entire web application.

Turning off the debug mode is pretty easy. Open the `settings.py` file and change the `DEBUG` variable to `False`:

```
DEBUG = False
```

Disabling debug information carries an additional benefit; you improve the performance of the website because Django doesn't have to keep track of the debug data in order to display it.

Changing configuration variables

There are many configuration variables that need to be created or updated for production. The production environment is a very hostile environment. The following is the checklist that you should go through for deployment. Check the `setting.py` file properly, as each setting must be defined in the right way to keep the project secure.

Settings can be environment-specific, such as when you run the settings locally. The database credentials might change and even the database can change according to the environment. While conducting the process of deployment, enable the optional security features.

Enable performance optimizations. The first step to do so is to disable debug, which enhances the performance of the website. If you have a proper error reporting mechanism, once `DEBUG` is `False`, it's difficult to know what went wrong, so you better have your logs prepared once you disable debug mode.

The following are the critical settings that must be taken care of while going for Django's deployment:

- `SECRET_KEY`: This key must be chosen large and randomly and should be kept as a secret. In fact, it is recommended that you should never keep this information in the `settings.py` file or in the version control repository. Instead, keep this information somewhere safe in a nonversion controlled file or in the environment path:

  ```
  import os
  SECRET_KEY = os.environ['SECRET_KEY']
  ```

  This imports the key from the current operating system's environment. An alternate suggested method is to import it from a file, which can be done using:

  ```
  with open('/etc/secret_key.txt') as f:
      SECRET_KEY = f.read().strip()
  ```

- ALLOWED_HOSTS: This must have a valid host configuration. When the debug mode is switched off, this is used to protect the CSRF attacks:

```
ALLOWED_HOSTS = [
    '.example.com',  # Allow domain and subdomains
    '.example.com.',  # Also allow FQDN and subdomains
]
```

- ADMIN: The ADMIN key holds the names and e-mail addresses of the site administrators. You will find it in the settings.py file, commented out as follows:

```
ADMINS = (
# ('Your Name', 'your_email@domain.com'),
)
```

Insert your name and e-mail address here and remove the # symbol to uncomment it in order to receive e-mail notifications of code errors when they occur.

When DEBUG=False and a view raises an exception, Django will e-mail these people with the full exception information.

- EMAIL: Since the e-mail server of your production server most likely differs from your development machine, you may want to update your e-mail configuration variables. Look for the following variables in the settings.py file and update them:

  - EMAIL_HOST

  - EMAIL_PORT

  - EMAIL_HOST_USER

  - EMAIL_HOST_PASSWORD

Also, your web application now has its own domain name, so you need to update the following settings to reflect this: SITE_HOST and DEFAULT_FROM_EMAIL.

Finally, if you use caching, make sure that you have the correct settings in the CACHE_BACKEND parameter (ideally, the memcached parameter); you don't want the development backend to be here while you are in production.

Setting error pages

With the debug mode disabled, you should create templates for the error pages, particularly these two files:

- `404.html`: This template will be displayed when the requested URL does not exist; in other words, when a page is not found, such as an uncaught exception.

  Create the two files with whatever content you like. You can, for example, put a `"Page not found"` message in the `404.html` template or a search form.

- `500.html`: This template will be displayed when an internal server error occurs.

It is recommended that you give these templates a consistent look by deriving them from the base template of your site. Put the templates at the top in your `templates` folder and Django will automatically use them.

This should cover the configuration changes that are essential for production. Of course, this section is not conclusive and there are other settings that you may be interested in. You can, for example, configure Django to notify you via e-mail when a requested page is not found or provide a list of IP addresses that can see debug information. For these and more, refer to the Django documentation in the `settings.py` file.

Hopefully, this section will help you make your transition from development to production much smoother.

Django on cloud

Deployment in web development has changed over the course of time. Most of the start-ups are moving to a cloud setup and away from traditional VPS hosting methods, due to reliability, performance, and ease of scalability.

The most popular cloud platforms that provide **IAS (Infrastructure As a Service)** are Amazon EC2 and Google Compute Engine.

Then, we have other well-known options, such as **Platform as a Service (PaaS)**, where you push your code, such as you push it to a normal repository so that is gets deployed automatically. These include Google App Engine, Heroku, and so on.

Let's get introduced to them one by one.

EC2

Deployment on **EC2** is simple. Follow the given steps to deploy your desired settings on EC2:

1. Create an account for AWS. Follow `http://aws.amazon.com` and click on **Create a Free Account**, as shown in the following screenshot:

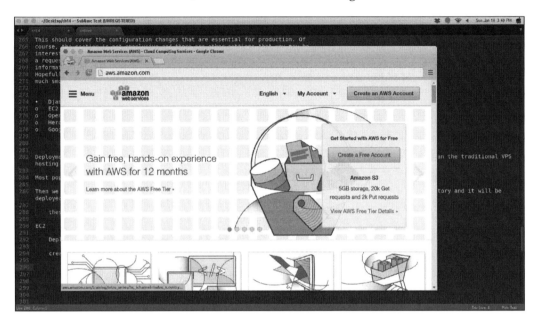

2. Sign up and add your credit card for the billing details. Once you are done, log in and you will see a dashboard. For deployment, we need to create a server called EC2 instances (it can be treated as a server) on AWS.

3. Click on EC2 (in the top-left corner), as shown in the following screenshot:

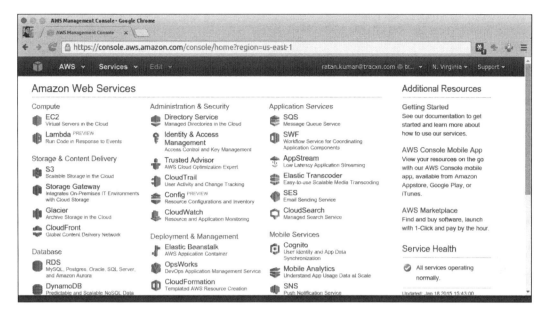

As you can see in the preceding screenshot, I already have an instance running (**1 Running Instances**). Click on **Launch instance** to create a new instance. This will show you the available AWS images (which is like a screenshot in VMware or the last backup disk available) for the instance:

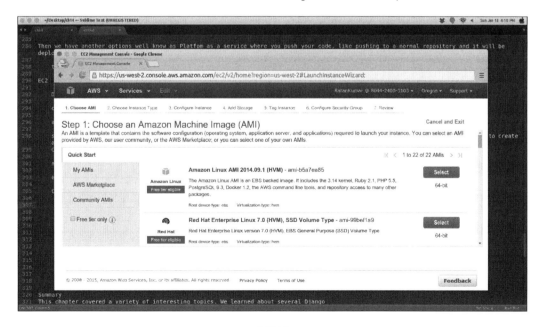

4. Scroll down to choose the Ubuntu 64-bit instance (the Ubuntu server).

   Next, choose an instance type; initially, choose the free tier, which is given to every new account that AWS calls the **t2.micro** instance type. Check for other settings as most of them are kept at default. Move to the **Tag** instance and give a name to your instance:

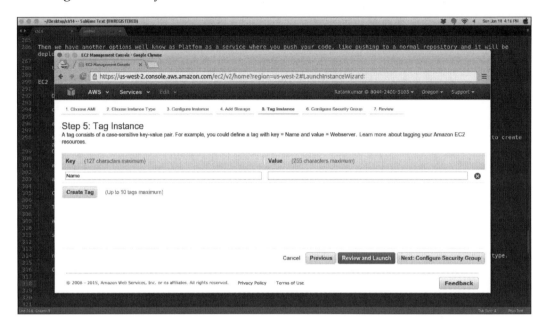

5. The next important thing to do is to choose a security group. AWS has this feature to protect your server from attacks. Here, you can configure which specific ports will be publicly accessible. Basically, you need to open two ports to make the tweets publicly accessible.

6. You should use SSH (Port 22) to connect the system from a local machine to deploy the code.

7. HTTP (Port 80) is used to run your Django server.

> As the database we will use runs on the same instance, we are not going to add the MySQL port to the security group.

Make sure that you have configured something like the following:

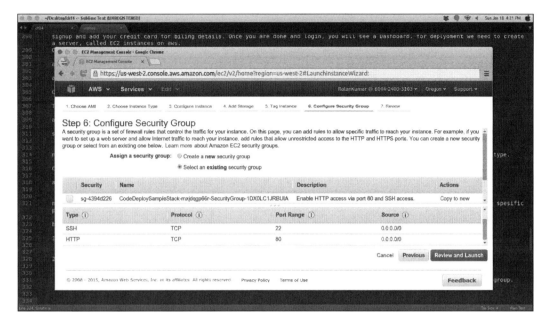

Next, review and launch the instance. Also, you must create a key pair to access your AWS machine through SSH. The key is a .pem file that you will use with SSH to log into your machine remotely. Create a key pair and download the .pem file.

Make sure that the PEM file has a specific permission of 400. Your key file must not be publicly viewable if you want SSH to work. Use this command if needed: chmod 400 mykey.pem.

It will take a while and will appear back on your dashboard as a running instance.

Click on the instances to the left of your screen. Then, you can see your running instance. Click on the instance row to get more details at the bottom of the screen, as shown in the following figure:

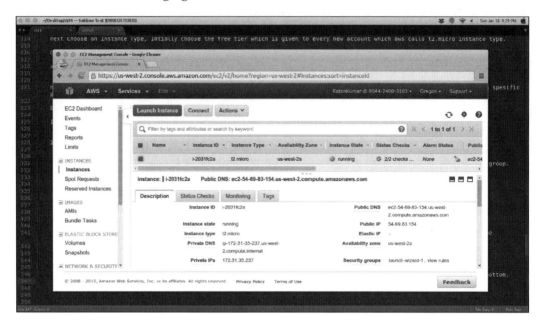

On the right-hand side of the details, you can see the public DNS: `<public DNS>` and the public IP: `<public IP>`. That is all you need (and the `.pem` file, of course, to log in to your instance).

On your machine, go to the folder from the terminal where you downloaded the PEM file and type `$ssh -i <pemfilename>.pem ubuntu@<pubic IP>` on your terminal.

Otherwise, type the following:

`$ssh -i <pemfilename>.pem ubuntu@<public Dns>.`

By doing this, you will be logged in to the remote server.

This is your online system from scratch. If you want to deploy the website on your own from your local machine, then you can go to the previous chapters and install everything required for a virtual environment. Django and Apache perform deployment on this server.

Once you have deployed, use the public IP we used for SSH and you should see the deployed server.

Google Compute Engine

Google Compute Engine works on the same concept as AWS EC2. Google Compute Engine, at present, does not give a free tier.

Google servers are known for their reliability and performance. So, if you are thinking of a project with such a need, go for them.

Google Cloud gives you a cloud SDK to use its instances, and most of its initial configuration can be done from the terminal.

To create an instance on Google Compute Engine go to:

`https://cloud.google.com/compute/docs/quickstart`.

This link will help you set up the instance that runs on an Apache server.

The open hybrid cloud application platform by Red Hat

Red Hat gives another solution for cloud deployment, which is free upto some usage limit, with a service called **OpenShift**.

You can create an OpenShift account and get a free basic 3 dynamo-based cloud server from `https://www.openshift.com/app/account/new`.

After you create your account, you can go to `https://openshift.redhat.com/app/console/applications` and add your account.

OpenShift gives a Django repository all set up for you with the version control pre-configured.

All you need is to make your changes and push the code. It will automatically deploy the code.

OpenShift also gives you the SSH feature to log in to your cloud server and some basic troubleshooting as well.

Heroku

This is also a good platform for deploying your Django code to the cloud smoothly. Like Google Compute Engine, Heroku also gives you an SDK tool to install and perform the configurational changes from a local terminal. You need to get a toolbelt (an SDK for Heroku).

Create an account on Heroku at `https://signup.heroku.com`.

The following are the steps taken from `https://devcenter.heroku.com/articles/getting-started-with-python`. Check it out for the latest updates. The following steps explain how to create and use Heroku:

1. First, we need to install **Heroku Toolbelt**. This provides you access to the Heroku command-line utility:

    ```
    $wget -qO- https://toolbelt.heroku.com/install-ubuntu.sh | sh
    ```

    The following screen will appear:

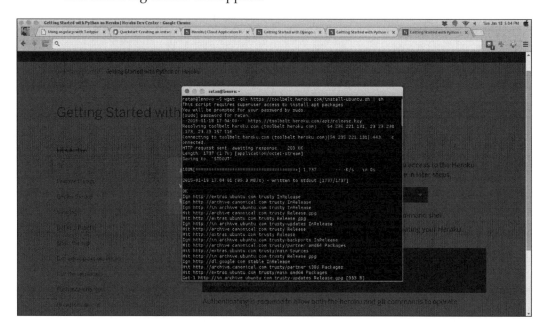

2. It will install Heroku Toolbelt on your local machine. Log in to Heroku from the command line:

    ```
    $heroku login
    ```

3. Use the same username and password as you did for the Web login. Let's take a look at the following screenshot:

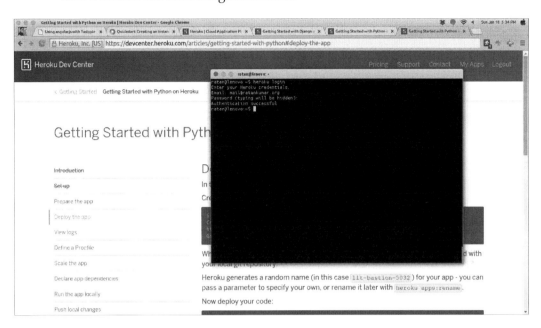

4. Now, go to `https://devcenter.heroku.com/articles/getting-started-with-django` to deploy Django on Heroku.

Google Application Engine

Google Application Engine works differently, it does not work on the traditional database, instead it has its own database. Thus, to deploy Django on Google Application Engine, we will use a separate project called **Django-nonrel**.

Django-nonrel is a project that allows developers to run native Django projects (including Django's ORM) on nonrelational databases, one of which is Google Application Engine's datastore. This is all in addition to the standard traditional SQL databases that were always supported by Django. Google Application Engine does come with some Django support, but the support is mainly regarding templating and views. For other tools that allow rapid development, such as forms, the built-in administration interface or Django authentication just won't run out of the box. Django-nonrel changes this for Django developers.

Summary

This chapter covered a variety of interesting topics. You learned about several Django-based deployment options that are useful while deploying Django. You also learned how to move a Django project from a development environment to a production environment. Notably, the frameworks that you learned about are all very easy to use, so you will be able to effectively utilize them in your future projects.

15
What's Next?

Web development has evolved over time and so have the devices where users consume information. The Web was designed for large-screen devices earlier, but recent trends show that consumption of the devices with small screen size and the devices that can be held in hand has increased. Thus, here arises the need to mold the Web to serve small-screen devices, but these devices are very power sensitive. So, there is the need to separate the backend functions from the frontend functions in Django.

One such most widely used solution is to use Django backend with an API enabled at the frontend to use it with Django. Using **AngularJS** for such a situation is most suited.

REST has been the future of web development and REST APIs are rather an integral part of the modern Web. As the fragmentation across a device increases, there arises a need of single minimal endpoint, which does not perform any presentation operation. For instance, the information retrieval or commutation could be as fast as possible and could also be scaled, and the presentation or business logic for this is left in the hands of modern browsers using a frontend framework.

AngularJS meets Django

AngularJS is a modern JavaScript framework used to create complex web applications within a browser.

Since the birth of AngularJS in 2009, it has been evolving very fast and is being widely accepted as a production-grade frontend framework. It is now maintained by Google.

AngularJS has a very interesting birth story. It got its big attention when one of the creators of angular recreated a web application in 3 weeks, which initially took 6 months to develop, by reducing the number of lines of code from 17,000 to 1,000.

AngularJS has many features over conventional web development frameworks. Among them, a few unique and innovative features are two-way data bindings, dependency injection, easy-to-test code, and extending the HTML dialect using directives.

For the server side, we can use the **Django REST Framework** or **Tastypie** for REST endpoints. Then, we can use AngularJS, which focuses on the MVC model, to encourage the creation of easily maintainable modules.

Web technologies have evolved from synchronous to asynchronous, that is, the website requests now heavily use asynchronous calls to refresh its content without reloading the page, an example of which is your Facebook wall.

AngularJS is one of the solutions for the asynchronous need in a better way for Django web development.

In the following example, we will use AngularJS to create a single page, which uses the tweet's API that we already created.

We will use AngulaJS to list all the tweets, but before that, we need to get familiarized with AngularJS's key terms:

- **Directives**: For this, the HTML file is extended with custom attributes and elements. AngularJS extends the HTML with **ng-directives**. The **ng-app** directive is used to define AngularJS's application. The **ng-model** directive binds the value of HTML controls (input, checkbox, radio, select, and text area) to the application. The **data.ng-bind** directive binds the application data to the HTML view.

- **Model**: This is the data shown to the user in the view and with which the user interacts.

- **Scope**: This is the context where the model is stored, so that controllers, directives, and expressions can access it.

- **Controller**: This is the main business logic behind views.

When we design an API-based web application, there is a high chance that both (the API's backend and the webapp frontend) of them reside on different servers. Thus, there arises a need to configure Django for **Cross-origin resource sharing**.

From the definition explained on Wikipedia:

> *Cross-origin resource sharing (CORS) is a mechanism that allows many resources (for example, fonts, JavaScript, and so on) on a web page to be requested from another domain outside the domain from which the resource originated.*

We need to alter our Django API to allow requests from other servers as well. We will now update the `api.py` file of the `tweets` application to allow the requests to the server cross-site request:

```python
class CORSResource(object):
    """
    Adds CORS headers to resources that subclass this.
    """
    def create_response(self, *args, **kwargs):
        response = super(CORSResource, self).create_response(*args,
        **kwargs)
        response['Access-Control-Allow-Origin'] = '*'
        response['Access-Control-Allow-Headers'] = 'Content-Type'
        return response

    def method_check(self, request, allowed=None):
        if allowed is None:
            allowed = []

        request_method = request.method.lower()
        allows = ','.join(map(unicode.upper, allowed))
        if request_method == 'options':
            response = HttpResponse(allows)
            response['Access-Control-Allow-Origin'] = '*'
            response['Access-Control-Allow-Headers'] = 'Content-Type'
            response['Allow'] = allows
            raise ImmediateHttpResponse(response=response)

        if not request_method in allowed:
            response = http.HttpMethodNotAllowed(allows)
            response['Allow'] = allows
            raise ImmediateHttpResponse(response=response)
        return request_method
```

After adding this class, we can create a subclass of any resource that we want to expose for a cross-domain request. We will now change our `Tweet` class to make it available for cross-site access.

Let's update the `Tweet` class to the following:

```python
class TweetResource(CORSResource, ModelResource):
    class Meta:
        queryset = Tweet.objects.all()
        resource_name = 'tweet'
```

Now, the tweet resource is ready for access from different domains.

The following is a basic AngularJS example:

Create a single HTML file called app.html (as this file is independent of our existing Django project, we can create it outside the project folder) with the following content. Currently, this page uses AngularJS from a local disk, you can import the page from a CDN as well:

```html
<html ng-app="tweets">
  <head>
    <title>Tweets App</title>
    <script src="angular.min.js"></script>
  </head>
  <body>
    <div ng-controller="tweetController">
      <table>
        <tr ng-repeat="tweet in tweets">
          <td>{{ tweet.country }}</td>
          <td>{{ tweet.text }}</td>
        </tr>
      </table>
    </div>
    <script src="app.js"></script>
  </body>
</html>
```

In the following code, the ng-controller directive is triggered at its render time, which processes any business logic and injects the calculated models inside the scope.

The <div ng-controller="tweetController"> tag is one example where the tweetController parameter is processed before its div is rendered.

We have our business logic completely in JavaScript in the app.js file:

```javascript
var app = angular.module('tweets', []);
app.controller("tweetController", function($scope,$http) {
  $http({ headers: {'Content-Type': 'application/json;
  charset=utf-8'},
  method: 'GET',
  url: "http://127.0.0.1:8000/api/v1/tweet/?format=json"
  })
    .success(function (data) {
    $scope.tweets = data.objects;
  })
});
```

This `app.js` file makes a request to the API endpoint of tweets and injects the `tweets` object to the scope, which is rendered by the AngularJS in view (`app.html`) with the `ng-repeat` loop directive:

```
<tr ng-repeat="tweet in tweets">
  <td>{{ tweet.country }}</td>
  <td>{{ tweet.text }}</td>
</tr>
```

The output of the preceding code is shown in the following figure, which shows the country and tweets:

This is just a basic AngularJS application, as advanced web development has moved from backend to frontend completely. An AngularJS-based application is best suited for a complete single-page application.

Django search with Elasticsearch

Search has become an integral part of most of the applications we deal with nowadays. From Facebook, to search for a friend, to Google, where you search the whole Web, everything from blog to log needs a search capability to unlock the hidden information on a website.

The Web is evolving at an exponential rate. A GB of data is now obsolete and hundreds of terabytes of both structured and unstructured data is generated every day.

Elasticsearch (**ES**) is better than other alternatives because, in addition to providing full-text search, it provides meaningful real-time data analytics and is highly scalable with a strong support for clustered data infrastructure.

Elasticsearch also gives you a simple REST API that can easily integrate with any custom application and a Django (and more broadly, Python) development environment gives a lot of cool, out-of-the-box tools to implement Elasticsearch.

The Elasticsearch website (http://www.elasticsearch.org/) contains a thorough documentation and there are lots of great examples online that will help you build any kind of search you need. By making full use of Elasticsearch, you can probably build your own "Google" with it.

Installing an Elasticsearch server

First, install Java. Then, download and extract Elasticsearch. You can either run ES as a service or you can start an ES server using the following Shell commands (change paths in accordance with your system):

```
set JAVA_HOME=\absolute\path\to\Java

\absolute\path\to\ES\bin\elasticsearch
```

If it is done correctly, you can call the following URL in your browser:

```
http://127.0.0.1:9200/
```

It will give you a response in the following way, but with a different `build_hash` parameter:

```
{
  "status" : 200,
  "name" : "MN-E (Ultraverse)",
  "cluster_name" : "elasticsearch",
  "version" : {
    "number" : "1.4.1",
    "build_hash" : "89d3241d670db65f994242c8e8383b169779e2d4",
    "build_timestamp" : "2014-11-26T15:49:29Z",
    "build_snapshot" : false,
    "lucene_version" : "4.10.2"
  },
  "tagline" : "You Know, for Search"
}
```

Elasticsearch comes with basic configurations for basic deployment. However, if you want to tweak the configuration, then refer to its online documents and change the Elasticsearch configuration in the `elasticsearch.yml` file.

Communication between Elasticsearch and Django

Django can be seamlessly integrated with Elasticsearch using basic Python programming. In this example, we will use the Python requests library to make the request from Django to Elasticsearch We can install requests by typing the following code:

```
$pip install requests
```

For the search functionality, there are mainly three operations that we need to execute:

1. Create an Elasticsearch index.

2. Feed the index with data.

3. Retrieve the search results.

Creating an Elasticsearch index

Before loading an Elasticsearch index with text and retrieving the search results, Elasticsearch has to know some details about your content and how data should be treated. Therefore, we create an ES index that consists of settings and mappings. **Mappings** are the ES equivalents of Django's models—data field definitions for your content.

Although mappings are completely optional, as Elasticsearch dynamically creates a mapping from the information that it has got for indexing, but it is advised that you predefine the data map for indexing.

A Python example for creating an ES index is as follows:

```
data = {
  "settings": {
    "number_of_shards": 4,
    "number_of_replicas": 1
  },
  "mappings": {
    "contacts": {
      "properties": {
        "name": { "type": "string" },
        "email": { "type": "string" },
        "mobile": { "type": "string" }
      },
      "_source": {
        "enabled": "true"
      }
    }
  }
}

import json, requests
response = requests.put('http://127.0.0.1:9200/contacts/', data=json.
dumps(data))
print response.text
```

The output of the preceding code is shown in the following figure:

```
ratan@lenovo: ~
>>> data = {
...                         "settings": {
...                             "number_of_shards": 4,
...                             "number_of_replicas": 1
...                         },
...                         "mappings": {
...                             "contacts": {
...                                 "properties": {
...                                     "name": { "type": "string" },
...                                     "email": { "type": "string" },
...                                     "mobile": { "type": "string" }
...                                 },
...                                 "_source": {
...                     "enabled": "true"
...                 }
...                         }
...                     }
...                 }
>>> import json, requests
>>> response = requests.put('http://127.0.0.1:9200/contacts/', data=json.dumps(d
ata))
>>> print response.text
{"acknowledged":true}
>>>
```

For every operation done with Elasticsearch, it gives a response message such as
{"acknowledged":true}, which means that our index has been created successfully
by Elasticsearch.

We can check whether the mapping has actually been updated or not by making a
query command such as:

```
mapping_response =
requests.get('http://127.0.0.1:9200/contacts/_mappings')

print mapping_response.text
```

The following figure shows that Elasticsearch has been updated with the new mapping:

```
>>>
>>>
>>> mapping_response = requests.get('http://127.0.0.1:9200/contacts/_mappings')
>>> print mapping_response.text
{"contacts":{"mappings":{"contacts":{"properties":{"email":{"type":"string"},"mo
bile":{"type":"string"},"name":{"type":"string"}}}}}}
>>>
```

After we created our first Elasticsearch index, we created the JSON dictionary with the information and dumped this information into Elasticsearch via Python requests. The **"contacts"** parameter is the index name we have choosen and we will use this name to feed and retrieve data from the Elasticsearch server. The **"mappings"** key describes what data your index will hold. We can have as many different mappings as we like. Every mapping contains a field in which data is stored, exactly, like a Django model. Some of the basic core fields are string, number, data, Boolean, and so on. The full list is given in the Elasticsearch documentation. The "shards" and "replicas" parameters are explained in the ES glossary. Without the "settings" key, ES would simply use the default values—which in most cases is perfectly fine.

Feeding the index with data

Now that you have created an index, let's store content inside it. An example Python code for our imaginary BlogPost model that contains a title, description, and content as text fields is as follows:

```
import json, requests
data = json.dumps(
  {"name": "Ratan Kumar",
  "email": "mail@ratankumar.org",
  "mobile": "8892572775"})
response = requests.put
('http://127.0.0.1:9200/contacts/contact/1', data=data)
print response.text
```

You will see the output, which is shown as follows:

```
>>>
>>>
>>> import json, requests
>>> data = json.dumps(
...     {"name": "Ratan Kumar",
...     "email": "mail@ratankumar.org",
...     "mobile": "8892572775"})
>>> response = requests.put('http://127.0.0.1:9200/contacts/contact/1', data=data)
>>> print response.text
{"_index":"contacts","_type":"contact","_id":"1","_version":1,"created":true}
>>>
```

This acknowledgment shows that our contact data has been indexed. Of course, indexing a single data and searching it does not makes much sense, so we will index more contacts before we make a retrieval query.

Elasticsearch also provides bulk indexing, which can be used as follows:

```
import json, requests
contacts = [{"name": "Rahul Kumar",
  "email": "rahul@gmail.com",
  "mobile": "1234567890"},
  {"name": "Sanjeev Jaiswal",
  "email": "jassics@gmail.com",
  "mobile": "1122334455"},
  {"name": "Raj",
  "email": "raj@gmail.com",
  "mobile": "0071122334"},
  {"name": "Shamitabh",
  "email": "shabth@gmail.com",
  "mobile": "9988776655"}
]

for idx, contact in enumerate(contacts):
  data += '{"index": {"_id": "%s"}}\n' % idx
  data += json.dumps({
    "name": contact["name"],
    "email": contact["email"],
    "mobile": contact["mobile"]
  })+'\n'
```

Let's take a look at the following screenshot:

```
ratan@lenovo: ~
>>>
>>> import json, requests
>>>
>>> contacts = [{"name": "Rahul Kumar",
...              "email": "rahul@gmail.com",
...              "mobile": "1234567890"},
...                  {"name": "Sanjeev Jaiswal",
...              "email": "jassics@gmail.com",
...              "mobile": "1122334455"},
...                  {"name": "Raj",
...              "email": "raj@gmail.com",
...              "mobile": "0071122334"},
...                  {"name": "Shamitabh",
...              "email": "shabth@gmail.com",
...              "mobile": "9988776655"}
...              ]
>>>
>>> for idx,contact in enumerate(contacts):
...     data += '{"index": {"_id": "%s"}}\n' % idx
...     data += json.dumps({
...         "name": contact["name"],
...         "email": contact["email"],
...         "mobile": contact["mobile"]
...     })+'\n'
...
>>> response = requests.put('http://127.0.0.1:9200/contacts/contact/_bulk', data=data)
>>>
>>> response.text
u'{"took":686,"errors":false,"items":[{"index":{"_index":"contacts","_type":"contact","_id
":"0","_version":1,"status":201}},{"index":{"_index":"contacts","_type":"contact","_id":"1
","_version":1,"status":201}},{"index":{"_index":"contacts","_type":"contact","_id":"2","_
version":1,"status":201}},{"index":{"_index":"contacts","_type":"contact","_id":"3","_vers
ion":1,"status":201}},{"index":{"_index":"contacts","_type":"contact","_id":"0","_version"
:2,"status":200}},{"index":{"_index":"contacts","_type":"contact","_id":"1","_version":2,"
status":200}},{"index":{"_index":"contacts","_type":"contact","_id":"2","_version":2,"stat
us":200}},{"index":{"_index":"contacts","_type":"contact","_id":"3","_version":2,"status":
200}},{"index":{"_index":"contacts","_type":"contact","_id":"0","_version":3,"status":200}
},{"index":{"_index":"contacts","_type":"contact","_id":"1","_version":3,"status":200}},{"
index":{"_index":"contacts","_type":"contact","_id":"2","_version":3,"status":200}},{"inde
x":{"_index":"contacts","_type":"contact","_id":"3","_version":3,"status":200}}]}'
>>>
```

As you can see in the preceding screenshot, the **"status": 201** parameter, which in the HTTP status means that the record is successfully created. Elasticsearch reads data line by line, so we used **"\n"** at the end of every dataset. Bulk operations are much faster than running the multiple single request.

This example is a simple JSON example. When we use Elasticsearch with our Django application, the same JSON object can be replaced by the Django model and to index the model, you can get all the Django model objects from the `ModelName.objects.all()` query and then parse and save it. Also, in the case of the manual ID, as we used in the preceding example, which is the index count, it will be much more convenient if you use a primary key to index it as an Elasticsearch ID. This will help us to directly query for a result object if we are not passing the object information as a payload.

Retrieving search results from the index

Searching an index is rather simple. Again, we use Python requests to send a JSON-encoded data string to our ES endpoint:

```
data = {
  "query": {
    "query_string": { "query": "raj" }
  }
}

response = requests.post
('http://127.0.0.1:9200/contacts/contact/_search',
data=json.dumps(data))
print response.json()
```

This gives a result, as shown in the following figure:

```
>>>
>>> data = {
...     "query": {
...         "query_string": { "query": "raj" }
...     }
... }
>>>
>>>
>>>
>>> response = requests.post('http://127.0.0.1:9200/contacts/contact/_search', data=json.d
umps(data))
>>> print response.json()
{u'hits': {u'hits': [{u'_score': 0.5036848, u'_type': u'contact', u'_id': u'2', u'_source'
: {u'mobile': u'0071122334', u'name': u'Raj', u'email': u'raj@gmail.com'}, u'_index': u'co
ntacts'}], u'total': 1, u'max_score': 0.5036848}, u'_shards': {u'successful': 5, u'failed'
: 0, u'total': 5}, u'took': 79, u'timed_out': False}
>>>
```

In the example, we are looking for the term **"raj"** in our contacts index. ES returns all the hits ordered by relevancy in the JSON-encoded format. Each of these hits contains an **"_id"** field that gives you the primary key of the concerned blog post. Using Django's ORM, it's now simple to retrieve the actual objects from the database.

> The ES search endpoint offers an unlimited set of options and filters; fast retrieval from huge datasets, pagination, and everything you need to build a powerful search engine.

This is just the tip of the iceberg. When you will build your Django application with Elasticsearch, you will explore many interesting features, such as aggregation, which can be used in the preceding example. It lists all the contact information of Ratan and autocomplete, which will be used to suggest a user the complete name from Elasticsearch, as they start typing in the search box for a contact.

Summary

In this chapter, we learned about the two important components that are used most often when the Django project is involved, namely, AngularJS and Elasticsearch. As frontend framework, AngularJS not only decreases the load from the server by pushing the render logic to a browser, it also gives a rich experience to the users when using an AngularJS-powered application.

Elasticsearch, on the other hand, is one of the most popular search engines used, which is open source as well. The ease of setting up and scaling Elasticsearch is what makes it the choice for any search engine requirement. You learnt a bit about Django as well. As the chapter started, we're sure that you'll had the aim of learning a skill and of becoming experts in it. Well, this is just the beginning; there are more things that you need to explore to reach at the expert level in each topic that was discussed in this chapter. We have reached at the end of this book. In this book, we went through the process of building a micro blogging application from scratch using Django as our framework. We covered a lot of topics related to Web 2.0 and social applications, as well as many Django components. You can always refer to the online documentation of Django. If you want to learn more about a particular feature or component, visit `https://docs.djangoproject.com`.

Thanks for choosing this book to learn the Django web development basics. We wish you all the success in your professional life.

Index

Bootstrap
  about 2, 47
  manual installation 49, 50
  URL 57
  using, with Django 48
branching, Git 42

C

C 28
C++ 207
caching
  configuring 185
  configuring, for specific views 186
  configuring, for whole site 185
  enabling 184, 185
  used, for improving site performance 183
caching backend, options
  Database Caching 184
  Filesystem Caching 184
  Memcached 184
  Simple Caching 184
CamelCase naming convention 32
class-based generic views
  about 197
  using 197, 198
class-based views
  defining 62-64
Client() class
  get method 188
  login method 189
  post method 189
closed source software 232
CMD 16
coding style
  about 28
  imported packages, grouping 31
  indentation, in Python 28, 29
  naming conventions 32
  package, importing 31
commands, Git
  $git add 41
  $git add <file-name> 41
  $git commit -m 41
  $git diff 41
  $git rm <file-name> 42
  $git stash 42

  $git stash apply 42
  $git status 41
commands, migration
  makemigrations 213
  migrate 213
  sqlmigrate 213
compatible databases
  MySQL 212
  PostgreSQL 212
  SQLite 213
components, grid
  column 59, 60
  container 58
  row 59
configuration variables
  changing 277, 278
content
  organizing, into pages 159-163
contributed sub-frameworks 198
CouchDB
  about 207
  benefits 207
  strengths 207
critical() function 256
Cross-origin resource sharing (CORS) 290
cross-site request forgery (CSRF)
        protection 201
custom filters
  creating 195-197
  escape string 197
  raw string 197
  safe string 197
custom template tags
  creating 195-197

D

database
  setting up 44, 45
database system
  installing 19
  setting up 208
data migration 219
data.ng-bind directive 290
Debian 14
debug() function 256

E

EC2 280-284
Elasticsearch
  about 233, 293
  communication, with Django 294, 295
  installing 294
  URL 294
Elasticsearch index
  creating 295, 296
  feeding, with data 297-299
  search results, retrieving from 300
error() function 256
error pages
  setting 279
event handler 110

F

fields, MongoDB
  BinaryField 225
  BooleanField 225
  ComplexDateTimeField 225
  DateTimeField 225
  DecimalField 225
  DictField 225
  DynamicField 225
  EmailField 225
  FileField 225
  FloatField 225
  GeoPointField 226
  ImageField 226
  IntField 226
  ListField 226
  MapField 226
  ObjectIdField 226
  reference link 226
  StringField 226
  URLField 226
flatpages
  about 199
  cross-site request forgery (CSRF)
      protection 201
  humanize application 199, 200
  sitemap 200
follower
  adding 145, 146
  removing 145, 146

form widgets
  FileInput 97
  HiddenInput 97
  PasswordInput 97
  Textarea 97
Foundation 2
function-based view
  defining 62, 63

G

generic views 197
Git
  about 40
  branching in 42
  setting up 41
  URL 40
  working 41
GitHub 41
GNU gettext
  about 179
  URL 179
Google Compute Engine 285
group permissions 157

H

hashtag data model
  about 92-95
  Django forms 96
hashtags
  about 91
  autocompletion, implementing 133-136
  tag page, creating 101
Heroku 47, 285, 286
Heroku Toolbelt
  about 286
  URL 286
humanize application
  about 199
  apnumber filter 199
  intcomma filter 199
  intword filter 199
  naturalday filter 200
  naturaltime filter 200
  ordinal filter 200

M

Mac OS X
  Django, installing 19
  Python, installing 14
main page
  creating 60, 61
  template, creating for 84-89
many-to-many relationship 73, 74, 92
many-to-one relationships 73
mappings 295
message system
  implementing 201, 202
migration
  about 210-212
  advantages 211, 212
  commands 213
  need for 210, 211
  new features 211
  performing 213-216
  working 216, 217
migration class
  dependencies list 219
  operations list 219
migration file 217-222
mixins 62
Modal Class 6
model, migration operation
  AddField 219
  AlteIndexTogether 219
  AlterModelTable 219
  AlterUniqueTogether 219
  CreateModel 219
  DeleteModel 219
  RemoveField 219
  RenameField 219
  RenameModel 219
**Model Template View (MTV)
    framework 52**
**Model-View-Controller (MVC)
    web framework 3**
mod_wsgi parameter 274
MongoDB
  about 5, 8, 207, 222
  benefits 207
  connecting, with Django 223

  strengths 207
  URL, for installing 222
MongoEngine 223
most followed user
  displaying 147
MS SQL Server 19
multilingual support 4
MySQL
  about 19, 205, 212
  benefits 206
  installing, in Linux 209
  plugins, installing for Python 209, 210
  setting up 209

N

naming convention 32
ng-app directive 290
ng-directives 290
ng-model directive 290
node.js 2
NoSQL databases
  about 207
  CouchDB 207
  MongoDB 207
  Redis 208
  versus SQL databases 205, 206

O

OAuth 233-235
Object-Relational Mapper (ORM) 71
offline access 235
one-to-many relationship 92
one-to-one relationships 73
OpenID 5
OpenShift
  about 285
  URL 285
open source 231
open source software
  about 232
  versus other software 232, 233
operators
  contains 116
  exact 116
  gt 116

Thank you for buying
Learning Django Web Development

About Packt Publishing

Packt, pronounced 'packed', published its first book, *Mastering phpMyAdmin for Effective MySQL Management*, in April 2004, and subsequently continued to specialize in publishing highly focused books on specific technologies and solutions.

Our books and publications share the experiences of your fellow IT professionals in adapting and customizing today's systems, applications, and frameworks. Our solution-based books give you the knowledge and power to customize the software and technologies you're using to get the job done. Packt books are more specific and less general than the IT books you have seen in the past. Our unique business model allows us to bring you more focused information, giving you more of what you need to know, and less of what you don't.

Packt is a modern yet unique publishing company that focuses on producing quality, cutting-edge books for communities of developers, administrators, and newbies alike. For more information, please visit our website at www.packtpub.com.

About Packt Open Source

In 2010, Packt launched two new brands, Packt Open Source and Packt Enterprise, in order to continue its focus on specialization. This book is part of the Packt Open Source brand, home to books published on software built around open source licenses, and offering information to anybody from advanced developers to budding web designers. The Open Source brand also runs Packt's Open Source Royalty Scheme, by which Packt gives a royalty to each open source project about whose software a book is sold.

Writing for Packt

We welcome all inquiries from people who are interested in authoring. Book proposals should be sent to author@packtpub.com. If your book idea is still at an early stage and you would like to discuss it first before writing a formal book proposal, then please contact us; one of our commissioning editors will get in touch with you.

We're not just looking for published authors; if you have strong technical skills but no writing experience, our experienced editors can help you develop a writing career, or simply get some additional reward for your expertise.

Django Essentials

ISBN: 978-1-78398-370-4   Paperback: 172 pages

Develop simple web applications with the powerful Django framework

1. Get to know MVC pattern and the structure of Django.

2. Create your first webpage with Django mechanisms.

3. Enable user interaction with forms.

4. Program extremely rapid forms with Django features.

5. Explore the best practices to develop applications of a superior quality.

Python Tools for Visual Studio

ISBN: 978-1-78328-868-7   Paperback: 122 pages

Leverage the power of the Visual Studio IDE to develop better and more efficient Python projects

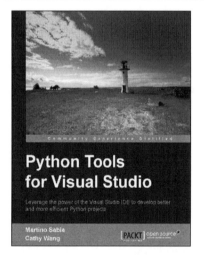

1. Learn how you can take advantage of IDE for debugging and testing Python applications.

2. Enhance your efficiency in Django development with Visual Studio IntelliSense.

3. Venture into the depths of Python programming concepts, presented in a detailed and clear manner.

Please check **www.PacktPub.com** for information on our titles

Mastering Object-oriented Python

ISBN: 978-1-78328-097-1   Paperback: 634 pages

Grasp the intricacies of object-oriented programming in Python in order to efficiently build powerful real-world applications

1. Create applications with flexible logging, powerful configuration and command-line options, automated unit tests, and good documentation.

2. Use the Python special methods to integrate seamlessly with built-in features and the standard library.

3. Design classes to support object persistence in JSON, YAML, Pickle, CSV, XML, Shelve, and SQL.

Python Data Visualization Cookbook

ISBN: 978-1-78216-336-7   Paperback: 280 pages

Over 60 recipes that will enable you to learn how to create attractive visualizations using Python's most popular libraries

1. Learn how to set up an optimal Python environment for data visualization.

2. Understand the topics such as importing data for visualization and formatting data for visualization.

3. Understand the underlying data and how to use the right visualizations.

Please check **www.PacktPub.com** for information on our titles